GLOBALIZATION
AND URBANIZATION

D1598668

GLOBALIZATION

Series Editors

Manfred B. Steger
*Royal Melbourne Institute of Technology and
University of Hawai'i–Mānoa*

and

Terrell Carver
University of Bristol

"Globalization" has become *the* buzzword of our time. But what does it mean? Rather than forcing a complicated social phenomenon into a single analytical framework, this series seeks to present globalization as a multidimensional process constituted by complex, often contradictory interactions of global, regional, and local aspects of social life. Since conventional disciplinary borders and lines of demarcation are losing their old rationales in a globalizing world, authors in this series apply an interdisciplinary framework to the study of globalization. In short, the main purpose and objective of this series is to support subject-specific inquiries into the dynamics and effects of contemporary globalization and its varying impacts across, between, and within societies.

Globalization and Sovereignty
John Agnew

Globalization and War
Tarak Barkawi

Globalization and Human Security
Paul Battersby and Joseph M. Siracusa

Globalization and the Environment
Peter Christoff and Robyn Eckersley

*Globalization and American Popular
Culture, 3rd ed.*
Lane Crothers

Globalization and Militarism
Cynthia Enloe

Globalization and Law
Adam Gearey

Globalization and Feminist Activism
Mary E. Hawkesworth

Globalization and Postcolonialism
Sankaran Krishna

Globalization and Media
Jack Lule

*Globalization and Social Movements,
2nd ed.*
Valentine M. Moghadam

Globalization and Terrorism, 2nd ed.
Jamal R. Nassar

Globalization and Culture, 2nd ed.
Jan Nederveen Pieterse

Globalization and Democracy
Stephen J. Rosow and Jim George

*Globalization and International Political
Economy*
Mark Rupert and M. Scott Solomon

Globalization and Citizenship
Hans Schattle

Globalization and Money
Supriya Singh

Globalization and Islamism
Nevzat Soguk

Globalization and Urbanization
James H. Spencer

Globalisms, 3rd ed.
Manfred B. Steger

Rethinking Globalism
Edited by Manfred B. Steger

Globalization and Labor
Dimitris Stevis and Terry Boswell

Globaloney 2.0
Michael Veseth

Supported by the Globalization Research Center at the University of Hawai'i, Mānoa

GLOBALIZATION AND URBANIZATION
THE GLOBAL URBAN ECOSYSTEM

JAMES H. SPENCER

ROWMAN & LITTLEFIELD
Lanham • Boulder • New York • London

Published by Rowman & Littlefield
A wholly owned subsidiary of The Rowman & Littlefield Publishing Group, Inc.
4501 Forbes Boulevard, Suite 200, Lanham, Maryland 20706
www.rowman.com

16 Carlisle Street, London W1D 3 BT, United Kingdom

British Library Cataloguing in Publication Information Available

Library of Congress Cataloging-in-Publication Data

Spencer, James H.
  Globalization and urbanization : the global urban ecosystem / James H. Spencer.
    pages cm. — (Globalization)
  Includes bibliographical references and index.
  ISBN 978-1-4422-1474-3 (cloth : alk. paper) — ISBN 978-1-4422-1475-0
(pbk. : alk. paper) — ISBN 978-1-4422-1476-7 (electronic) 1. Urban ecology
(Sociology)—Cross-cultural studies. 2. Urbanization—Cross-cultural studies.
3. Urban policy—Cross-cultural studies. 4. Cities and towns—Cross-cultural
studies. 5. Globalization—Cross-cultural studies. I. Title.
  HT241.S67 2015
  307.76—dc23
                                                                   2014006349

∞™ The paper used in this publication meets the minimum requirements of
American National Standard for Information Sciences—Permanence of Paper
for Printed Library Materials, ANSI/NISO Z39.48-1992.

Printed in the United States of America

To my father, who taught me to see
connections beyond those in my line of sight

CONTENTS

PREFACE

As I sent this manuscript to press while sitting on the edge of my bed in Honolulu, awaiting the birth of my first daughter, my father lay dying of lung cancer in his bed in New York City, a nine-hour direct flight away. Globalization and the distance it can create are hard. This book is dedicated to him.

The past couple of decades of globalization have enabled families and friends to disperse across the world, but my father's life provides an opportunity to reconsider our connected globe. Born in 1931, Jim Spencer saw his father leave for World War II in Europe and grew up hearing stories from his mother, an Englishwoman who was born and grew up in China, of fleeing across Siberia from the Xinhai Revolution. As an adult, he married a Vietnamese woman and forged a life in New York City, with regular visits to family in Pennsylvania, Michigan, and France. In the 1970s, his mother's family was personally invited by Prime Minister Zhou Enlai to return to China to visit the place where his uncle, Henry C. Whittlesey, was killed in World War II as part of the famous Dixie Mission. In the 1980s, they returned to receive an award on his behalf. Later on in life, my Dad's brother moved from Detroit to retire in Mexico to spend his final several years. The particulars of my father's life illustrate numerous, seemingly accidental, global connections concealed beneath an exterior of local embedding.

My Dad didn't like to travel much; he loved to spend time with his family and friends, wherever they happened to be, but our home in New York City was the source of his strength and excitement. At first glance, few would have labeled him a "globe-trotter." At the same time, he was the smartest person I have ever known because he had an intellectual curiosity unencumbered by conventional boundaries and informed by a vast network of historical and contemporary connections across the known world. His focus was deeply local, but because he recognized the deeply interconnected parts of all the people and things he saw around him, his outlook—and therefore his experience—was profoundly global. It was only as I concluded this book manuscript that I was able to retrospectively realize the profound influence that my father's ability to see the global aspect of every single local particularity has had on my thought process. He was not only a man ahead of his time but also a man committed to recognizing and cultivating the global connections that lie—not so deeply—beneath the surface of everyday life.

This book is underlain by a dense network—or ecosystem, to be consistent with the theme—of personal and professional relationships, without which I would never have been able to share my ideas with you. First and foremost, I must thank my family. My wife, Meron Girma Tsige Spencer, has been an emotional and intellectual foundation for me ever since I began this project. In addition to her tolerance with my prioritization of the researching and writing of this book, her own personal experiences and thoughts have intimately shaped my own. Our son, Yohannes, and daughter, Sabah, have also provided a reason for sharing these ideas. Meron and I will see only the first act of the global urban ecosystem unfold, but it is Yohannes and Sabah who will grow into adults much more global than we. My mom, Nguyen Xuan Dao Spencer, has also provided me much of the historical perspective and interest in pursuing these ideas about globalization, and she has also been a source of personal and professional inspiration.

The seed for this book came at the suggestion of Manfred Steger, one of my coeditors, and as conversant with the literature on globalization as anyone on the planet. As a colleague, Manfred was the one who first encouraged me to shape my incoherent musings on globalization into something more. More than anyone else, Manfred is the one who encouraged me to pursue the idea of globalization and urbanization as a scholarly project. His editorial partner, Terrell Carver, was an excellent sounding board, corralling my sometimes confused thinking into a set of ideas focused on the details of the case studies that follow, and

Susan McEachern at Rowman & Littlefield always provided focused advice on relating to potential readers. On the research side, Nguyen Thi Phuong Thao, Hoang Thi Mai Huong, Solomon Bamidele Oluwaseyi, and Michel Pisetta all provided unique windows into some of the contemporary aspects of globalization that rarely make it into the public eye. Learning about their lives through this project has been a real gift, even beyond the confines of this book. Bewketu Kassa, Hokulani Aikau, and Noelani Goodyear Ka'opua each provided particular insights into my writing of the case studies from perspectives that I will never be able to attain, and they served as tolerant sounding boards for complicated issues for which I needed to make editorial decisions. While their keen eyes and thoughtful suggestions were invaluable, the responsibility for any misperceptions and inaccuracies is mine alone.

This ecosystem of friends and colleagues has made my life richer, and I hope that it will do the same for yours.

Honolulu's city in the country

New York's Freedom Tower

Saigon, old and new

Sprawling Addis Ababa

INTRODUCTION

Urbanization is one of the defining characteristics of the twenty-first century and planning for it is the major challenge, with 90 percent of urbanization occurring in the developing world.[1] Most of this urbanization is occurring in Southeast Asia, China, and Sub-Saharan Africa and presents numerous challenges for planners to develop creative responses in the provision of basic services such as transportation, electricity, water supplies, and sanitation. Although contemporary urban studies and planning have tended to focus on local participation, local activism, and local solutions in the resolution of urban problems, many of the characteristics of contemporary global urbanization are nonlocal.

At the same time that fast-changing cities of the South face highly localized challenges of urban services provision, political development, and cultural change, many of these very same cities exhibit surprisingly new global characteristics. The fact that daily flights occur between Dubai and Beijing, and Addis Ababa and Bangkok, as do other connections that reflect the regularity of contact between Asian businesspeople and technical development experts and the capitals of Uganda, Nigeria, and elsewhere illustrates a growing reality that former colonial and neocolonial centers in Europe and North America no longer mitigate globalization. A decreasing centrality of the traditional "world cities," or "global cities,"[2] extends beyond trade in simple commodities, as shown by the growing practice of health-care tourism, for example, and shopping sprees to Thailand by wealthy Africans and Middle Easterners.

1

Cases of twenty-first-century urbanization cannot be divorced from the types of globalization that have enabled this rapid acceleration. Even as the nations of the world have become "flattened" in their engagement, cities have become increasingly "spiky," showing—oftentimes—sharper distinctions from their domestic hinterlands than from other cities around the world. In other words, nations have deconcentrated power and influence, while cities are busy concentrating it.

This acceleration of urbanization was enabled by the breakdown of colonial and Cold War political fault lines based on nation-states. Prior to 1945, when formerly colonized parts of the world began to liberate themselves from (mostly) European empires, cultures and societies were as globally connected as today. Vietnamese subjects in Southeast Asia attended school with French children, and Vietnamese schoolteachers taught West Africans French grammar, all in the name of France's supposed Mission Civilisatrice. Likewise, there are important historical reasons for the high number of South Asians living in England and the excellent English spoken throughout the subcontinent. Without romanticizing these kinds of connections, a recognition of such national affinities, which were often characterized by brutality and violence as well as love and respect, reflects deep global interconnections rarely seen today.

However, these global connections were politically defined notions of citizenship and efforts to cultivate cultural affinities across sprawling empires in the name of political power and commerce. Urban settlements were simply the crucibles within which these national affinities and aspirations played themselves out. The liberation of colonial societies brought an abrupt end to such connections, releasing the junior partners from sometimes hundreds of years of oppression. Empires along different political, cultural, and social fault lines eventually reestablished themselves as the United States, the Soviet Union, and, to some degree, the People's Republic of China, vied to define new supranational entities. Hence, Ethiopian engineers and doctors braved Russian winters to earn their degrees at the top Soviet universities and performers from across Africa frequented China to demonstrate their arts, while Vietnamese military personnel went to flight school in Texas.

The decline of colonial empires post–World War II, and the ending of the Cold War in the early 1990s, enabled the growth of new fault lines of global economic, social, and cultural connectivity that allowed new kinds of direct contact between urban societies unmitigated by national politics, and it was not until the post–Cold War era that the interrelated nature of globalization and urbanization became obvious to many people. Before the 1990s, economic, social, and cultural transactions between global cities such as Shanghai and New York were mitigated by national political institutions. The remarkable lessening of national and supranational restrictions led to a new kind of contemporary "urban pioneer," driven by direct economic interests sometimes mitigated by national interests, but often motivated by uniquely individual perceptions of where economic opportunity lies. The scale and depth of these new connections are just now coming to be recognized and form the basis of this book.

Today, almost one million Chinese technical experts, workers, and others live in Sub-Saharan Africa (SSA).[3] It is not just the Chinese who are directly exporting technical experts to every country in SSA and Southeast Asia (SEA) regardless of their national politics, however. A different kind of expert from the African continent is currently finding new and lucrative global markets. For avid fans, it is common knowledge that over the past decade, African soccer players have become de rigueur personnel on European professional teams. Less well known is that less skilled African players have gone on to make professional careers not only in financially lucrative—though less prestigious— leagues in Japan, for example, but also in very-low-income countries such as Thailand, Cambodia, and Vietnam.

It is not just these new forms of technical expertise and specialization that are leading to the globalization and urbanization of people. Interestingly, for example, Japanese retirees have begun to create expatriate communities in Thailand with high-end services in tropical resort–like locations, in the same way that Americans have "colonized" parts of Mexico and Central America to serve out their final years in retirement communities. One of the trends that have made many of these unlikely connections possible is the globalization of health care, which supports a medical tourism industry of over US$20 billion. Bumrungrad Hospital in Bangkok exemplifies how this health-care mobility has introduced far-off cities to patients and their families seeking services and procedures either unavailable or too expensive in their home countries.

The cost-quality differentials (ranging from 200 to 800 percent), combined with demographic and development trends, simply make this inevitable. Because of these cost differentials, for example, Saudi princes rub shoulders in the Bumrungrad-lobby Starbucks with British National Health Service patients and wealthy Sudanese businesspeople, all waiting for family members to receive procedures from physicians trained in the United States. Of particular relevance to urbanists and planners, however, is that these trends have spillover effects onto the local neighborhood of Sukhumvit, where Middle Eastern, African, and Muslim hotels, restaurants, and other services now complement the older ones targeting North American and European tourists.

These diverse, and seemingly fanciful, examples illustrate surprising global intersections and transactions rarely explored and documented beyond the popular media. During the age of European imperialism or the Cold War, it would not have been surprising to find British and Nigerian leaders negotiating over land, trade, and education. Today, the descendents of these Nigerian politicians are negotiating with Vietnamese mayors over how to deal with a perceived immigration racket on the streets of Saigon. The emerging twenty-first-century political economy is characterized by such new kinds of connections at the urban scale, with implications for cities, the nodes that make them possible.

Attention to deep economic complementarities involving urban environments can shed light on these unlikely global connections. These new connections, I illustrate in this book, are underlain by three existing trends likely to accelerate in the near future: the growth of agro-industrial processing regions in Southeast Asia, and to some extent Africa; the growing social and economic development links between Africa and Asia; and the growing global market for tourism, especially new forms of tourism popular among diaspora communities and the aging populations of the West and Far East.

No doubt, the world is becoming more urbanized. The Global South is driving most of this change, even as the developed countries remain largely static in terms of overall urban growth. While fascinating in a descriptive sense, the numbers alone cannot explain *why* the cities in the Global South have grown so quickly, and why this has been sustained over a period of twenty years and is projected for decades into the future. The growth of these cities cannot be explained simply by internal growth and migration dynamics because the development of the

Global South—given its colonial histories—has rarely been driven by autarkic means. Rather, the current long-wave spurt of global urbanization has been driven by growth dynamics that connect the Global South to its northern counterpart. The much-publicized mobility of diasporas and retirees is but the tip of an urbanization iceberg that might best be thought of as demographic globalization: new movements of people across the globe, facilitated by cities with numerous pathways and multiple ports of entry. Examining and analyzing these remarkable dynamics with a strong emphasis on the Global South, this study seeks to contribute to the growing literature on globalization and urbanization from an uncompromising transdisciplinary perspective. After all, understanding the increasing complexity of extensive urban systems in the age of globalization—what some have begun to call the "Global Anthropocene"—requires a multifaceted approach that goes far beyond the confines of a single discipline.

Chapter 1

Urbanization and the Construction of the Global Urban Ecosystem

The Bowling Green stop is the last chance to exit the New York subway system in Manhattan before the 4/5 train burrows down under the East River on its way to downtown Brooklyn. Upon reaching the top of the staircase leading up from the platform, it is difficult not to feel that you have only ascended halfway out of the station. The top of the stairs is the bottom of a massive, 3-D built environment, and towering cliffs of office buildings and mid-level residential condominiums give the impression that there may be even more subway lines hiding above, somewhere around the tenth floor.

If you miss your stop at Bowling Green, the next chance is Borough Hall on the other side of the East River. While only about two miles separates the two stations, they occupy different environments that can be viscerally felt even more than can be the historical and cultural distinctions separating Manhattan and Brooklyn. At the top of the station stairs, one is greeted with an open sky, limited only by five-story walk-ups that allow you to keep an eye on a setting sun after a long workday. To traverse this underground space between Bowling Green and Borough Hall is akin to driving from the Badlands of western South Dakota up onto the midwestern plains of the eastern part of the state. They are part of the same place, but completely different in their feel. When you sense this noticeable widening of the urban horizon, you realize that the built environment is a visceral, tangible environment that defines much of your world.

This book draws out the characteristics of this difference and how it defines a way of living that is fast becoming the norm for people around the world, and the cultures, habits, economies, and identities conditioned by these environments.

Globally speaking, few will ever ascend the staircase at Bowling Green, but about 650 million have experienced a similar difference over the past several years in other ways. That is the number of people around the world who have come from rural communities to live in the world's cities.[1] As of 2010, these migrants can clearly call themselves part of the global majority. Not fifty years ago, observers might have called cities the nodes of elitism and the 25 percent minority. This tipping of the balance from a nonurban to an urban global society has come with both hand-wringing and boosterism, with special series and issues initiated by outlets ranging from the *Financial Times* to the *Atlantic Monthly*. From a more analytic standpoint, *Scientific American* devoted an entire issue to understanding the city in August 2011. Each interesting in its own right, as collections of essays rather than comprehensive lenses onto the contemporary world, they offer limited insight into making sense of this comprehensive and global shift. In the following pages, I suggest that an emergent term—the "global urban ecosystem"—is a useful and more comprehensive lens for understanding the global connections among cities as well as the changing human norms that characterize globalization.

THE TRENDS: A NEW POLITICAL ECONOMY OF GLOBALIZATION IN THE DEVELOPING WORLD

The UN estimates that the world has become over 50 percent urban in the past several years, with the share of the world's population liv-

Table 1.1.   Urban Share Growth Rate by Region, 1990–2005

	Southeast Asia	Sub-Saharan Africa	Latin America and the Caribbean	Europe	North America
2005 Urban Share (%)	43.8	35.2	77.4	72.2	80.7
1990–2005 Urban Share Growth Rate (%)	38.6	25.3	9.2	2.3	7.0

Source: United Nations, Department of Economic and Social Affairs Population Division, *World Population Prospects: The 2005 Revision* (New York: United Nations, 2006).

ing in urban areas growing by 13.2 percent between 1990 and 2005.[2] Table 1.1 shows the extent to which urbanization in Southeast Asia and Sub-Saharan Africa has outpaced all other regions of the world. What is immediately apparent is that since the late 1980s, Southeast Asia and Sub-Saharan Africa have accelerated their urbanization almost as fast as China, but that the developing countries of Latin America and the more developed regions of Europe and North America have not.

Some have called this kind of urbanization in the developing world "periurbanization,"[3,4] and scholars have come to recognize that the patterns of uncoordinated development can lead to serious problems of equality and fairness in the distribution of basic infrastructure,[5] especially in the Global South. A planetary term such as the "global urban ecosystem" can help contextualize rapid change in the Global South with contemporary trends affecting the Global North. It can serve to deconstruct a decreasingly central divide between these two sociopolitical spheres, and reconstruct an increasingly relevant distinction between the urban and its opposite.

While the growth of urban areas means the challenges that people face across the Global South are immense, there *are* some promising trends. Examining these same data a bit more closely, figure 1.1 suggests that many of the developing countries of SEA and SSA are approaching a slowdown in urbanization; it suggests that SEA is really decelerating and SSA is somewhat decelerating. This deceleration is important for urban planners and managers because it suggests that the overall transition to global urban settlement may have reached a midpoint maximum and the characteristic of settlement stability has begun to set in globally. This trend puts additional pressure on city-level decision makers and professions such as planning, architecture,

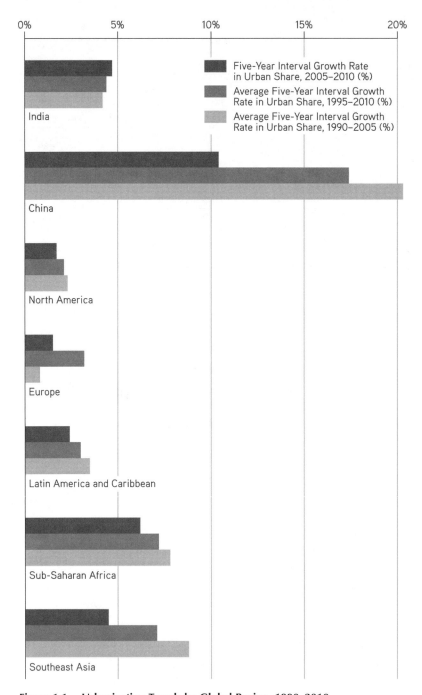

Figure 1.1. Urbanization Trends by Global Region, 1990–2010.
Note: In figures 1.1–1.3, five-year-interval moving averages were used where both pre- and post-data were available, to minimize variation. Thus, figures across the periods are conservatively estimated. "Urban share" is defined as the percentage of the national population living within urban-designated areas.

engineering, and management to invest in material and social structures, knowing that such investments are decreasingly undermined by
demographic fluctuations.

Figures 1.2 and 1.3 show that at the national level, such dynamics
vary somewhat, but remain largely the same. In SEA, for example, both
Cambodia and Indonesia—which showed extremely high growth in
urban share between 1990 and 2005—had slowed significantly by the
most recent five-year interval, while Thailand has remained steadily
at low-moderate levels. Vietnam, on the other hand, has remained
relatively steady in its five-year-interval growth rates at about 11–12
percent. In SSA, overall rates of growth are lower than in SEA and show
somewhat less of a range. The smaller countries such as Kenya and Senegal seem to be accelerating somewhat, growing from 4.6 percent to 7.2

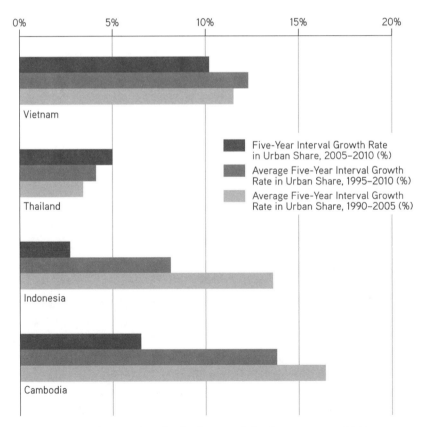

Figure 1.2.   Southeast Asia Urbanization Trends by Country, 1990–2010

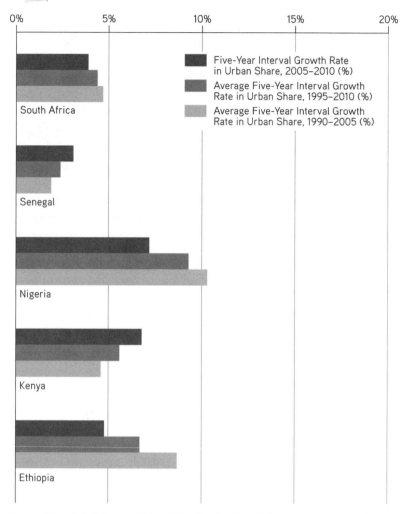

Figure 1.3.   Sub-Saharan Africa Urbanization Trends by Country, 1990–2010

percent and 1.9 percent to 3.2 percent respectively, while larger countries such as Nigeria and Ethiopia seem to be decelerating somewhat, at
10.3 percent to 7.8 percent and 8.7 percent to 5.0 percent respectively.
With this relative stabilizing of the rate of increase in global urbanization, the time for a comprehensive effort to understand its significance
is as important as ever.

Urbanization is not necessarily a naturally occurring shift arising
out of a deep-seated human evolutionary instinct. The question of

what is happening in Southeast Asia and Sub-Saharan Africa behind the urbanization trends is discussed in the following chapters and focuses on as-yet-unnoticed trends affecting the two regions: the growing social and economic development links between Africa and China, the growth of agro-industrial processing regions in Southeast Asia and to some extent Africa, and the growing global market for tourism, especially new forms of tourism popular among the aging populations in the West and Far East. On the other hand, "urbanization" more broadly is the socio-physical form resulting from innovation and social reorganization of human societies that began in prehistory and eventually led to the market economy, the Industrial Revolution, and postindustrial consumerism. This latter history of urbanization provides long-wave context in the following chapter, and the contemporary global political economy of the developing world framing each of the case-study chapters illustrates how global urbanization is unfolding.

But before delving into the specifics driving global urbanization, one must first address why this particular form of human settlement matters. Certainly, observers of all types have written volumes about cities, describing the looming crisis of slums[6] or how poor residents are constructing cities right under our noses.[7] Insightful as they are, few delve extensively into why cities exist and how they have evolved: questions that help us define what "urban" actually means. Even economists, those fussily precise analysts behind much of urban-development strategy have a difficult time pinning this construct down. One of the most oft-quoted, Ed Glaeser,[8] in his 2011 tribute *Triumph of the City: How Our Greatest Invention Makes Us Richer, Smarter, Greener, Healthier, and Happier*, calls the city modern man's most important technology, illustrating all the ways in which it enriches the human experience through economic efficiencies, competitiveness, and even quality of life. All of these qualities from a technology that we cannot quite define and therefore awkwardly use as a placeholder term for something we suspect is much more important than it appears.

Perhaps most significantly, Jeb Brugmann's *Welcome to the Urban Revolution: How Cities Are Changing the World* attempts to define a global system of cities and how this has changed everyday life. He refocuses on urbanism as a characteristic of people and the types of innovation they are capable of when they live in close proximity. While useful as a strategic approach, we are still left trying to understand how cities came about in the first place. This seems to be important if we are to understand what will continue to make them attractive into the latter parts of the twenty-first century.

WHAT IS A CITY? THE CASE FOR A GLOBAL URBAN ECOSYSTEM

Missing, from both the doomsday and triumphant depictions about how the statistical growth of cities is changing the world, is an analysis of the broader social, cultural, political, and economic significance of the shift; how urbanization changes our personal identities, and how people adapt their behaviors to cities. The totality of how urban life changes human life is seen in the growing understanding that cities are indeed changing the nonhuman biota around us.[9] Studies showing the effect of urbanization on infectious-disease reservoirs, the eating habits of deer and bears who increasingly feed on human garbage, and the loss of immunity to deadly viruses among urban flying foxes compared to their rural brethren all point toward the fact that the human urban technology is shaping a much larger ecology.[10] If these complex human technologies are transforming the biota under our noses, surely the urban environment is changing us humans too. This simple fact compels us to know what urbanization means.

The city is both a physical and a social entity influencing and reflecting humans in their physical shape and their social composition. To understand this socio-physical environment, one must recognize its prevalence and dynamics, as well as the importance and significance of human settlement—or urbanization—throughout human history. To understand why the scale and culture of urbanization is so compelling as a public topic, one must move beyond the "wow" factor of descriptive statistics. In this book, I argue that the core fact of contemporary urbanization demanding attention and analysis is that cities are the new ecosystem of daily human life, regulating, supporting, and reflecting a period that some have come to call the "Anthropocene"—a planetary age in which geologic and natural systems of the earth are best understood by understanding human behavior.[11] A focus on cities emphasizes that this "Global Anthropocene" is the inevitable result of the growth of a global urban ecosystem, which is, in turn, the result of a long history of global integration of humans and their associates, and the physical construction, rearrangement, and adaptation that accompany it. In a sense, we as humans have arrived at a new way of living that is *marked* by the global urbanization statistics rather than *defined* by them. This passage into a time of urban life generates the type of excitement and fear often accompanying major human encounters and transformations, giving substance and human meaning to the raw statistics. To understand the global urban ecosystem and its parallel to the structure and management of natural ecosystems, one must first review how previous scholars have seen the city. Thus, an understanding of this global-urban transformation begins with a simple question.

What is a city? What is "urban"? These are deceptively simple yet difficult questions, given the seeming diversity, historical trajectories, and geographies of urban centers worldwide; nevertheless, writers, conversationalists, scholars, marketing gurus, and hip-hop artists have all continued to use the term as if we share a precise definition. We see it every day, we ask new friends which one they call home, we complain incessantly about how it cramps our style with traffic, pollution, and crime, but also how it frees us from the constraints of small-town life, provides the "edginess" to shock us out of comfortable and boring lives, and provides the convenience of everything from theaters, to corner stores, to playgrounds. The city is a strange focus of analytic attention; other disciplines focus on discrete, identifiable targets such as people, political parties, nations, and businesses, while urbanists are left eternally answering the basic question that all know is important, but few can define coherently: what is a city?

What makes an administrative settlement of fifty thousand inhabitants—the U.S. Census Bureau's definition of the smallest possible "Metropolitan Statistical Area"—more like one of one hundred thousand than one of twenty-five thousand? Moving beyond simple population numbers, need a city have basic infrastructure such as a public transit system? Water and sanitation services? By these measures, many of the developing world's cities and megacities—those areas so remarkable in their statistical growth—fail to meet the standard. And what about density? Does the city of Detroit, with all of its population decline over the past two decades, become less urban over time? We think we know what urban is, but it is very difficult to narrow down to any simple metric. Importantly, without a shared understanding of urbanization, how can we know what to make of its ascendance? To

meet the challenge, we need to step back a bit from the metrics, important as they are; we need to think of them as complex and multifaceted
collections of people and things bumping up against one another like
so many asteroids pulled into the gravitational orbit of a new star.

Here on earth, human beings respond to a more complex manifestation of gravity than simple mass, however. As I hope to convey in
the following pages, cities' gravitational forces lie at the intersection
of engineering and poetry where science contrasts with aesthetics,
creating a powerful pull, able to draw billions of people to live at the
crowded intersection of many individual and personal trajectories—to
the places we call cities. It is this density of human trajectories in particular places that makes urbanization so complex, thereby enhancing
the need for further engineering and an ever more complex aesthetic.
The gravitational force grows with each additional resident and each
new building. This pull has persisted in fits and starts steadily over the
millennia, drawing humans into the density, noise, and chaos of cities,
even when they strive for order and control of their surroundings. Why
do these forces persist even as technology allows us to live in increasingly disparate locations, far from urban pollution, slums, and crime?

For many, urbanization is a bittersweet experience. In the 1995
comedy *Blue in the Face*, Lou Reed quips, "I don't know very many
people who live in New York . . . who don't also say, 'But I'm leaving.
And I've been thinking of leaving . . . for, uh, 35 years now.'" Should
urban residents be seen as eternally caught between the inward pull of
excitement and convenience yet simultaneously repelled by the outward push of congestion and stress?

Others have tried to make sense of this kind of painful attraction,
perhaps most eloquently captured by E. B. White's essay "Here is New
York," posted throughout the New York City subway system under
the Metropolitan Transit Authority's (MTA) Subtalk, Train of Thought
program:

> There are roughly three New Yorks. There is, first, the New York of
> the man or woman who was born there, who takes the city for granted
> and accepts its size, its turbulence as natural and inevitable. Second,
> there is the New York of the commuter—the city that is devoured by
> locusts each day and spat out each night. Third, there is New York of
> the person who was born somewhere else and came to New York in

quest of something. . . . Commuters give the city its tidal restlessness, natives give it solidity and continuity, but the settlers give it passion.

Old-time New Yorkers give the city stability, those who choose to "do their time" early on in their careers give it an economy (both at the high and the low end), but it is really those who commit to the city for all of its chaos, life, and energy that truly give the place its identity.

Literature from around the world romanticizes and anthropomorphizes the city. Gabriel García Márquez, in his masterpiece *Love in the Time of Cholera*[12] romanticizes an unnamed colonial city by the sea suggestive of his native Cartagena, Colombia, describing the return of "the prodigal son" to his hometown:

> He was still too young to know that the heart's memory eliminates the bad and magnifies the good, and that thanks to this artifice we manage to endure the burden of the past. But when he stood at the railing of the ship . . . only then did he understand to what extent he had been an easy victim to the charitable deceptions of nostalgia.

Likewise, Ghanaian novelist Ayi Kwei Armah's *The Beautyful Ones Are Not Yet Born*[13] depicts the oppressive grime, noise, and crime of the city as a metaphor for corruption and social dysfunction in postcolonial African life—a physical manifestation of the nameless protagonist's frustrations that, ironically, holds out the promise of a better life.

The city remains a character in most people's lives, though perhaps today it is more of a friend than an archenemy. Many make personal choices based on them and cultural references about how their home cities reflect their values even though cities themselves—as distinct from their inhabitants—are dominated by inanimate objects and impersonal technologies. Because humans build, occupy, and transform them, however, cities come alive and develop personalities that represent the many people, objects, and technologies in continuous negotiation and symbiosis within places. More poetically, cities are the canvas upon which the collective history, relationships, and aspirations of its residents are painted.

The complexity of these interacting forces in cities and the distinct identities they represent clouds our attempts to focus clearly on an acceptably defined target of analysis. What is it that Detroit shares with Mumbai? Iowa City with the city of Osaka? Making sense of urbanization requires a meso-analysis distanced from the immediacy of human experience, and a level of abstraction beyond individualism, beyond national, state, or even municipal governments, and beyond the concept of businesses focused narrowly on efficiency and profit. On the other hand, study of the city is more focused than that of "society" or "culture," which allows the analyst to be blissfully unbound from the constraints of management, policy, and other immediate decisions of practical relevance. This tension between the material and the philosophical makes the study of cities, why they grow, and how individuals, businesses, and governments should engage with them a very thorny question. Nevertheless, this tension mirrors the basic "experimentality" of human life in which people make choices to maximize their benefits and achieve material security, but also long for larger meaning in the form of altruism, thrill seeking, and their love to know that life is more than simply an accounting game.

An understanding of this tension begins with the question of how people connect with places. Urbanists have taken theoretical inspiration from geographers identifying the importance of physical, political, and economic proximity in explaining development outcomes. John Friedmann,[14] one of the fathers of the urban planning discipline, identifies the central role of "placemaking" in determining contemporary identity, while David Harvey[15] has theoretically pointed to the importance of residence and location in the provision of justice in industrialized societies, and Ed Soja[16] describes how location and proximity can nurture a "thirdspace" in which creativity, innovation, and/or dysfunction are likely to take root. Clearly, whether one comes from a sociological, political, or economic perspective, the deep connections between people and places matters. But why do we choose to live in the places we have come to call cities? Why not live in rural places?

Some offer the promise of economic growth as the explanation. For them, cities offer a sufficient scale of production to salve humans' need for material improvements. Regional development theorists would have us see cities as simply the places where a global economy is produced. They convincingly use neoclassical economic theory to explain the development of areas as diverse as Silicon Valley[17] and Northeast Brazil,[18] leading to important questions of governance that highlight tensions between the nation-state and localities.[19]

However, such economic explanations of why a city exists ring only partly true. Regional economic clustering seems to explain only those dynamic urban economies such as Detroit in the 1950s, Silicon Valley in the 1990s, and Shanghai in the twenty-first century. What explains—economically—all those urban losers in the global economy? While many have rightly claimed that dense, polluted, and dangerous cities of the Global South, such as Mumbai, Jakarta, and Lagos, generally offer better economic and social opportunities than do their rural alternatives, in the developed world the argument breaks down. Even as cities in the Global South are known as the lands of economic opportunity, many North American cities struggle to attract businesses and residents or simply have modest economic ambitions. Does this make them any less urban? If they are simply rusted-out shells of their former glory days, how can we explain the persistence of cities such as Pittsburgh, Madrid, or Saint Petersburg, each of which has survived both the booms *and* the busts? A simple economic explanation cannot explain the existence and persistence of the city in both contexts; it lacks the neatness and logic of scientific explanations, an approach attempted by other scholars.

For decades, more scientifically oriented scholars have proposed a "science of the city." In 1935, Zipf's Law became popular as a mysterious predictor of city populations, and the subfield of "city systems" became popular as an explanation of urban population distribution. Such valiant analytic efforts, however, foundered on purely mathematical empiricism that—while necessary for generalization—was fundamentally limited by the absence of a compelling logic behind the statistics; they lacked any explanatory argument and thereby remained "mysterious" relationships, even to economists.[20] Happy to leave such theoretical speculation to fanciful architects and designers, such analyses could make no realistic projections about trends arguing for what cities might look like in the future. Contented with a narrowly focused backward look, these efforts could never break through to a sharply generalizable characteristic of what a city was within the larger urban systems, and therefore never caught on beyond their narrow disciplinary boundaries.

More recently, physicist Geoffrey West and his colleagues at the Santa Fe Institute have tried to develop a science of cities that takes a scalar approach to urbanization, in which cities—much like biological life itself—gain efficiencies of economics, politics, society, environment, and a whole host of other characteristics the larger scale they become. While empirically interesting in their ability to predict commonalities of even cultural attributes such as walking speed based on unemployment, for example, the commonalities found by this approach—like those of the city systems analysts before them—are devoid of complex human agency and a discernable human logic relentlessly increasing the scale of human life. Their interesting work is more in the vein of the application of "emergence theory" to cities and neighborhoods, in which urban residents are akin to army ants ever on the search for food. The collective intelligence of thousands of ants—like a city neighborhood—creates sophisticated analysis, beauty, and order out of simple logical decisions replicated millions of times. Again, while fascinating as a component of urbanization, surely we are more than a collection of ants looking for food. What is it that we are looking for when we find cities?

Both efforts to bring scientific order to the study of cities gloss over potentially different and important second-order characteristics that likely influence what can be observed, and mask differing goals, habits, and motivations. Just as the scientific study of humans must account for fundamentally different second-order categories such as gender, race, age, and culture, a scientific approach to urbanization must incorporate a meso-level of analysis to be credible. In this book, I attempt to define a global urban ecosystem by giving preliminary shape to this meso-level of analysis, characterizing a variety of urban types that shape the decisions and motivations of all the ant-like humans creating and sustaining cities around the world.

Pragmatically, we as observers have, so far, dutifully pushed forward using the term "cities" without being able to fully explain why. Without a real definition, however, we are left only to "know it when we see it," which leaves a naggingly frayed edge to our use of the concept. As an alternative to the overly prescriptive "science" of cities and the "I know it when I see it" approach, I find an ecosystem approach most useful. I find this approach to globalization as the growth of a single global urban ecosystem of mutually supportive urban types a useful and generally demonstrable framework for making sense of the statistics. Therefore, my definition of "contemporary globalization" begins with an understanding of the ecosystems within which humans have always lived.

Ecosystems: Patches and Corridors

Beginning in the 1970s, an emerging discipline of ecosystem science came to be accepted among scholars concerned with natural resources and the environment. This science, however, was largely silent on the built environment, focused narrowly on the existence of small-scale human ecosystems existing in largely separate corners of the world. These ecosystems were punctuated by periodic engagements with other systems, resulting sometimes in catastrophic consequences and disruptions. In retrospect, it is hard to ignore the fact that even at that time, much of human civilization was quietly cultivating their spaces far from the frontiers of these natural ecosystems.

Despite its general silence on the questions of human civilization, ecosystem science was useful for the study of people because it focused on complex natural relationships in defined spaces. It called these spaces "patches," and chose to focus on dense and diverse interactions in them, a lens that had a convenient parallel in urbanists' visions of the city. During the early twentieth century, amidst the turmoil of the Industrial Revolution, a group of thinkers emerged with distinct beaverlike inclinations to change their surrounding environment. Beginning in 1902 with Ebenezer Howard's *Garden Cities of Tomorrow* and culminating today with the New Urbanist movement, utopian planners have long dreamed of an ideal society in which cities and settlements achieve human-scale interactions, social equity, and connections to the environment. Some, such as Frank Lloyd Wright's Jeffersonian ideal of a fully developed agrarian society, never moved from concept to plan, while others, such as Howard's Garden Cities and the New Urbanists' transit-oriented developments, have periodically attracted investors, residents, and theorists alike. The important concept running throughout these various ideas and experiments is the powerful impulse of humans to transform their physical environments to meet material and cultural needs and aspirations based on an understanding of complex relationships between humans and their local built and natural environments, to control the functioning of local ecosystems.

Howard's Garden City patches, for example, proposed concentric street systems in which open space was interspersed with housing, light and heavy industry, and extractive forest gardens, all to be

developed from pristine wildlands. His plans went so far as even to locate "homes for waifs" and "mental institutions" in strategic locations
within the city boundaries. In Howard's and his backers' minds, every
parcel was planned to maximize the city's overall "efficiency, equity,
and environmental quality," to use contemporary lingo. The urban
ecosystem was completely planned out a priori, even down to the concentric streets, which were bounded on the outer ring by "1st Street"
so that outward expansion was limited by the needed creativity to come
up with appropriate new street names![21]

Today, one can watch patches of five-hundred-hectare developments
in China, Vietnam, India, and Abu Dhabi sprout up almost overnight
out of what only months before were pristine wetlands, hillsides, and
deserts. Observers often note that Shenzhen, one of the most productive
and busy urban agglomerations in the world today was only an isolated
fishing village surrounded by farms as late as the 1980s.[22] Such centrally
planned projects often share the comprehensiveness of a utopian planning approach that ranges from Howard's Garden Cities, to Abu Dhabi's
ultramodern Masdar City of the early twenty-first century. While each
is utopian and visionary, both the Garden Cities and Masdar pale in
comparison to the more outrageous efforts to create complex and multifaceted places. Projected to lie twenty meters below the Persian Gulf,
Hydropolis, like the Garden Cities of their time, was an ambitious effort
to start anew; to escape the confines of a seemingly overly industrial,
polluted, and dysfunctional world into a new, planned, rational, and
functional human-dominated ecosystem cut from whole cloth. A futur-
istic vision for living under the sea, Hydropolis was a project to re-create
human environments completely anew, and lay at the extreme end of
the irrepressible human determination to shape environments suitable to
their material and aesthetic needs based on the newest science, technology, and finance. This determination of central and local authorities in
partnership with private finance and visionaries to create whole physical
ecosystems oriented around the material and spiritual needs of humans
has now encompassed the global scale.

Humans' inclination to shape and build their ecosystem patches is
visible not only through planned "starchitect" developments and master
plans but also in the intricacies of street-level neighborhoods and architectural designs. For twenty years, architect Peter Calthorpe[23] and other
New Urbanists have argued that human settlements require deep social

interactions possible only through spatial proximity and shared residential spaces. Their premise rests on the work of Jane Jacobs, who famously and vigorously opposed centralized efforts to reshape the environment to fit the needs of contemporary human settlement. The persistence of her idea that deep social interactions in places and a sense of community are facilitated and possible only at the street level is remarkable. Even in an age of the Internet and global travel, her ideas show up in the work on urban poverty where social ecologies of poor neighborhoods are seen to independently limit the opportunity structure of poor minority youth, and in the reinvigoration of her intellectual tradition championed by the University of Chicago's School of Urban Ecology.

While the planners of Shenzhen and Jane Jacobs' neighborhood protégés fight tooth and nail over what the built environment should look like and the process to construct it, they share an assumption that it matters. Both sides struggle to shape the physical environment—the human ecology—into their own visions of the ideal and good life. In some places, such as New York City, such battles are ancient history and used by contemporary analysts as ammunition for current political battles. In fast-developing parts of the world such as China, these battles between those who see the human and urban ecosystem at the city scale and those that see it at the neighborhood scale are very material and immediate, even though oftentimes one-sided.

Understanding these urban patches of human-defined ecosystems is critical for discerning any given case of urbanization, but is it sufficient as a framework for defining the *global* urban ecosystem? Surely we are now more than just isolated settlements. It is not as if Shenzhen and New York exist as autarkies. Rather, it is precisely because they are connected to other cities and rural areas that allows them to generate the financial and other resources necessary to shape the urban environment, which in turn sparks a political battle over how to create, manage, and control space. As important as the complex patches of cities are, it is the corridors connecting them that allow them to transform.

Recently, John Kasarda and Greg Lindsay focused on the global transportation infrastructure network that has enabled an increasing frequency and depth of contact across vast spaces: the airport. In *Aerotropolis: The Way We'll Live Next*, Kasarda and Lindsay describe a global system of cities centered on the nodes of air transportation, enabling global circumnavigation on a daily basis.[24] The compression of time and space facilitated by the airplane now makes possible monthly business ventures between New York and Bangkok, overnight trips between Nairobi and Amsterdam, and computer repair services from virtually anywhere with a post office. Just one rung down from the airport is the globalization of containerized shipping, as described by Brian Cudahy in *Box Boats: How Container Ships Changed the World*.[25] Combined with cheap telecommunications and the Internet, the infrastructure supporting cheap transport of people and goods has laid down a spider's web of corridors connecting urban patches across vast distances.

This dialectic between patches and corridors, between urbanization and globalization, simultaneously produces uniqueness and difference. It can best be explained not only by an ecosystem approach that rests on unique collections of forms and relationships in locations, but also by common elements that tie together these forms through networks at the larger scale. These forms and networks allow for a kind of global-urban division of labor and land use plan in which cities connected through transportation, communications, and other networks play different material, cultural, and political functions in a system that extends across the globe, but does not yet encompass all forms of settlements.

A narrow definition of human relationships locked in patches rings somewhat hollow in today's world of lightning-fast and global financial transactions and seventeen-hour flights. One cannot understand those social, political, and economic relationships without a peripheral vision to other clusters of settlement as well as to the nonurban areas of human life. The former connect the dense ecosystems of daily human transactions to one another in space, and the latter defines the boundaries of the "known world." It is the existence of settlements outside of this network of forms that makes the contemporary pressures for urbanization so global, and so powerful. Only when we conceive of the global ecosystem and its patches and corridors does the differentiation of cities and unique urban identities begin to make sense.

ECOSYSTEMS: PUNCTUATED EQUILIBRIUM AND THE RISE AND FALL (AND RISE) OF CITIES

Ecosystem thinking focuses on process and dynamism, so one cannot simply say that these urban spaces are atemporal. They exist in specific places and at specific moments. Cities don't modernize, develop, and then rest on their laurels; they are in constant motion, traversing hospitable periods and hostile ones alike, but ever in motion. This motion comes in fits and starts, marking cyclical, nonlinear changes to which city populations and their physical forms must adapt.

Ecosystem science was turned upside down when scholars began to propose that natural ecosystems were not inherently stable; instead, natural environments underwent major changes and disturbances such as fires and invasive species that periodically transformed the basic arrangement of species and interactions found in those places.[26] This insight pointed out not only the obvious fact that places change over time, but that these changes can be quite sudden. Moreover, it implied that these changes might be understood in some systematic way, giving rise to the study of "punctuated equilibrium."

This aspect of the science of ecosystems allows us to respect our understanding of the obvious—that cities change over time, and often in very rapid and nonlinear ways, while at the same time providing conceptual space for us to define what they are in today's moment. Such a recognition leads to questions of why new people settle in cities, what kinds of changes do politics, economics, and society undergo in these new settlements, and how long do they last? Additionally, what are the kinds of forces that disrupt the stability of cities as they mature?

The advantage of an ecosystem approach is that it is a more sophisticated approach to understanding the relationship between stability and disruption in the spatial geography of human evolution. As forest ecosystems are periodically riven by wildfires, cities are periodically transformed by global forces beyond any kind of internal controls. These changes can, but do not always, represent progress from a human development standpoint, however. Unlike more normative definitions of change related to urbanization, such as development or modernization, the ecosystem approach is not blinded by unrealistic assumptions of social agency in the improvement and evolution of places. Stripped of these well intended, but ultimately obfuscating, distractions, the ecosystem approach of patches and corridors periodically shifting their equilibrium can provide a more insightful lens that is not just theoretically interesting and confirmed through observation but also suggestive for policy makers, planners, and others facing key decisions about the public future.

GLOBALIZATION IS URBANIZATION:
REVISITING THE GLOBAL CITY

One of the main points I make consistently in the ensuing chapters is that globalization *is* urbanization and urbanization constitutes globalization. Lewis Mumford has written that "[w]hat men (*sic*) cannot imagine as a vague, formless society, they can live through and experience as citizens in a city. Their unified plans and buildings become a symbol of their social relatedness; and when the physical environment itself becomes disordered and incoherent, the social functions that it harbors become more difficult to express."[27] While his focus was primarily on the built environment, I use Mumford's trope that one can only see (and live) the vague, amorphous global social relationships by living through the global ecosystem of patches, corridors, and difference to understand the new social (and political and economic) relationships known as "globalization."

If globalization is an economic, social, political, and cultural phenomenon, then it must have a physical form. In this book, I argue that this form is the city—in all its types, shapes, and locales. Only through a tour of the four types of cities illustrated in the following chapters can one actually visualize the abstraction of global relationships that so many have written about in recent years. Through my focus on a network of spaces, cities within a global ecosystem of cities, I hope that readers will be able to better visualize the ways in which residents of this "global urban ecosystem" are connected. The physical definition of "globalization" presented here is distinct in its focus on the micro spaces of global networks rather than on disciplinary themes—such as global culture, economy, or politics—allowing us to visualize the ways in which these important global forces of social life interact in city spaces. A focus on the material production of global environments can not only do justice to the complexities and diversities of human integration but also provide enough simplification and categorization to help us understand a phenomenon almost universally recognized as important.

Contemporary studies of globalization begin in the nonphysical world and have tended to focus on economic and cultural phenomena. Thomas Friedman famously declared the world "flat," within a neoliberal understanding of international trade and migration. Even Marxist

Saskia Sassen, in asserting that cities were the "command and control centers" of the "New International Division of Labor" illustrates global connectivity primarily through the economic relationships among individuals and businesses that happen to be in cities. Manfred Steger, in his thoughtful analysis of "globalism," has focused on other aspects of globalization such as ideology, and Jan Nederveen Pieterse has focused on the creation of a global "mélange" of culture through the movement of demographics across space.[28]

Perceptive as these arguments about globalization are, such understandings are no longer sufficient, as the globalization process has progressed unabated over the past two decades. It is now standard teaching that diaspora communities, global finance, and transnational corporations shape our everyday lives in very real, but often intangible, ways. They change particular individuals and businesses, but what has been their long-lasting imprint on societies? Are they anything more than ephemeral trends certain to fade away once the Internet is interrupted, political conflict limits migration, rising fuel costs limit global transportation, and global companies go out of business? My perspective on globalization is that its effects are not ephemeral; that it does not disappear once the pressures for global human integration abate. Rather, globalization as a framework for understanding human relationships becomes important precisely when the trend—ephemeral or not—has shaped long-standing structures, physical arrangements, and institutions irreversibly. It is for this reason that the rest of this book centers on the globalization of the city, of the urban human ecosystem. The globalization of the physical and social infrastructures of human society marks a point after which the term "globalization" takes on a staying power all its own, independent of political decisions, economic trends, and cultural change.

Steger's argument that the national state as the primary political form may be disintegrating in favor of something—as of yet undefined—can be illustrative.[29] In 1848, after the Western European nation-state became the primary negotiating framework among vibrant cultures and societies, the world began to reshape itself into nations, precisely bounding societies and geographies. Once beyond a critical threshold, this fundamental shift in human organization—largely forged out of city-states themselves—had tremendous staying power. No matter how poorly the Greek economy performs, for example, few challenge its premise of sovereignty; despite the breakup of the Soviet Union, the result is a collection of nation-state entities; and even where national boundaries are coterminous with urban boundaries, as is the case in Singapore, states seek representation among nations.

Nevertheless, globalization of the economy, culture, and the arts has begun to shape new boundaries of daily life, centered less on the boundaries of language, territory, and culture but more on the physical and social institutions of cultural urban life. These new boundaries of daily life—a kind of global urbanism—are recontouring human existence around cities. Philip McCann and Richard Florida among others have contextualized Freidman's claim about nations that the world is flat by accurately stating that relationships within nations have simultaneously become more "spiky," with new topographical contours of inequality being largely along urban/rural lines.[30] More concretely, the proliferation of "sister city" agreements and supporting international municipal agencies such as the Seattle Trade Development Alliance, and a nascent movement for "charter cities"[31] as semiautonomous partnerships between nations, for example, all indicate that cities are acting more and more like city-states, comfortable with international diplomacy, sidestepping their national governments, and connecting with complementary economic, social, cultural, and political entities for mutual benefit across vast oceans. While still in its infancy, the trend of urbanization described earlier represents a form of globalization that is changing the macro political context—a world in which metropolitan regions constitute the highest (and most powerful) form of political organization and the sites of most effective negotiations across political, economic, and cultural interests. Recognizing these shifts long before they become fully embodied can help us to prepare for a far more global and urban world.

The development of this kind of new political order requires a foundational set of assumptions that allow political constituencies to recognize one another and enter into negotiations. The Treaty of Westphalia began the process through which nation-states came to recognize political constituencies labeled "republics," "constitutional democracies," and "monarchies" as different forms of a shared set of assumptions and exemplars regarding territory, human constituencies, and decision-making hierarchies empowered to represent communities. As human society moves into dense settlements and clusters, these shared assumptions and exemplars of constituencies are also changing, and toward a more urban and agglomerated form. My concept of the global urban ecosystem allows such mutual intelligibility across global political constituencies; such mutual intelligibility is likely to shape the political future of global-scale negotiations.

Take the example used at the beginning of this chapter as a starting point for my concept of globalization. Subway travel between Bowling Green and downtown Brooklyn is remarkable not only for the stark contrasts of physical environments between its varied stops but also for the fact that a metropolitan transportation system *exists* in the first place. Think about it: the diversity of streets and neighborhoods made physically accessible to anyone in a metropolitan region through the simple purchase of a MetroCard shrinks space much in the same way that global air travel and container shipping have transformed accessibility around the planet. For the right price—a price that decreases steadily with new technology and economies of scale—any person can move out of their familiar space (figuratively) at the drop of a hat. However, were this ability to transport across space purely individualized, like some *Star Trek* transporter, trips to new places would be difficult indeed. Imagine being transported halfway around the world onto an island in the middle of the South Pacific. How about onto a Southern California freeway? How would we even begin to get our bearings and start to get to know our destination? We would want to be transported only to sites that we already knew, such as your grandmother's house or your college dormitory; our ability to experience new global places would be very limited if this were all we could do. Without some kind of mediating system to ease these transitions across distance, it is hard to imagine this kind of technology compressing space in a useful way; global connectivity without a local road map is useless. In many ways, globalization is the creation of a global urban *system* of patches and corridors, subway stops and lines.

Think about what a metropolitan transportation system is good at. Whether you enter the system from the outermost point on a New York commuter rail or bus network, or drop down into the subway in Times Square, once you are in the system, familiarity abounds. Physical structures and signs beckon from each corner at every stop, indicating transfers, waiting times, and ticket prices. Your seatmates give you confidence about where you are and where you are going; headed to the airport, you are more likely to follow a fellow traveler sporting a suitcase than one with a briefcase. The formal and informal cues that comprise the system not only efficiently allow us to overcome great distances in the metropolitan context but, more important, provide an infinite number of physical and social reference points for negotiating an unfamiliar space. It is the city—with its physical technologies, urban institutions, and even its problems—that allows individual humans to negotiate vast global physical spaces effectively. In this way, the urban form is the greatest technology driving globalization.

Understanding the complexity of Addis Ababa, I argue in this book, helps an Ethiopian intent on coming to the United States because—different as Addis and New York are—they share the same urban signs, institutions, and norms. Similarly, a Saigonese negotiating the United States will feel largely at home in Honolulu but like a fish out of water in rural Texas. The kinds of systems making intra-metropolitan accessibility convenient are diverse, with multitudes of transit authorities interacting with taxi fleets, "gypsy" cabs, and rail lines, just as the technologies and institutions for compressing global space run the gamut from the Internet to air flight to container shipping. It is the interoperability of these systems in formal and informal ways that comprises a global urban ecosystem central to understanding contemporary globalization and urbanization. It is these kinds of systems that constitute a mutually intelligible global urbanism.

Once these different urban spaces become familiar enough to be considered part of the same system, their differences take over. In *Who's Your City*,[32] popular urbanist Richard Florida specifies the self-segregating characteristics of American cities that increasingly attract residents of like backgrounds, ages, and aspirations. In his framework, San Francisco is the retirement city, Des Moines is best for price-conscious families, and San Diego is second only to the southern Connecticut metro area for gay or lesbian singles. Of course, this is not to say that San Francisco has no gay community and that people in San Diego don't retire, but it is to draw the distinction that cities have distinctive characteristics that allow mobile people to pick and choose where to nest based on the match between their personalities and that of their cities.

The literature on globalization and urbanization has similarly sorted cities into different identities, focusing on the "economies of agglomeration," "slum proliferation," and "Global Cities," almost as if they exist completely separate from one another. Scholarship in economic geography and urban economics has focused on the factors that make some cities dominant in the global economy. Allen Scott, Michael Storper, and AnnaLee Saxenian, for example, have focused on how the division of labor for higher-level industrial products has driven new economic agglomerations associated with new "technopoles" and centers of global economic development.[33] More recently, other economically oriented thinkers have championed the city as both the future of global economic development and the world's most important environmental technology,[34] as well as economically "sorted" centers of consumers.[35] While important explanations of how the largest megalopolises and most dynamic economies have come to be, such approaches usually ignore major categories of cities. In particular, other than the big centers of Mumbai and Shanghai, for example, cities of the Global South are often invisible from this vantage point. If economic growth and innovation were the only relevant factor of global urbanization, we would not see much urbanization in countries that will likely never play a major role in the global economy, such as Cambodia or Kenya, or even the existence of cities with minor economic roles to play, such as Portland, Oregon, or Honolulu.

Simultaneous with this focus on macroeconomic positioning, other analysts have focused on a range of cities in the Global South, but they have done so from a primarily Marxist or systems-theory stance in which global urbanization has led to dysfunction and social problems. Some suggest that migration and urbanization lead to insider/outsider dynamics that threaten to change spatial and, therefore, personal identities.[36] Others have drawn attention to the explosion of slums as either the physical manifestation of global inequality,[37] the sites of remarkable social and economic innovation,[38] or the crucibles of a global urban future.[39] While important efforts to document the slum areas of the urban Global South, such "doom and gloom" versions of global urbanization overly champion the "disadvantaged" urban at the expense of viewing urbanization as a dynamic between those slums, more privileged elements of that urban society, and the generally less privileged rural hinterlands.

Finally, the study of globalization and urbanization is full of what might best be seen as "case studies in urbanization." John Friedmann provides an excellent review of the particularities of how urbanization has transformed Chinese society,[40] Aprodicio Laquian provides a similarly comprehensive view of how urbanization has affected the particularities of Asian countries,[41] and Toyin Falola of the commonalities of urbanization in Africa.[42] In the same vein, countless studies of globalization and particular cities from Los Angeles,[43] Jakarta, and Dakar,[44] to Accra[45] comprise a large collection of unique case studies without theoretical or empirical connective tissue. While fascinating in their detail and complexity, such case studies are ultimately unsatisfying because they leave the reader with no framework sufficient to perceive truly "global" urbanization. Their focus on rich details comes at the expense of a more generalizable approach to global urbanization.

While it is incontrovertible that each city has its own identity, character, and narrative, it is also true that there are similarities of urban life that remain intact across cultures, oceans, and environments, mitigating each city's uniqueness. These commonalities found from New York to Seoul to Johannesburg set urban residents apart from their rural counterparts and mark a distinct urbanism relatively easily transferred from city to city. Negotiating Rio's commuter rail—for example—is likely easier for a Chicagoan than a Northeast Brazilian farmer, just as both the Mumbai slum dweller and a Parisian see the value of tenants' associations, while rural French farmers might lose patience with the ongoing prospect of community management meetings. Moreover, as natural hazards and climate change transform the kinds of environmental challenges facing planners, the difference between city residents and rural residents becomes even more stark. It is the practice of urbanism in these daily forms that connects city residents across oceans, nations, and cultures. When seen through the lens of global urbanism, the stark divisions between the Global North and South become less compelling.

Since the 1980s, scholars have been concerned with globalization and world cities,[46] and during the 1990s it seemed that one need understand the global cities that "commanded and controlled" the world economy.[47] Each strand of thought outlined a vertically differentiated literature and ultimately portrayed a, perhaps, overly dualistic world in which cities in the Global South are at a permanent disadvantage, or in which migrants from the South occupy permanently disadvantaged positions in the North. While useful when it was first formulated, the model seems a bit dated, as the quality of life in many cities in the

Global South has improved and—arguably—surpassed that of some in the Global North.

Rather than using these subfields of economic growth, inequality, or area studies to guide our understanding of cities in a way that usefully includes both what we have characterized increasingly inaccurately as the "Global South" and the "Global North," an alternative view is to apply a more vertically integrated framework across a wide range of city types. Seeing them all as part of a single global urban "ecosystem" in which each city occupies a mutually dependent ecological niche, performing different but related and intertwined functions, is the starting point for truly understanding contemporary globalization and urbanization.

John Rennie Short has attempted to better vertically integrate this stark dualism across Global North and South cities to match contemporary realities. However, without extensive discussion and elaboration, he ultimately proposes the integration more as a hypothesis than as a useful framework. Short's grouping of New York, Sioux Falls, and Havana certainly advances beyond the limitations of many studies of globalization and urbanization but simply identifies cursory characteristics rather than drawing out tangible, realistic, and future-oriented trends.[48] To do justice to this kind of "selection on the difference," one must dig into the details of diverse cities and identify broader global trends driving unlikely connections across them.

IDENTIFYING THE PITCH:
FRAMING GLOBAL URBANIZATION IN THIS BOOK

This chapter began with the question: why is global urbanization important? With over 50 percent of all humans living in urban ecosystems, understanding them will have tremendous consequence. As of 2004, 600 million[49] urban residents lived with no access to sanitation, and even as the Millennium Development Goal efforts suggest progress on the provision of clean water, many questions of urban water security remain. With 530 million European urban residents—72 percent of the total population, the European Union's 11 percent[50] unemployment hits cities hardest, and Japan and Korea's population declines are sure to transform those countries' cities most profoundly, as this very same phenomenon is currently transforming the physical shape of Detroit today.

It is these long-term problems that loom large in the twenty-first century, however, without adequate solutions on the horizon. In part, this is because urban planners, policy makers, and analysts have yet to ask the right questions—what I call "identifying the pitch." Any evolving problem has a life cycle and trajectory; likewise, every solution to that problem is time dependent. An analogy from American baseball can illustrate this problem of timing. Any successful batter facing a pitch must have lightning-quick reflexes, but more important, a quick and observant eye. For each batter, there is a moment at which he[51] is able to judge the nature of the pitch thrown at him and prepare his body to swing. Once his judgment is made, his whole body kicks into action with little chance of significant adjustments; in sports, this is the nature of commitment. The earlier his correct perception of the pitch, the more effective his swing. If his perception is incorrect or too late, even the most powerful and thunderous swing results in an embarrassing whiff.

Global urbanization is changing the physical and social characteristics of the world in which we live. Cities are complex entities requiring vast amounts of construction, management, and coordination if they are to be more than just chaotic jumbles of people, animals, and things stepping all over one another. The particulars of effectively managing global urbanization start with an accurate and early perception of twenty-first-century-city problems. In this way, urbanists with a keen eye for perceiving the global forces reshaping contemporary urbanization can position themselves well before it is too late.

Lewis Mumford, the patriarch of American urban planning, once wrote that the city is the essential organ for expressing humanity.[52] Following his universal and—to use a more-contemporary term—"global" metaphor provides unique insights into urban society and its unique characteristics. On the other hand, one of the points of examining any given city—at least for the declared "outsider"—is to make an effort to perceive where there are similarities and differences from the observer's counterpart. Unique, in-depth case studies of cities provide detailed ecologies of urban space, often paying homage to the uniqueness of a city, but in the process necessarily eschew efforts to generalize across urban contexts. Understanding the details common throughout Mumford's view of urbanization—the expression of humanity—is a major challenge in seeing contemporary globalization.

The intent of comparing the cases from Southeast Asia, Sub-Saharan Africa, the developed Pacific, and North America presented here is not to assert universal principles, but rather to explore and illustrate the kinds of urbanism that may be defining today's urban century. The mutually intelligible urbanisms characteristic across these geographical and cultural diversities reflect a global urban ecosystem in which the local ecologies of daily urban life are becoming more universal while, at the same time, maintaining enough of their differences to create an urban "edge"—the elusive quality of cities that makes them exciting, yet familiar. The intent is to find both commonalities across disparate cases—what Robinson has called "positive difference."[53] This unlikely comparison, therefore, does not argue for particular policy prescriptions on urbanization and globalization, but rather points out how planning and policy, scholarship and pedagogy, might make more coherent sense of the urban century.

In many ways, such an approach is anathema to contemporary trends in regional studies and planning that emphasize local knowledge, unique contextual factors, and bottom-up forms of development. This approach to planning in the twenty-first-century's rapidly urbanizing regions, however, is often undermined by both the central role that nonlocal actors (e.g., foreign direct investment, diasporas, climate change) play in driving or facilitating urbanization in developing countries, as well as the frequency of underdeveloped and "differently-developed" local planning education.

The limitations of nonlocal scholars, researchers, and teachers are well known, as language deficiencies and cultural/political naivete become immediately apparent as such scholars dip their toes into the very immediate challenge of urbanization in developing countries. On the other hand, nonlocal perspectives play an essential role in finding our commonalities, as Janet Abu-Lughod has done so well for North Africa and Europe.[54] As importantly, they indicate new handles for mutually productive policy development.

Understanding global urbanization is a bit like understanding how human society makes major changes seemingly at the drop of a hat. The precipitous drop in crime in U.S. cities over the 1990s, the fad for Hush Puppies shoes, and even the American Revolution were all events, as argued by Malcolm Gladwell in *The Tipping Point: How Little Things Can Make a Big Difference*, that only appear comprehensible when a meso-level of analysis is applied.[55] Gladwell classifies people into "connectors," "mavens," and "salesmen," each of whom interact with society and one another to achieve thresholds of social change that burst onto the scene, seemingly out of nowhere. His explanation of how these epidemics—both good and bad—emerge classifies ideal types, but only at a level that is deep enough to allow most of the other, sometimes more superficial characteristics (age, race, language, location) to vary. His extensive description of salesmen, for example, obviously ignores important aspects of their other individual characteristics but does help us understand how change suddenly ripples through society.

The question of making sense of global urbanization similarly defies simple metrics of classifications and must dig down deeper into individuals' and individual cities' characters, their "DNA." Such conceptual clarity about heuristic types can refine our thinking about cities, urbanization, and urbanity in a way that facilitates decision making, and sensitizes us to the range of possible changes that may spring suddenly out of nowhere and seem comprehensible only once they have happened and have changed society in ways both good and bad. I believe that a similar meso-level of analysis of cities in a global world will help us better understand a rapidly changing global society.

At the broadest scale required to understand the global urban ecosystem, however, one must engage in a calculated ignorance of local details to give shape to that essential organ of today's humanity: the city. Contemporary geopolitical economics has combined with unique local trends to shape and define what it means to be a global city. It is not simply the size and economic connections that define today's global cities, but, rather, their contributions to the *growth* of contemporary global connections define them. In this way, those cities where roughly equal proportions of global and local activities coexist are where the action is. Some might consider Mumbai a global city because its massive economy incorporates elements of the global economy, but the vast majority of residents exist in a local economy. On the other hand, even a small U.S. city such as Honolulu has a relatively large proportion of residents connected to a much broader Asia-Pacific and global economy. Which can more legitimately hoist the label of "global city"?

The global urban ecosystem defined through the case studies in this book identifies a set of emerging global trends shaping cities, before they overrun them. Chapter 2 briefly reviews the natural history of the city—a history whereby nature and human civilization have become increasingly and irrevocably intertwined, and which blurs the distinctions between the rural and the urban forms.

Considering the obvious connections between the urban and the rural, it is the surprising non-megacities where globalization can be seen most starkly, and where the global urban ecosystem is most clearly seen. While not yet among the top tier of cities in terms of population size, Saigon and Addis Ababa are dynamic centers within fast-growing nations: Vietnam, with a steadily high state of urban growth, and Ethiopia, with a high, but slightly decreasing one. The reasons for this ascent stretch, in equal proportions, to their rural hinterlands and to their points as regional and global nodes.

I call these cities "do your timers" because they are fundamentally about working hard and improving material lives. Like climbing a corporate ladder, establishing a scholarly niche for untenured faculty, or serving a prison sentence, doing this kind of time is unsustainable but necessary. And that is okay, because these cities are all about the future.

Honolulu, on the other hand, is a city strangely caught between a time when it was—and is—a center of vibrant global agricultural and tourist economies, and an uncertain future. The city now faces a challenge of pulling itself, kicking and screaming, into a twenty-first century in which abundant natural resources and beauty are insufficient as the basis for continued growth. I call this city one of "old-timers" championing those community elements anxious about discarding the past—and in particular an agrarian-, community-based past—and a deeply "local" world and worldview. If it successfully transcends the challenge of reconciling a globalizing economy with this deeply felt and valued local connection, Honolulu will be a city at the leading edge of experiments on how globalization can proceed without destroying the past and traditional local communities.

Finally, I describe New York City, the most urban of all. New York is much more than a work site to develop material wealth. It has also come to terms with the specifics of its historical identity, unself-consciously preserving stories about the (supposed) $24 sale of Manhattan by the Lenape people to the Dutch settlers,[56] the Harlem Renaissance, downtown Negro burial grounds, and the Triangle Shirtwaist Factory fire—all chapters of its historical identity. The city's history and identity, unlike the others presented here, is not directly contested, a quality that makes it both open to new reinterpretation and able to move forward in self-consciously creating new history. Instead, New York is a "for-all-timer" city of those who love it—like a spouse—through thick and thin, those committed to it whether it provides them jobs, quality of life, security, culture, even happiness, or none of the above. It is a city that comprises a force in and of itself, able—so far—to grow, decline, transform, and reinvent itself, for itself, over centuries.

The seventh and final chapter uses these disparate cases to revisit the global urban ecosystem connecting them all, identifying the "DNA" and building blocks that they share and that make them mutually intelligible and therefore globally connected. By framing global urbanization in these terms—"old-timer cities," "do-your-timer cities," and "for-all-timer cities"—I hope to describe a range of urban sub-identities that allow us to immediately see, and communicate to others, how our local contexts relate to a global network of shared challenges. It is ultimately this heuristic language that will allow us to identify challenges from a distance close enough to be definable, yet far off enough to be actionable.

My stylized naming of city types in this global urban ecosystem as "do your timers," "old timers," and "for all timers"—based on my qualitative and unsystematic observation and research—will never be confused with a "science of cities." At the same time, I do hope it will open up a substantive debate on urban development and on how cities share much more than they differ. One of the recent debates among urbanists, planners, and scientists has been about the significance of the city as an analytic construct. If each city is unique, then of what value is the term? Why not just talk about Boston, Rio, and Accra and jettison the use of a significant generalizable pretense. Certainly, there are urban-studies, planning, and politics disciplines, but mostly they assess and categorically analyze discrete disciplinary phenomena *within* cities, not across them. Even across Boston, Rio, and Accra, we can find similar issues of traffic engineering, administrative reform, and the arts; however, in such an analysis, the city is merely a setting for engineers, economists, and anthropologists to ply their skills, carving out sub-urban topics. What about the city as an organic, complex entity itself—more than just a transit system, a governing structure, or culture? With some cities and metropolitan regions reaching the size of twenty-thirty million inhabitants, surely the category is worthy of study as an independently functioning organism, as Mumford last did.

CHAPTER 2

URBAN HISTORIES: ARRIVING AT THE GLOBAL URBAN ECOSYSTEM

This trope of the city constituting a uniquely human environment characterized by an underlying urbanism—a human ecosystem—is the conceptual hook upon which the following chapters hang. In colloquial use over the past two decades, the abstract process of globalization has begun to more concretely dominate these environments. At this moment, with global urbanization comprising over 50 percent of humanity, one would not be overstepping bounds to say that we stand on the edge of an Anthropocene; we stand on an urban edge.

Calling this human ecosystem the "Anthropocene" invokes a global and planetary scope warranting a historical overview of globalization, nature, and the city. While many of us have become comfortable distinguishing the human-oriented sphere from the supposedly natural one, it is not clear what is "natural" and what isn't. Stone Age societies did not obsess about this analytic problem, but surely with every technological advance and repurposing of the natural resources around them, they built up a more complex social environment and blurred the line between nature and its opposite. Today, we would see such societies as marginal players in the functioning of their ecosystems; for them, Mother Nature usually won out. On the other hand, modern society has become accustomed to imposing its will on the same adversities faced by the ancients; most storm surges, earthquakes, volcanoes, and floods are easily managed through simple technologies and planning. Today, it is only the rare case of an extreme event that threatens to disrupt the everyday rhythms of human life. And even now, we are coming to the realization that the "natural" events—especially those associated with global climate change—are themselves largely driven by human behavior. How did humans assume the position of global ecosystem manager from that of bit player?

As we will see, the distinction between nature and the human environment is difficult to define, but largely has to do with the extent to which human processes dominate, for better or worse, other biological and physical forms on the planet. With this new global-urban-ecosystem approach, a brief history of humans' "nature" is in order.

A NATURAL HISTORY OF THE CITY

PREHISTORY: MAGNETS, PERFORMANCE, AND HOUSE PETS

Few urbanists have considered the universal forces driving urbanization and human settlements as deeply as Lewis Mumford. In 1961, Mumford wrote *The City in History: Its Origins, Its Transformations, and Its Prospects*, an attempt to understand the existence of the city in all its complexity and the diversity of its countless forms found around the globe. This one-thousand-page tome remains the definitive work on what cities are and why they exist. Mumford's thoughts provide three insights particularly important for understanding the contemporary city, as economic, cultural, and spatial globalization unfold: 1) the city was a meeting place before it was a container; 2) the city was a stage for performance and population control; and 3) the city was born of a desire to bring the ecosystem under human influence.

As Mumford tells it, the city began as a fixed place to which premodern societies were able to return periodically to meet both sacred and material needs. As mobile hunter-gatherer societies developed and strayed further from well-worn paths, their desire to pay respects to ancestors and past kin nagged at them. To fulfill this innate need to honor such community memories, mobile primitive societies required periodic visits back to places where important past events occurred, and the sites of death rituals where their forebears were buried, cremated, or otherwise ceremonially laid to rest. As Mumford insightfully argues, "In the earliest gathering about a grave or a painted symbol, a great stone or a sacred grove, one has the beginning of a succession of civic institutions that range from the temple to the astronomical observatory, from the theater to the university."[1]

Like a flag planted on virgin territory, such symbolic locations facilitated the material benefits associated with social gathering. These symbolic locations soon began to serve as meeting places for the living to exchange goods, ideas, and mating (later marriage) partners that served to improve their material conditions in a world of scarce resources. In this way, the city was a meeting place before a place of residence; as Mumford aptly argues, "The magnet comes before the container."[2] One can see this powerful magnetic force in effect today around the world, as 180,000 people move to cities globally each and every day, resulting most acutely in 60 million new urban residents in developing countries each year.[3] Importantly, these new residents are attracted to cities, regardless of the available housing stock, services, and employment opportunities. At root, they come to be part of a connection to social past and present, as well as to engage in the material and emotional transactions with new people that will improve their lives for the future.

As human settlements evolved with these simultaneously sacred and functional roles, they necessarily became places for performance— the place to perform rituals associated with death, courtship, and marriage, to perform advertising of new technologies and ideas, and to perform leadership. From a social perspective, the people found in these places served as willing and perhaps unwilling "captive" audiences for bachelors, businesspeople, and leaders to connect with potential constituents. More specifically, Mumford argues, as social organization increased during the fourth millennium BCE, and leaders of religion, politics, and other emerging social institutions achieved prominence, their worship and homage required increasingly prominent physical monuments to their power and significance, which also became enshrined in ever-expanding human settlements in the form of churches, palaces, and other structures denoting authority over increasingly complex societies. Over the generations, these religious and political actors presided over increasingly large audiences, which were found only in cities. Thus, the performance of religious, political, and other forms of leadership took advantage of this new technology known as "the city" and transformed it from an ephemeral site of periodic congregation into a long-term site for human residence and ongoing engagement between performers and audiences.[4]

With the rise of secularism and democracy, monuments to great leaders have changed in design, materials, and even functions, but the need to enshrine ideals and collective human aspirations into a concrete form remains. Today, the worldwide need to build the tallest office tower,[5] construct the most innovative and architecturally sophisticated stadium,[6] or shape the most environmentally and technologically sophisticated neighborhood[7] hints of the persistence of this human desire for cementing collective human aspiration into the concrete urban structure, whatever the cost.

Mumford's final observation is—perhaps—the most relevant to the contemporary global urban ecosystem. According to his description of global history, the domestication of animals was the first step toward dense urban living. He argues that the dog and the pig served as symbiotic partners enabling human settlement, as they scoured yards, streets, and fields for scraps of food like a proto–sanitation department, a situation that persisted even through the nineteenth century, when formal sanitation systems began to take root in places such as London and New York. Without such functions, humans would never have been able to tolerate the inevitable health and sanitation problems that come with denser living. Similarly, with the rise of agriculture and storage of grains in urban centers came the problem of rodents carrying disease and posing other health risks to humans, thereby necessitating the domestication of cats.[8]

In this interpretation of urbanization, Mumford's ideas suggest that the city represents an innate desire for humans to control their environment: to control their connection to the past and to their people, and even to control ecological relationships. Like movie producers, these proto-urbanists developed a cast of urban characters and sets playing mutually supportive roles that allowed humans to establish their fixed symbolic and economic gathering places and the monuments for leaders to perform for their constituents. This cast included humans, animals, structures, and all the spaces in between; a cast of characters comprising a new kind of ecosystem driven by human desires and intentions that seamlessly integrated humans with their partner animals and organisms as well as with the foundational bedrock of fixed structures. This integration could not simply fit precut pieces into a well-defined puzzle but required their gradual coevolution into a new kind of human ecosystem seen in modern cities.

The next major shift in human ecosystems came millennia later, when countless human actors began to see themselves as individuals with broad human agency as much as parts of localized collectivities.

FROM MANOR TO MARKET: THE ECOLOGY AND ECONOMY OF SOCIAL INTELLIGENCE

In *The Nature of Economies*, Jane Jacobs joins others who have pointed out that the links between economic and ecological life are inseparable.[9] For starters, both share the Greek root "eco," meaning "house" in its contemporary use. If "logy" means "knowledge" and "nomy" "management," then we can clearly understand the intertwining of understanding and managing the human "house"—a society existing with certain spatial boundaries that define humanity. Thus, the next step toward the global urban ecosystem is marked by a change in the way we think about managing the human house; a change in economic thinking.

In 1776, the much-quoted Adam Smith articulated that the baker selling bread to a customer is what makes society function effectively and provides for the material welfare of human society. Rather than through planning and collective action, it is the simple transaction between two individual parties with differing needs and productive capacities finding one another—and identifying their mutual interests—among the mass chaos of humanity that characterizes efficient and productive human interaction and that performs an important social task of meeting social needs. In his straightforward expansion on this basic concept, Charles Lindblom's *The Market System* details this basic observation in the contemporary globalized world of Starbucks supply chains and corporate outsourcing. For him, a market economy *is* society; it is the primary mechanism through which individuals and family units engage with one another.[10] This was not always the case; in Lindblom's telling, "markets" have always existed, but it is the development of an underlying system that allows markets to coordinate over vast spaces and cultural differences that allows for a quid pro quo—a set of universal assumptions guiding interaction—that operates at a global scale.

Smith's writings came as the political system of large English manors and medieval aristocratic society was coming to a close. An old quid pro quo of local royalty extracting labor and tribute from serfs and peasants based purely on social standing was coming to an end, giving way to a an era of different norms of behavior. As Lindblom describes it, today we share a basic assumption that labor and time have monetary value—a principle not often recognized during a period when princes and queens could extract labor from their people at will. This key quid pro quo of money—or shells, beads, and any form of abstract social value—as the medium for exchanging goods and services of value transformed human society and provided the "DNA" for globalization. Amartya Sen, in his foreword to the twentieth anniversary edition of Albert Hirschman's convincing explanation of capitalism in historical perspective, *The Passions and the Interests: Political Arguments for Capitalism before Its Triumph*, succinctly describes this shift in human thinking:

> The basic idea is one of compelling simplicity. To use an analogy (in a classic Hollywood form), consider a situation in which you are being chased by murderous bigots who passionately dislike something about you—the color of your skin, the look of your nose, the nature of your faith, or whatever. As they zero in on you, you throw some money around as you flee, and each of them gets down to the serious business of individually collecting the notes. As you escape, you may be impressed by your own good luck that the thugs have such benign self-interest, but the universalizing theorist would also note that this is only an example—a crude example—of the general phenomenon of violent passion being subdued by innocuous interest in acquiring wealth. The applause is for capitalism as seen by its pioneering defenders studied in this penetrating monograph.[11]

With the establishment of a universal currency, the ability of individuals to venture out and broaden their scope without the slow-moving and laborious task of diplomacy heretofore necessary for overcoming language, cultural, and class barriers freed individuals and small family units from their larger political organizations, to act universally. Thus, following Lindblom's emphasis that "economy *is* society," these individuals' expanded scope of economic activity expanded their social community. With this shift from manor to market, the number and scope of transactions among individuals boomed as the mitigating political structures were dismantled. In many ways, this shift was the birth of modern society, where collective human intelligence—everything from technological innovation, to issue-oriented activism to industrialization—profited from the exponential boom in human interaction, and transactions cumulatively led to "development." As a form of collective human progress, development implies a kind of transformation achievable only through the social embedding of changed thinking. In many ways, the shift from manor to market allowed human society to learn what ants had known for eons.

The science of "emergence"[12] seeks to understand how large numbers of individual actors in biological populations are able to achieve complex collective intelligence even when the capacities of any individual actor within the social organization are surprisingly simplistic. The substitution of population numbers for cognitive capacities of any individual actor in a given society, the theory goes, allows for collective intelligence to "emerge" from countless simple transactions and subsequent adaptations that, for example, lead ants to find hidden food sources across vast jungle landscapes. It is the same phenomenon that allows huge crowds of pedestrians to cross a New York rush-hour street in opposite directions with a minimal amount of jostling and without any kind of centralized a priori plan. It is this combination of individual transactions, learning, and mutual adjustment that created a kind of social ecology driving global human development.

As Jacobs has it, "learning economics from nature"[13] is best. Social development requires the complexity and diversity achievable only through the intensive interaction of very large numbers of humans. It is intensive and extensive social cooperation that leads to the innovations, institutions, and public infrastructures necessary for development; without it, we are constrained to a closed, manor-like society. Just as human beings develop by splitting cells and growing new functional

organs, human society splits and diversifies itself to create ever more complex organizations, technologies, and built environments of mutually dependent parts.

Jacobs, of course, is best known for her views on the city as an organic entity.[14] The density of people, institutions, politics, technology, and other aspects of human life present in cities drove her interest. Yes, while some technologies and innovations originate in dispersed human settlements, it was mostly in cities where the critical mass of transactions, adaptations, and diversifications could combine to create a kind of "secret sauce" for human development. In the end, the knowledge of the market and "emergence" explains how the interior dynamics inside the human "house" operate, and the city is the primary way in which it is managed.

The creative and innovative aspects of the city, however, cannot alone explain how we now find ourselves in a globally connected system rather than in numerous agglomerations coexisting in relative isolation. The next major shift in our journey to the global urban ecosystem came when the scope of that biology, both literally and figuratively, expanded well past the limitations of a medieval European world.

THE COLONIAL WORLD: A GLOBALIZING BIOLOGY

Environmental approaches to understanding urban issues often look for the "natural" environment in the city (e.g., urban agriculture, park space, air quality). While these are central policy and planning questions, ecological *science* provides a clearer window into understanding cities as more than merely a set of practical issues to address; rather, it provides a framework for understanding the changing nature of those places humans call "home."

In 1977 William McNeill wrote a book, called *Plagues and Peoples*, that transformed the way we think about historical globalization and how human involvement with other species has determined the shape of the contemporary world. He described a kind of European biological superpower in which human bodies acted like unwitting supersoldiers, carrying disease and plagues around the world through colonial and other exploratory ventures. Because of their inclination toward venturing out into new territories, McNeill argues, Europeans had a head start on gradually adapting to diseases and microbes not found in

Europe. It is—sadly—a known truth that this gradual adaptation had disastrous consequences for formerly isolated societies on islands from the West Indies to Hawai'i, and perhaps most notably on the North American continent, with the decimation of native populations.

McNeill's work was not alone in positing the central role of micro-human ecosystems in shaping contemporary social, political, and economic relationships. In *Ecological Imperialism: The Biological Expansion of Europe, 900–1900*, Alfred Crosby[15] explains that the biological adaptations and expansions of the physical European body served as more than just an unwitting carrier pigeon for dangerous microbes and parasites. Rather, he argues that settlers consciously brought with them animal species, biological cultures, and plants to make their new physical surroundings more like home. Like North America's formerly ubiquitous beaver, European colonists from New England to New Zealand were not content to simply carve out a space within a new natural ecosystem but, like the beaver, instead "improved" it to conform to their social needs. European settlers, for example, took great care to bring pigs, plants, and—yes—even flies to New Zealand in an effort to re-create the familiarity of farming life back in Europe. What they saw as crops, livestock, and pollinators back home were seen by locals as weeds, vermin, and pests.

More recently, Charles Mann argued that this process was not limited to European settlers in distant lands. An inward-looking nation of enthusiastic traders, China was very effective at closing its borders to people but much less effective at policing its porous borders regarding goods. Prior to the European presence, for example, China was colonized by North American foods such as maize and potatoes.[16] To be not only on the receiving end of colonization, Chinese cultural expansion into Southeast Asia, it is very likely, embodied not just a political and social conquest but also an ecological one in which a Chinese system of wet rice cultivation became the local norm and ultimately assumed prominence as an identifying regional—and "indigenous"—cultural characteristic.

Scholars of property and natural resources have long made the argument that where humans live, there is no pristine natural environment. Traditional healers and "medicine men" from the Central American and African jungles to the temperate forests of North America and Europe manage the plants, shrubs, and trees in their surroundings in ways that few of us would be able to visually perceive, making management decisions to improve the quality of their respective tribes' lives. To locals, small marks on trees, collections of species, and other purposefully arranged materials mark both ownership patterns and functional assets for community life. In this way, as legal scholar Carol Rose points out, we make small arrangements in our physical environment to mark our social, economic, and political relationships and communicate rights and investments to our peers.[17] Conventional history tells us that European adventurers to the New World found "noble savages" living in harmony with their natural environment, but recent evidence suggests otherwise. While vast tracts of wilderness greeted the European colonists, what they failed to perceive was that the decimation of native populations by European disease that served as the vanguard for human colonization had secondary impacts on the physical landscape. With disease riddling the human population of North America, the widespread and traditional Native American practice of clearing land with controlled burns stopped, allowing for the reforestation of massive parts of the continent.[18] Even the "pristine" New World—it turns out—was a human-managed environment.

If colonization expanded the scope of transacting individuals into a more globalized market system, it was the *in situ* intensification of transactions that marked the next shift in our march to the contemporary global urban ecosystem.

THE INDUSTRIALIZATION OF NATURE: SCALING UP THE CITY

So far, this natural history of the city has focused on the moment dispersed bands of mobile humans first began to mark and occupy settlements and to repurpose the natural fauna around them to manage the problems of settled life, the moment at which medieval society realized that universal systems of currencies allowed markets to connect over distances and social barriers, and the moment during which largely European mercantilist ambitions leaped across vast spaces and cultures/societies to connect biological and economic systems on a global scale. After colonialism in the Americas, the opportunities for scaling up human society by *extending* the market across space were largely expired, leaving the *intensification* of market transactions in places within that global system as the only pathway toward growth and development.

Colonial ventures into Africa and Asia had yet to unfold, but stronger political entities, less local susceptibility to disease, and challenging topographies made continued expansion a costly prospect indeed.

From the beginning of the Industrial Revolution forward, development was to come increasingly from industrialization of those sites within the global economy and biology and further complexification of the economy in dense places. Gone were the days in which overseas conquest and settlement could simply exploit greater amounts of natural resources and labor; the low-hanging fruit harvested through brutal force had been taken. In some ways, the late nineteenth century marked a return to the focus on the internal dynamics of place. If Mumford's city was a centrifugal force defining a gathering place before it became a vessel, the shift from manor to market and global colonization faced outward from the locality, creating powerful centripetal forces that brought large portions of the globe into a single system. From the industrial period on, gains to human development once again returned to the centrifugal forces of cities and their role in advancing human development.

Urbanization and industrialization pose two important connections to an understanding of the global urban ecosystem. First, the natural world has played a central role in the actual creation of cities: without the natural resources upon which industrial production boomed in the nineteenth century, most major urban centers would not exist. This is the "why" of industrial urbanization. Second, the scale of industrialization and urbanization at this time created ecological problems way beyond anything seen before, requiring the creation of urban infrastructures and controls for efficient and tolerable functioning of the economy and societies of the growing cities and, therefore, nations of the time. This is the "how" of industrial urbanization, without which cities would have naturally collapsed under their own weight.

Why do cities exist where they do? The ancient cities of Europe and Asia are not particularly good illustrations of why contemporary cities exist where they do. Many are preindustrial political centers that operated primarily for the purposes of defense and political control. Others, such as those located on major transportation routes and ports, however, belie an economic rationale. The early industrialization of manufacturing processes was largely based on the raw materials found in nature, and early economic geographers often predicted the location of cities as those places midway between raw materials and markets.[19] Such economic rationales for the site of a city address the "why cities exist" question.

No one more masterfully illustrates this link between country, city, and location than does historian William Cronon in his masterpiece *Nature's Metropolis: Chicago and the Great West*.[20] Trying to understand why a struggling Chicago won out over an, at the time, better-positioned regional competitor such as St. Louis, and how it has become so large, Cronon ventures out into descriptions of the grain, lumber, and meat industries, and the industrialization and modernization of the Midwest's agrarian economy.

Beginning with extensive historical overviews of how the standardized railway system and improvements in navigation along the Mississippi River connected the natural hinterlands of the Great Lakes region to the commercial centers of the Northeast, Cronon quickly documents how this increased continental connectivity created powerful incentives for Chicago's boosters and capitalists to innovate greater efficiencies in how the natural forest, agricultural, and livestock resources of the Midwest could be controlled and sold to the large consumer markets on the country's Eastern Seaboard. To understand why Chicago won out over its regional competitors, according to Cronon, one must understand the importance of standardized packaging at the farm according to grain quality, the ability to "store the winter" (i.e., refrigeration) so that butchered meat could be shipped across vast distances without spoiling, and the demands placed on the forests to meet the needs of a fast-growing urban construction market in Chicago and the East.

His description of how midwesterners, centered in Chicago, controlled nature flows seamlessly into his description of the origins of the industrial city. For him, Chicago was the site for concentrating the Midwest's vast agrarian resources into a single and efficient marketplace, which required vast stockyards, grain elevators, and eventually, a complex agricultural-commodities exchange called the "Chicago Butter and Egg Board," where investors and traders could purchase standardized amounts of commodities in bulk based on continental—and eventually global—supply and demand. In time, these physical and organizational architectures of Chicago became the institutions for heavy manufacturing and the Chicago Mercantile Exchange. For Cronon, the midwestern natural environment was standardized and prepackaged on the farm, shipped efficiently to Chicago, and drove a complex, market-based social and economic organization that attracted vast numbers of people and firms to the city. Moreover, the city still retained the descendants of these urban organizational structures long after the region's forests were depleted and transportation systems allowed for more direct links between midwestern farms and their markets.

From a different discipline, but a similar standpoint, Nobel Prize–winning economist Douglass North sums up the theory behind Cronon's deep historical description: North America and other regions that have come of age during a period of raw capitalist exploitation of resources grow their regions based on the types of products they produce and export—either overseas or to other regions. "The early town centers were located not only so as to service the agricultural stratum, but so as to implement the export of the region's staples. The prosperity of the region depended on its success in competing with other areas producing the same staple exports."[21] In a market economy, the city is the springboard for locals to compete with other metropolitan regions as they seek to sell their goods on ever-increasing spatial scales. Back then, agricultural commodities were some of the most profitable; today, automobiles, silicon chips, and complex services have each subsequently repurposed the urban infrastructure as an updated platform for competing in larger, increasingly global markets.

If industrialization and the scaling up of the market economy into mass production capitalism drove urban growth, what enabled these cities to sustain themselves as places to live? Nineteenth-century descriptions of Chicago, New York, London, and other growing industrial centers abound with descriptions of putrid smells from unregulated factories and human waste, slimy streets covered in mud and horse dung, epic traffic jams, and unplanned, unserviced housing susceptible to fires and collapse. The resulting landscape of daily urban dangers and inconveniences would have undermined the growth of the industrial city had it not been for the mass production of urban services and the governments and organizations to provide them. Industrialization required the creation of an urban infrastructural backbone to ensure a minimal efficiency and security from disease and other hazards of dense living. Dogs and pigs were no longer sufficient.

Perhaps most famously, the urban cholera epidemics of the mid-1800s illustrate how a new urban ecology required to control natural resources and the built environment transformed the daily lives of urban residents. In its popular revisiting of the story of London physician John Snow and the Broad Street Pump, Steven Johnson's *The Ghost Map: The Story of London's Most Terrifying Epidemic—and How It Changed Science, Cities, and the Modern World* documents the origins of the first mass-produced urban service: water supply.[22] The story of Snow's discovery of the origins of biological epidemics and how it led to the germ theory of disease is well known; less well known is the implications his work—in cooperation with a local pastor named Henry Whitehead—had on how cities manage the elevated risk posed by dense living. With human proximity hundreds, if not thousands, of times greater in the industrial cities of Europe and North America than in their rural counterparts, it is inevitable that the risk of epidemics is comparably elevated. In the 1800s, residents still drew water for daily use from ground pumps, and threw their waste and excreta in pits oftentimes in the basements of their multistory buildings. Over time, this kind of unorganized water source and waste disposal system allowed deadly pathogens such as cholera an easy pathway from an infected individual into a healthy one, leading to over fifty-five thousand deaths in London in 1832, for example. With Snow and Whitehead's discovery of water's and sanitation's role in the cholera epidemic, it became crystal clear that the density associated with mass urbanization required mass provision of basic services to meet even elementary human safety benchmarks. For this reason, after the cholera epidemics, London and other cities invested in massive public works projects to clean and transport water and sewage over great distances to maintain an adequate separation of humans and pathogens, thereby allowing for the continued functioning of the growing urban economies.

While water and sanitation were the most dangerous "externalities" of the growing urban industrial economy, traffic, fire, and other aspects of daily urban life argued for further comprehensive reforms in the mass production of a physical environment that would minimize human risk and allow for the functioning of an economic system depending more and more on the concentration of natural and other resources in metropolitan areas.

These challenges were the focus of urban reformers and utopians who eventually gave rise to the field of urban planning. In *Urban Utopias in the Twentieth Century*, Robert Fishman reviews the flourishing of innovative ideas to rectify these dangers of urbanization with the comprehensive design of an urban environment.[23] From Ebenezer Howard's Garden Cities in which green areas, factories, and public services were all planned out prior to development, to Frank Lloyd Wright's designs for de-urbanization of the North American landscape based on a Jeffersonian ideal of the gentleman farmer, to Le Corbusier's "Contemporary City" in which unorganized and dangerous urban slums would be destroyed in favor of vertically dense high-rises with modern services, ample natural light, and open green spaces, the urban-utopian ideals fell upon the deaf ears of financiers and policy makers unable to completely plan the urban ecosystem. Where greater governmental control was the norm, as was the case in many European cities, the ideas of Baron Haussmann, similar in their innovative efforts to plan the urban ecosystem, gained greater relevance, transforming the built and social environments of cities such as Paris and Barcelona in the mid-nineteenth century.

A walk along the boulevards of Paris, a tour of the London water supply and sewer system, or a tour of Chicago's Mercantile Exchange will illustrate the tight connection between capitalism, industrialization, and urbanization. With vast parts of the agrarian world developing under the rules of a market- and export-driven economy, cities became powerful local ecosystems of new economies and technologies; as they grew beyond "natural"—that is, unmanaged—sustainability, these local ecosystems required ever-increasing levels of human design and management. The natural and physical topography needed ever-greater human direction and attention.

URBAN SEDIMENTATION:
THE LAYERED AND REPURPOSED CITY

The age of rapid industrialization and urbanization of North and South America is largely over, with major cities established and deindustrializing. Contemporary urbanization is a process mostly relevant to agrarian countries—mostly in Asia and Africa—currently undergoing an urban transition. Whether they follow a similar trajectory as those in the Americas is yet to be known and occupies the attention of multitudes of development economists and planners as we progress into the urban century.

However, what happens to cities once they pass their manufacturing heyday? Do they disappear as rapidly as they arise? Anyone familiar with construction will know that this is not the case. Both construction and demolition are costly, but the former is motivated by the prospects of a future of productive and profitable use, while the latter is followed by precious few opportunities to recoup costs. This basic fact is the challenge of many contemporary cities that are downsizing after decades of building a physical environment targeted for a particular kind of economy and society that has moved on.

According to the U.S. Census Bureau—and reported popularly by CNN and other popular media—between 2000 and 2010, the city of Detroit lost roughly 25 percent of its population. About 240,000 residents picked up and left or died off without being replaced during the course of the decade—needless to say, they didn't bring their houses with them. Run-down and abandoned housing is the stereotypical image of the former Motor City, which once placed the American economy on the global map with its automobile industry as well as the cultural flourishing of the Motown generation that defined a landmark cultural moment for Americans. The story of "deindustrialization" as articulated so well by Barry Bluestone and Bennett Harrison[24] hit manufacturing cities across the United States and other industrial countries hard. Left in its wake was an overbuilt urban ecosystem with far too many rail yards, factories, and houses for the level of economic activity held within their boundaries by the late 1980s. Likewise, the theaters, parks, and restaurants that serviced these cities fell into disuse as productive activity shifted out of the city due to the rise of outsourcing, technological change in production, and changes in transportation infrastructure. This macroeconomic shift had devastating consequences for people and places,[25] but some cities emerged from the crisis, having made a shift from the manufacturing city to the consumption city.

Like Detroit, the North Rhine-Westphalia region of Germany had seen explosive industrial growth during the nineteenth century that eventually declined in the mid-twentieth century. Facing a markedly depressed regional economy and a rusting industrial built environment, public and private entities developed a strategy for repurposing the industrial urban infrastructure to adapt to a growing tourism market. Their development plans provided a model often repeated, and even more attempted, by cities around the industrialized world to transform a productive city into one for consumption.

Through innovative financing mechanisms and design, the region's Emscher Landscape Park took a long-term view by regenerating coalfields and stockpiles into a network of regional open spaces for bikers, picnickers, and other recreational users. The current park incorporates a variety of design elements: a water park based on the ecological regeneration of the old Emscher Canal transport system; promenades and parks along railway lines that help connect the park with adjoining cities; gardens that both document industrial history and serve as open parks; and preservation of the steelworks as an active museum of the smelting process and technical history of the blast steel furnace.

Possibly the most innovative conversion project is the city of Oberhausen's Gasometer. Built in 1928 to store the gaseous by-products of iron ore processing, the round structure is 360 feet high by 223 feet in diameter, and currently is used as an exhibition hall and theater, hosting astronomy educational exhibits and world-renowned artists. Through adaptive reuse, one of the largest industrial tank structures in the world has become a luxurious cultural icon for the region, attracting tourists from across the region. It is perhaps the most visible and stark change in use of the built environment to adapt to shifting economic realities.

This layering of new uses on top of outdated infrastructures is a kind of social and historical sedimentation process inherent to the urban ecological environment. Every city is the social equivalent of a geologic record of what its national, regional, and global economy was doing during a certain time. Such deposits have often defined the most recent shift on our road to the global urban ecosystem. With the rise of postindustrial cities from the ashes of deindustrialization, old factories had to find new uses. A walk through New York's Tribeca neighborhood, Los Angeles' downtown, or Honolulu's Chinatown shows just how central the adaptive reuse of industrial urban structures have been for the revitalization of these metropolitan economies. Factory workshops have been converted to lofts for housing young professionals and artists, theaters for regional consumers of the arts, and restaurants for the growing "foodie" revolution. In due time, these converted uses will be converted again into structures and designs that serve new economic needs.

ON THE EDGE OF A GLOBAL URBAN ECOLOGY

While few would argue that forest management is the equivalent to building Times Square, the notion that human agency and management is part and parcel of "natural" ecosystems has gained recognition over the past twenty years. If this is true, then the big-city mayor lies on the other end of the spectrum from the Central American forest managers; city sanitation departments are inheritors of dogs, pigs, and cats; and supersized shopping centers are the trading posts for natural resources on a global scale. While they differ in target markets and prices, Safeway, Whole Foods, and Pathmark all encapsulate the globe, even in the poorest of neighborhoods. Freezers will hold piles of frozen *basa* filets from Vietnam, and cans of macadamia nuts from Australia, the United States, South Africa, or Guatemala perch hopefully on shelves near the checkout of even the most "local" grocery store in any North American city. Increasingly, an equally wide array of products—Nike sneakers, Italian canned tomatoes, and Chinese dishware—is to be found in foreign-oriented mini-marts of very poor cities in Africa and Asia as well. Today, the globe is really in the city, and the city—through the global urban ecosystem—defines the globe; of course, many of these products exist in rural areas as well, but the scale and diversity pale in comparison to their urban counterparts.

For thousands of years, forests, mountain valleys, and savannahs were the physical environments that humans called home; they were driven by their respective naturally occurring ecosystems and, to the extent possible, managed by people to meet their needs and mitigate risks. Today, these ecosystems *do* exist, but are largely devoid of the vast majority of humanity. Today, people live in physical environments defined by the imprint of human societies and history. Some live in agrarian ecosystems defined by agriculture, others live in ecosystems defined by industry, and yet others live in ecosystems defined by the products they consume. In each case, though, we live in an ecosystem highly structured and managed by human agency. With the global majority of humans now living in cities, the physical environment and ecosystem inherent to the city is the primary ecosystem representing human dominance of the natural world, and this ecosystem is surrounded by vast tracts of human-managed environments relatively devoid of people but in service to the needs of the majority of society, which is increasingly found in cities.

The environment has changed from one in which humans make purposeful and small changes to a physical environment where animals, plants, and natural hazards dominate the ecosystem, to one in which human behavior dominates the system. Humans drive large landscape-level dynamics such as deforestation, climate change, and even other species' survival, as the tiger, the panda, and bees have come to be primarily managed through human agency. Within cities, we ever re-create natural environments, such as parks and waterfronts, so as not to completely divorce ourselves from the more organic elements of our contemporary ecosystem, but these are just small elements of a much more complex human-structured environment. This approach to urbanization is not so far from early ecosystem scientists who described the importance of both patches and corridors linking microscale environments across landscapes.[26] The important difference, however, is that their view saw humans making only minor—if any— adjustments to a functioning natural system. Contemporary globalization, however, is much more akin to an urban ecosystem of patches and corridors where human bodies, materials, and structures transform the ecological environment around them.

To truly understand the global urban ecosystem, one must understand this natural history of the city that takes human interactions as its core. In prehistory, nomadic tribes periodically gathered together for social purposes and brought nature into these proto-settlements to manage the problems inherent in denser living. Growth of the market economy in the eighteenth century brought scale-order change to human intelligence by promoting openly oriented interactions and transactions among widely ranging people and institutions, which led to diversification of and complexification of the societies found in cities and allowed for great leaps in social intelligence and innovation. During the Industrial Age of the nineteenth century, mass production and standardization of goods for export brought natural resources and raw materials into cities, vastly expanding their size and economic activity. Of course, the externalities of such dense living and production required the mass production of urban services to maintain minimal standards. In the penultimate chapter of this history, outsourcing, technological change, and an increasingly knowledge-based economy led to deindustrialization of the industrial city and industrialization of agrarian regions in the developing world. The urban layering of social and historical sediments on the enduring built environment of postindustrial cities gave birth to a new kind of consumer city in which amenities assumed an importance equal to production. Of course, these postindustrial cities coexist globally with industrial ones and make up a planetary system of cities and urbanity; and the global urban ecosystem is the backbone from which a coming Anthropocene will eventually grow.

The following chapters flesh out this global urban ecosystem by describing how it plays out under four very different urban contexts. Each provides some historical context followed by a detailed description of the various local communities that incorporate and define distinct forms of the urbanism that connects the locality to the globe. Three components are central to this urbanism and deserve further elaboration before delving into the particulars of the case studies: mobility, development, and experience.

It is well known that telecommunications advances such as the World Wide Web, videoconferencing, and e-mail have enabled global-scale communication at virtually no cost. Further, containerized shipping, express mail services, and long-haul transportation have enabled goods and service exchange on a global scale. The simple existence of these technologies, however, does not provide any explanation of why people have taken such advantage of them and brought them to their current scale of affordability. They are technologies that *allow for* the global urban ecosystem, but do not *require* it.

Certainly, it is not easier to traverse vast distances to secure simple goods or services than to secure the same ones at home, all other factors being equal. One simple motivation requiring the use of these new global transportation and communications technologies is simple economics. Cheaper shoes made in China, after accounting for transportation costs, are worth buying in Paris, for example; and better quality education in the United States is worth paying for if you live in Zimbabwe. This explanation of globalization is about development focused on securing a better material life in which revenues are maximized and expenditures minimized. This drive to globalize and urbanize is fairly straightforward, following a general logic of supply and demand for basic needs. But why do Thai restaurants exist in New York? Why do people travel halfway around the world to take a week off from work? Simple economics of need cannot explain these choices: green curry is usually not cheaper than a hamburger, and most localities have some-place to relax nearby.

The global urban ecosystem is characterized by not only the ongoing need to improve human material life but also a drive to develop human intelligence; to develop based on diversification and complexification, articulated so succinctly by Jane Jacobs in her celebration of the city as a form for human living. Most accept that producers are constantly at-tempting to diversify their offerings if they are likely to profit from do-ing so. Few recognize the deep need for consumers to diversify as well. Some have begun to call this phenomenon the "experience economy," in which contemporary consumers attempt to collect a vast array of diverse experiences ranging from rock climbing for the first time to eating an unfamiliar cuisine. Through such diverse experiences, con-sumers educate themselves, diversify their perspectives, and satisfy in-herent urges for development and self-improvement of a less-economic type. But this kind of individual development is limited in scope when compared to the broader social development inherent in globalization and the turning of the consumer's desires outward beyond the locality.

Nonlocal consumption creates new and unfamiliar transactions of exactly the kind described earlier as the ecology of intelligence—a kind of complexification of society based on new transactions, relationships, and conflicts. Such complexification is the source of innovation and social development on a global scale. And this is the crux of the global urban ecosystem: if we believe that globalization and technologies al-low us to operate on a daily basis at the global level, and we believe that both individual and social innovation happens with diversification of human transactions and experiences, then cities where such diverse transactions can occur are the future of a global humanity ever on the lookout for innovation in technology, society, and culture.

In a simple definition, the global urban ecosystem approach sees a globally connected world in which both consumption and produc-tion operate according to the search for new markets and experiences. But it is not a search through a completely unfamiliar terrain. Rather, it is an outward search facilitated by a quid pro quo of global urban-ity that underlies the very distinct local cultures to be found around the planet. Without the common markers of urbanism, the search would end frustratingly in miscommunication, insurmountable differ-ences, and a retreat back into locality and autarky. The global urban ecosystem allows us to continually experience the "edge" that is often used to describe urban life. An "edgy" neighborhood presents just enough difference to be exciting, but at the same time, enough familiarity to be comfortable. It is an "edge" we experience halfway around the world, but we can also experience it right at home, if we live in a city within this global ecosystem.

The following chapters elaborate on what this evolving world actually looks like, why a city's size is not an accurate marker of globalization, and how the ecology of the urban built environment is intimately tied up with the ecologies of experience, innovation, and social intelligence.

CHAPTER 3

SAIGON'S "DO-YOUR-TIMERS": RURAL TRANSFORMATION AND THE URBAN TRANSITION IN SAIGON

The Vietnamese term *"nha que"* voices a tension haunting today's Vietnam. Roughly meaning "home back in the village," it is often a derogatory term used to describe residents generally living in cities who still follow rural habits. These are the people who squat on toilet seats and cook on open fires inside the house; they live in cities, yet their rural habits and practices have not yet transformed into an urban culture.

In 2007, I participated at a symposium of local leaders and architects in Saigon organized by the Ho Chi Minh City branch of the Institute for Economic Research on the urbanization and development of Ho Chi Minh City. After giving an innocuous policy analysis of water supplies and periurban development, I nestled in for an interesting talk on urban design and housing by a prominent architect advising the Ho Chi Minh City People's Committee on how to develop the city. After some introductory generalities, the speaker went on to explain the difficulties presented by narrow residential lanes for the provision of important urban services such as transportation as well as emergency response functions such as fire and ambulance. These reasonable design limitations, he continued, formed the rationale for a multiyear strategy to convert all of the city's traditional narrow lanes into modern boulevards with high-rise residential towers. Prominent urbanist John Friedmann, who also happened to be in the room during the presentation, piped in with the innocent question: "About what percentage of the city's residents live along these kinds of lanes?" The architect replied "about 75 percent." The room silenced momentarily as the visitors absorbed the scale and scope of what was being proposed. Like the utopians of their time, this architect could envision a perfectly functioning physical and social environment planned and developed—at whatever cost—for a city of more than six million. This kind of determined view of the future and growth characterizes many of the city builders in history—from Robert Moses to William Mulholland—that have laid the concrete foundations for a global urbanism.

Saigon is a city on the move, and for good reason. Vietnam's national GDP growth topped 7 percent between 2002 and 2008,[1] and currently is positioned behind only China in the sustained rapidity of its economic rise. With roughly 20 percent of this GDP generated from Saigon and its surrounding metropolitan region—home to over 1.12 million trained workers and three hundred thousand scientific and technical professionals, 35 percent of foreign direct investment projects, and 28 percent of the country's industrial output[2]—it is no wonder that displacing the roughly five million people living on traditional lanes and relocating them to high-rise towers seems an eminently reasonable proposition. Saigon is on the move, and today's physical form will look quaintly obsolete within several years, according to local planners. It is a city where stability is sacrificed on the altar of economic growth and physical improvements and adaptations.

Fortunately, five years after the proposal, Saigon's intricate system of lanes and low-rise housing remains as vibrant as ever, continually pointing out to government planners that the life of the city cannot be suppressed or guided in ways discontinuous with its past. This tension between a relentless development agenda and an irrepressible local history characterizes the kind of urbanity defining the global urban ecosystem: an edginess of unresolved questions about the future. The story of Saigon illustrates the dynamism and excitement palpable in the city's air and how this excitement bumps up against nha que and a largely agrarian past. This city, the organ expressing Vietnam's "humanity," will—no doubt—be rebuilt along more-modern design principles, whether by local planners or, more likely, by the millions of daily transactions that are newly being conducted by its residents. As Saigon does so, it cements its position as Vietnam's primary node to the global economy and as the country's niche in the global urban ecosystem.

The story of Saigon is the story of conflict, agricultural intensification, and national policy reform. At the conclusion of the war with the United States and the reunification of the country in 1975, the newly unified Socialist Republic of Vietnam embarked on a major effort to increase production in the Mekong Delta and to take advantage of the modern infrastructure present in what was renamed "Ho Chi Minh City." The renaming of the city coincided with its reconstitution as the national economic center, freed of national political responsibilities of a newly unified Vietnam intent on rebuilding its society through rapid economic development and material improvements for a citizenry having suffered over thirty years of continuous war.

Like nineteenth-century Chicago, the city cannot be divorced from its hinterlands. The region surrounding Saigon became a global agricultural commodities producer in key staples such as rice, fish, and shrimp in 2000, with major bilateral agreements promoting trade. The cultivation of export markets for higher-end agricultural products and manufactured goods transformed Vietnam into a global source of quality, cheap products centered around Saigon's capacity for agricultural export. This exporting led to major demographic changes that might best be seen as an "urban transition" coupled with an agrarian transformation, which underlie the city's contemporary social, economic, and physical fabric.

Saigon's urbanization process is a "textbook case" of rural transformation and "urban-ward" migration that development economists hope for and prescribe through policy and planning recommendations but rarely observe in its pure form. The country's transition to a market economy with all of its quid pro quo, the mechanization of agriculture that released young laborers from farm employment, and a global export market for cheaply manufactured goods such as shoes and polar fleece jackets all drew rural residents and natives of smaller towns toward the city for higher paying jobs and the promise of advancing their, and their children's, economic and educational opportunities for the future.

These initial economic factors, however, have diverged from historical precedent because they cannot explain the extent to which the city has drawn in adventurers from all corners of the world, even when the pathways to employment and the economic gains are much less clear. Saigon is driven by the agricultural workers from the Mekong Delta seeking work in the booming manufacturing trades, professional managers relocating to the city to provide management services to local branches of global corporations, Hanoi professionals seeking new economic opportunities in the booming city of the South, Cambodian migrants to the city struggling to find a place in a new-language and cultural environment free of the political chaos of Phnom Penh, African journeymen carving out new markets, and overseas Vietnamese following their hearts but justifying their choices with arguments about their pocketbooks. This surprising diversity suggests that the urbanism of everyday life in Saigon is much more than farmers becoming factory workers.

Whatever the motivations for moving to Saigon, however, the growth of the city embodies social trends that have made the city grow in a way that identifies it as an "experience" more than anything else. The experience is something to be consumed, "done," and memorialized in stories, essays, and tall tales for residents who come from across the globe. For both local and global migrants, Saigon is truly a "do-your-timer" city: whatever you come for, it is unlikely to last in its current form. The local urban fabric in which these residents engage is one expression of the global urban ecosystem.

Beginning in the early 1990s, when national and regional experiments in land collectivization were abandoned,[3] migrants were attracted to jobs in the garment and textile factories popping up around Saigon. The number of former agricultural workers from the Mekong Delta seeking work in the booming manufacturing trades and making the short move to Saigon accelerated in 2000, when Vietnam negotiated a trade agreement with the United States, thereby opening up a vast consumer market for Vietnamese consumer goods and agricultural products and greater demand for factory labor. In that same year, National Assembly Law No. 60-2005-QH11 legalized nonagricultural, and predominantly urban, enterprises and invigorated a nascent, largely underground private-sector urban economy, leading to over a million new jobs in its first three years.[4] While most of these migrants entered the factories and started new businesses, a number of them turned toward the illicit services trades that included "haircut," "massage," and other quasi-illegal services for new urban consumers.

On top of this nationally sourced and lower-skilled workforce, cohorts of Vietnamese managers and professionals, diaspora returnees, and entrepreneurs from Atlanta to Africa realized the potential opportunities in Saigon and upped stakes to try their luck. This constellation of actors that evolved during the first decade of the twenty-first century is vertically integrated, ranging from the economically struggling Cambodian migrant to the hardworking Vietnamese factory hand to the professionals from Hanoi, Korea, and France—an integration that has made Saigon an exciting place for entrepreneurial and adventurous young people from around the world. Graduate students and well-educated former corporate professionals striking out on their own, as well as others hoping to cash in on being a "first mover" in Vietnam, began to arrive from North America, Europe, and Australia in the 1990s. One of the leading edges of this class of adventurer-students and entrepreneurs was the Vietnamese diaspora, who—by the mid-2000s—had become not only economically comfortable in their adopted countries but also confident that the personal risk of political imprisonment in Vietnam was largely a thing of the past.

How did an agricultural backwater become such a dynamic city? In retrospect, it should not be surprising. For decades, consumers from Los Angeles to Lagos have—when they stopped to ask—learned that basic food items are global. Jasmine rice from Thailand, New Zealand lamb, and Mexican mangos are packed together with Ethiopian coffee on any shipping container or transcontinental flight connecting the world. These products are part of what I have come to call the "Second Green Revolution."

THE SECOND GREEN REVOLUTION: GLOBAL TRADE AND AGRO-INDUSTRIALIZATION

One major Heckscher–Ohlin (H-O) model factor endowment complementarity unfolding on a global scale can be seen on any dinner table.

Communities in agrarian regions of the world currently grapple with a number of interrelated processes related to global trade integration, privatization, changing consumer preferences, and food security. Underway is a socio-environmental transformation of these regions, such as Southeast Asia and Sub-Saharan Africa to some degree, that dominate traditional agrarian areas, and this change marks societies undergoing a rapid shift from largely agrarian to predominantly urban societies, economies, cultures, and physical spaces. This transformation can be seen as a kind of "Second Green Revolution" that has evolved from agricultural production for national food security to industrial commodity in a global marketplace. It has pushed many of the countries of Southeast Asia, in particular, to the forefront of a global food processing industry.

In the 1980s, Southeast Asia was busy cultivating an infrastructure to become a production center for Asia and other parts of the world. In the 1970s, Africa and Southeast Asia were peers in terms of standards of living and position within the global economy. By the time the Vietnam War ended in 1975 and local Communist insurgencies had either succeeded—as in the cases of Vietnam, Cambodia, and Laos—or been quelled by national governments—in Thailand, Indonesia, and Malaysia—Communist as well as non-Communist nations of Southeast Asia were positioned to take advantage of the growing interconnection of global trade. First Malaysia in the mid-1980s, followed by Indonesia and Thailand in the early 1990s, came to be known as attractive sites for foreign direct investment and exports. By 2000, the region's Socialist and former-Socialist countries fell into line as Vietnam, Cambodia, and Laos made significant moves toward harnessing their economies to secure hard currencies through aggressive export strategies.

In addition to finding their niche on the value chain of complex products such as computers and mass-produced garments, the larger countries of Southeast Asia turned to their bread-and-butter commodities: agriculture and aquaculture. With the exception of Singapore and Brunei, relatively small regional labor-market players, the vast majority of people in Southeast Asia were engaged in the agricultural-, or natural-resource-based, economy prior to the 1980s. While textiles, manufacturing, and industry were the darlings of development theorists and foreign investors, it was in the natural-resource-based industries that Southeast Asia had a comparative global advantage[5]—and maximize this advantage it did. The big challenge at the time was to find lucrative export markets and develop high quality goods that met the demands of nonlocal consumers in North America, Europe, and East Asia. By the mid-1990s, Southeast Asia had established itself as the rice bowl not only of Asia but of the world. Fish, shrimp, fruit, and other food products followed not far behind. The rapid entry of these countries into the food export industries can be illustrated by the case of basa catfish exported from Vietnam.

On June 28, 2002, the Catfish Farmers' Association of the United States attempted to sue the Vietnamese Association of Seafood Exporters and Processors for "dumping" cheap catfish on the American market. This conflict between locally based American fish farmers and Vietnamese producers was emblematic of a larger process of globalization in foodstuffs that pit small-scale producers against one another and prompted "grassroots" political activism to protect unlikely products not usually discussed in a free-trade debate that focuses on garments, computers, and call centers. This process put the U.S. and Vietnamese governments in awkward positions regarding trade liberalization, and it opened many questions on the definitions of food products, patents on natural resources, and the renaming of Green Revolution technologies and supports as unfair government subsidy.

On August 7, 2003, the U.S. Department of Commerce announced antidumping duties on catfish fillets exported from Vietnam to the United States under the labels "*tra*" and "*basa.*" In response, the Vietnam Association of Seafood Exporters and Processors planned to submit legal proceedings against the Department of Commerce for its "unreasonable decision" at the U.S. Court for International Trade. In addition, the U.S. Department of Agriculture awarded $34 million to U.S. catfish farmers for losses due to bad weather and natural calamities in 2001 and 2002, apparently contradicting arguments that losses were due to Vietnamese catfish farmers dumping in the U.S. market and perpetuating the idea that the United States employed unfair trade protectionism against Vietnam. Contrary to the economic disaster this protectionism might have suggested for the Vietnamese producers, the Viet Nam News Agency reported that tra and basa catfish farmers found new markets in Japan and Europe, compensating somewhat for their losses in the United States.

This story has larger relevance, as trade liberalization became the standard for how governments, producers, and consumers related to one another across national borders. As an increasing number of refined natural resource products beyond the basic cereals and commodities—basa catfish from Vietnam, Basmati rice from India, or cut flowers from Kenya or Ethiopia—search for global markets, vaguely defined cultural products such as "catfish" (which informally describes a wide range of bottom-feeding fish with whiskers), "Basmati" rice (a strain that has recently been grown in and marketed from Texas, prompting resistance from Indian farmers), and a range of other products that benefit from a type of locally oriented "branding" have become particularly susceptible to protectionism.

Rather than prompt a clear nationalistic backlash in the United States, as would happen in a purely "flat" world of undifferentiated nations, urban consumers called for continued cheap imports of exotic foods, revealing the fact that the dispute was not so much between the Vietnamese and the U.S. producers but between the U.S. producers and the U.S. consumers. So much so that the leftward-leaning *New York Times*, in an editorial,[6] "urge[d] the International Trade Commission to . . . decide this case [of the *basa* catfish] on its merits." If not, they warned, "Vietnam will become yet another case study in the way the United States, Europe, and Japan are rigging global trade rules so that they remain the only winners." From the right, Senator John McCain concurred with the *Times* editors, saying that "much more is at stake here than trade in a strange-looking fish with whiskers."[7] In fact, this dispute embodies the "spiky" nature of globalization, in which urban and rural divides are as important as national ones.

The economic processes lying beneath this dispute also illustrate this divide within Vietnam. Within two years, Vietnamese catfish exports from the Mekong Delta to the United States had more than doubled to $21.5 million, and the number of enterprises engaged in this production had grown to two hundred thousand farmers and fifty-three processors and exporters[8] served by a wide range of business associations, brokers, buyers, and university extension programs.[9] Simultaneously, from 2000 to 2004, the two main producing provinces, An Giang and Dong Thap, showed a doubling of output (in tons) from river-based aquaculture (those fish farmed under rafts floating in the Mekong River) and roughly a 30 percent increase in the surface area of land devoted to aquaculture.[10]

The rapid growth of this indigenous industrial production of catfish required significant domestic capital invested by farmers and the reforming state-owned enterprises using Vietnamese bank credit, university-led technical expertise (research and development, outreach), and a strong preexisting artisanal industry of small catfish farmers. Many of these capital and intellectual resources were drawn to the zones developed in the region's largest city, Can Tho, and surrounding towns. Thus, the rapid rate of urbanization and industrialization of the Mekong Delta, one of the largest wetland ecologies in the world, is in large part the result of trade integration and the urban consumer preferences in the cities of the United States, the European Union, and Japan.

Because Vietnam became a member of the WTO in 2007, the country's production for export—especially in the food industries—stands to increase rapidly, and such trade conflicts will increase unless there are fundamental changes in Vietnam's planning and policy environment. And this phenomenon is not limited to Vietnam. Soon after the antidumping suit was brought against Vietnamese basa producers, Vietnam joined Indonesia and Thailand in a joint lawsuit challenging trade barriers erected in the United States to slow the importation of farmed shrimp from the three producing countries. Increased exports to the United States and Japan have prompted similar accusations, as well, in the Vietnamese coffee and leather shoe export industries,[11] all of which rely on natural resources.

The trade dispute over basa and other processed natural resource products are examples illustrating factor endowment complementarities of agriculture-rich developing countries, like many in Southeast Asia, with countries such as the United States that consume vast amounts and diversities of food products. With cheap and experienced natural resources, Vietnam has been able to provide an increasing number of high-quality food products to countries such as the United States, putting native and local producers out of business.

Although WTO entry has offered Vietnam some degree of protection from the most frivolous charges, it exposes these countries' highly productive, but lightly regulated and coordinated production systems in the food export industries to closer scrutiny.

The 1960s' and 1970s' Green Revolution sparked a major development push immediately relevant to the newly independent states of

Southeast Asia, enabling historically poor and food-insecure nations to feed their populations and ensure security. By the 1990s, these countries had begun the transformation into exporting economies, prioritizing the steady progression of their way up the development ranks by building ever more complex and value-added products. Much has been made of these moves up the industrial manufacturing chain, even though observers from across the political spectrum see such countries' comparative advantage as being in agriculture.[12]

Because of its preexisting comparative advantage in the food and natural resource processing industries and global urban desires for affordable and exotic foods, Southeast Asian countries have, like nineteenth-century Chicago, used vast agricultural hinterlands to improve living standards while simultaneously depopulating their countryside and creating nonagrarian economies in rural areas. Unlike Chicago, however, their markets and driving forces lie outside their national borders, placing the producers in a very different, more global and less clear, structure of governance.

The resulting urbanization, internal migration, and foreign direct investment in urban areas caused by this Second Green Revolution has created a new class of rapidly growing cities that are the leading edges of Southeast Asia's national economies. At 14.6 million residents, comprising about 22 percent of Thailand's population, Bangkok has become synonymous with the country's future. Almost as important in relative terms, at 28 million residents in the metro region, comprising 11.9 percent of the population, Jakarta serves a similar role. This disproportionate urban influence, however, is not limited to the major cities alone, and economic globalization is making each nation quite "spiky" indeed. Saigon is an exemplary case of how this Second Green Revolution and the global market for food has transformed cities and their rural hinterlands across the globe.

FROM RICE BOWL TO FAST FOOD: SAIGON, THE MEKONG DELTA, AND THE URBAN TRANSITION

Statistics show that in the early mid-1980s, Vietnam was a net importer of its rice; by 1989 it was a net exporter; and by 1996, it was the world's second largest exporter.[13] What is also documented, however, is that in 1961, nine million tons of rice were produced in Vietnam (both North and South), but by 2009, production had reached thirty-nine million tons.[14] That increase, from 0.26 tons produced per person to 0.42 tons per person, enabled Vietnam to produce an exportable surplus through a 66 percent increase in production. Agriculture was clearly one of the ways the country was poised to develop.

In the postwar (post–American involvement) period, the Mekong Delta aggressively developed as one of Vietnam's centers of global production, with its food processing and agricultural products finding lucrative markets in the United States, the European Union, and Japan. By the early twenty-first century, numerous lawsuits from U.S. and other industrial countries' producers against Vietnamese farmers resulted in trade disputes—such as the basa case described above—over trade "dumping" of fish, shrimp, coffee, and other agricultural commodities. With the globalization of agriculture and food processing in Vietnam, national leaders realized that participation in the global economy and all the wealth it promised required a much more sophisticated cluster of professionals to ensure benefits to the country. An army of lawyers, economists, accountants, agricultural scientists, and business association managers needed to stand at the ready to escort those agricultural commodities out into the global market. Farming was no longer just a family and its field; and more than just growing, packing, and shipping. To improve the region's logistics to a global export capacity required a fundamental restructuring of the local industry not just to produce more, but also to ensure industry-wide quality, regulatory compliance, and adequate research and innovative capacities. This kind of industrialization of agriculture brought the country into the city. For this reason, in order to understand contemporary Saigon, perched on the edge of the Mekong Delta, one must first understand the Mekong Delta's recent history.

Macroeconomists have hailed the Delta's turnaround as the triumph of capitalism, whereby a change in land law that gave greater private rights over agricultural management to families sparked both the industrialization of the agricultural economy and the need for higher-level skills and professions. While partially correct, to attribute the turnaround to privatization and land reform alone risks overlooking some important longer-simmering dynamics of how a remote farming region has gradually become a dynamic urban center on the surface, but with deep agrarian roots.

THE ROOTS OF THE CITY:
LAND REFORM, ENTERPRISE, AND TRADE

At the conclusion of the war with the United States and the reunification of the northern and southern parts of the country, the Vietnamese government embarked on a major effort to increase production in the Mekong Delta and to take advantage of the modern infrastructure present in the metro region now called "Ho Chi Minh City." Beginning in the late 1980s and accelerating in the early 1990s, national policy reforms on land ownership propelled the Mekong Delta and its urban center, Saigon, into a position of global agricultural commodities producer in key staples such as rice, fish, and shrimp. With major bilateral trade agreements in place with the United States, the European Union, and Japan, by the year 2000, export markets for higher-end agricultural products and manufactured goods had begun to transform Vietnam into a global source of quality cheap products. This ushered in a rush of regional and global managers, entrepreneurs, and adventure seekers hoping to find their place in this dynamic, and promising, growth. Thus, Saigon's contemporary urban trajectory began on the farm.

Land use was particularly affected by the Socialist Republic of Vietnam's passage of Doi Moi in 1986, an effort to integrate selected market principles into its national policy framework. One of the first policy reforms implemented concerned land and an effort to maximize grain production. The Law on Land Reform of 1993[15] provided secure tenure rights to land and placed crop selection and long-term land-use rights in the hands of farming families, under the assumption that individual rather than collective decisions would maximize yields. With collectives, each farming family had been allocated between one-tenth and one-seventh of a hectare of land without long-term tenure rights, and land was frequently reallocated at the will of the collective officials.[16] Agricultural inputs were provided by the collectives, outputs were distributed through them to meet preset national production goals,[17] and shared labor was mandatory.[18] Neither inputs nor outputs were controlled directly by the farmer.

In response to resistance to these collectivist policies, especially resistance in the Mekong Delta provinces,[19] 1981 saw the implementation of the "contract" system, which granted farmers greater independence from the collective on which they farmed their land. Each family was now in charge of farming their own plot subject to local restrictions set by the collective. No longer would the collective use a simple blueprint to distribute the inputs and buy up the harvest. While production quotas for the individual plots remained, the *manner* in which they could be achieved changed, since the responsibility for agricultural choices now lay with the family rather than with the collective. This change also meant that mutual aid requirements for working neighbors' fields were lifted.[20] Under the contract system, the collective retained its monopoly on fertilizer and its monopsony on harvesting, maintaining fixed prices at both ends of the agricultural cycle. The exception to the collective's control was the product from 5 percent of a farm family's land allocation, which could be sold on an open market free of taxes and was not subject to the production quotas required for the other 95 percent of the allocated land.

In 1986, the Vietnamese Politburo decided that family-based farming rather than collective-based farming would form the foundation of Vietnam's future agricultural development. This policy shift took the form of Resolution No. 10 in 1988[21] and confirmed earlier indications that the country was moving to privatize land resources. Resolution No. 10 is seen as a watershed in Vietnam's land-reform process, coming in the same year as several other macro policy reforms. In essence, this first step in Doi Moi, land reform, increased relative autonomy over land and created greater incentives for individual farmers to increase productivity. It is seen as the spark behind Vietnam's subsequent rapid improvements in agricultural productivity.[22]

In addition to lifting the 5 percent restrictions on private sale of output, Resolution No. 10 allowed family inheritance rights for the allocated plots. Perhaps most important, it allowed the sale of exclusive rights to the land allocated by the collectives and the sale of the farmer-collective relationships associated with these plots. In effect, this act created a market for exchange of use-value rights. Under this new policy of controlled "privatization," individual farmers, not collectives, selected fertilizer, technology, capital inputs, suppliers, and buyers.[23]

By 1993, long-term tenure rights and titles for family farmers were promised in exchange for repayment on the collective's investment prior to 1992. One million hectares of collective land was to be distributed to farming families in this way, and the role of the state shifted from one of land supervisor and planner to one of land broker. The promised "titles" guaranteed small farmers twenty-year leases. While stopping short of allowing absolute private property in perpetuity, this reform in land tenure instituted a system of land certificates that could be transferred, inherited, or mortgaged, as long as taxes from a government land price list were paid. These initial efforts saw production success beyond expectations, and in 1993, Vietnam became one of the world's largest exporters of rice.

Shortly after the granting of long-term land rights, Vietnam embarked on a transformation of private markets beyond land reform with its Law on Enterprise. This decree allowed private sector businesses of all sizes to operate free from state-mandated input and output regulations, and effectively created a class of market institutions to buy, sell, transport, and process all this new agricultural product. After 2001, individuals were free to register businesses to sell, buy, and service this Second Green Revolution targeted at export markets rather than basic food security. At the time, the decree hardly seemed necessary, since state-owned enterprises occupied all the productive niches with the ability to earn hard currencies, and small private producers and service providers were limited to a largely domestic market. During that same year, however, trade agreements began to expand possibilities for this nascent sector of private enterprise—an expansion that set loose the players who would transform Saigon from a relatively quiet administrative backwater into a bustling hub of urban commerce.

In the mid-1990s, the scale of Saigon's urbanization was modest at best, driven by production and export markets targeted at the former Soviet Bloc countries and selected other developed countries. This limited export market was largely due to a postwar economic embargo led by the United States (that ended only in 1994) that had walled off North America and much of Europe from Vietnamese products. Coming in the same year as the Law on Enterprise, Vietnam negotiated a bilateral trade agreement with the United States in 2000 that provided Most-Favored-Nation trading status. The former created an environment in which large numbers of privately acting firms could locate, hire, purchase, and supply goods and services independent of state quotas and subsidies; the latter opened up an enormous market for exported Vietnamese goods.

By granting Vietnam Most-Favored-Nation status, the agreement opened up the world's largest consumer market to the fields and factories surrounding Saigon. Between 2000 and 2010 Vietnam's exports of goods and services grew by over 360 percent.[24] While it did lead to awkward trade disputes such as that over basa catfish, it injected the traditional agrarian economy of southern Vietnam with an economic vibrancy and dynamism never seen in the region before.

It is within this context of gradually simmering policy reforms and market development that growth in and around Saigon must be understood. While the Mekong Delta's fields provided the fodder, it was the factories, processing plants, and trading markets of Saigon that attracted migrants worldwide and that drove a new, diverse hub of economic activity that has come to be a cosmopolitan mix of people, economics, and culture well tailored to an increasingly integrated world.

MIGRANTS TO THE NEW CITY:
LOCAL DREAMS WITH A GLOBAL REACH

Four distinct communities in Saigon illustrate the surprising global reach of a relatively small city. Their histories, diversity, and proximity all embody a growing political economy of globalization, and their interaction in everyday life shows just how vertically integrated globalization can be. Young professionals from Hanoi looking for a more open social environment, economic opportunities, and milder weather in the southern regions of Vietnam; laborers from the Mekong Delta seeking work, struggling to find housing, and living apart from their traditional families; a small but growing expatriate community of investors, NGO staff, students, and corporate managers from the United States and Asia seeking the opportunities of a new environment are the usual suspects of a rapidly growing city in the Global South. Additionally, however, a surprisingly large, but unlikely, expatriate community of African soccer players and small-business people plying their trade and building up relationships in an environment with better opportunities than they would find at home reinforces just how cosmopolitan and global this city has become.

THE LOCALS: STAFFING AN
INDUSTRIAL MANUFACTURING ECONOMY

Urban Saigon's lifeblood flows from the rural Mekong Delta. It is the residents from the Mekong Delta, combined with national and global investment capital, where contemporary Saigon's story begins.

According to one study, since 1984, over 30 percent of all migrants to Saigon have come from the Mekong Delta,[25] with young men and women leaving the rural poverty of the Delta to take positions in post–Doi Moi factories. In 2000, 16.4 million people called the Delta home, but by 2004, it was 17.1 million,[26] and by 2012, it had blossomed to 17.3 million.[27] While a reasonable rate of growth in absolute terms, this 6 percent increase in the Mekong Delta over twelve years pales in comparison to the national growth rate over the same period of over 17 percent. The issue was that during this period a lot of the region was moving to be closer to Saigon, as told by Le Van Thanh and Vu Thi Hong's *Les Chemins Vers la Ville*,[28] which describes the growth of migratory paths taken by poor and young workers to Saigon. Their movement was driven by an industrializing economy around Saigon. In 1988, only US$9 million of foreign direct investment had been invested in Saigon, but by 1997, US$1.182 billion had been cumulatively invested, and by 2007, US$2.11 billion representing over 2,500 projects. Between 1998 and 2007, the number of private enterprises grew by over 1,100 percent to 18,395, and investment capital by over 7,000 percent. To say that the city was growing during this period is a serious understatement, and the attractive force of this growth to potential workers cannot be understated. From 1996 to 2007, the GDP per capita of Saigon grew by about 120 percent, presenting gains to potential farmers in moving to the city to take up industrial jobs, a choice that promised to accelerate with rapidly increasing wages and other benefits.[29] These workers settled on the city outskirts in District 12, Thu Duc, and Binh Thanh, which grew in population by 77 percent, 64 percent, and 58 percent between 1999 and 2005, according to one study,[30] often squeezing into tiny shared apartments and sleeping in shifts throughout the day. Those going into the construction industry often slept on the work site, further reducing their costs. Such a housing squeeze was often worth the trouble because the city represented a better future, one in which constructing the base for future personal and family success was far more important than personal enjoyment and relaxation.

Even at what might be considered "poverty wages" in Ho Chi Minh City, the 7-million-Vietnam-dong national average urban household income beat out the 3.6 million[31] Vietnam dong they might expect back on the Mekong Delta's farms. Much of these funds, however, were simply sent back to provincial hometowns in the Delta to support parents, subsidize friends and family members to buy property, rebuild their homes, and start new businesses such as fruit plantations, aquaculture, hotels, and restaurants, which were also booming industries at the time.

As part of the middle- and upper-level management associated with these factories, Korean, Taiwanese, and Singaporean managers flew in to take up residence in a booming long-term-stay hotel industry, and newly gentrifying neighborhoods. As the need for managing this new economy grew, the need for market-based, but Socialist, regulation and economic participation also grew, thereby creating incentives for administrative and political staff from the northern provinces to migrate, as well as for a cohort of Hanoi-area professionals to fill higher-level positions in an urban economy dominated by state-owned enterprises and large public bureaucracies. Because these professionals held essential social connections to the northern power and administrative center, their important position in Saigon was quickly established. The interweaving of migration, politics, and business in Saigon is reflected in many of the new professionals who now call it home, and this mix is one of the reasons the city holds the promise of material improvements for those able and willing to seize its opportunities.

By 1996, Huong was on track to become a significant player in the increasingly media- and publicity-savvy center of Vietnam, Saigon. A decade before, this story would have seemed inconceivable due to personal reasons as well as the larger politico-economic changes driving Vietnam's development.

During the late 1980s, Huong had been a rising star in the Vietnamese foreign ministry, with a highly respected degree from the Moscow Institute of International Relations in 1986 that secured her a coveted position within the Vietnamese Ministry of Foreign Affairs, possessing excellent English-language skills just at the time that Vietnam's relationship with the United States was beginning to thaw after a decade and a half of severed diplomatic relations and an economic embargo. On top of impeccable personal abilities, Huong came from a well-connected Hanoian family, which enabled her to exercise those qualities within the personal-history-conscious Vietnamese political hierarchy. This combination catapulted Huong into a master's degree program at a prestigious U.S. university where she studied market economics, public policy, and American culture. Although it was a challenging social and academic experience, she graduated in 1993 and returned to Hanoi to resume her position in the foreign ministry's press department.

Not one to forget her lessons learned in the United States, Huong chafed under the hierarchy and formal constraints of diplomatic service, a discomfort that became increasingly acute as a paralyzed sister required ever more expensive and high-quality medical care, a public good best provided in Socialist Vietnam—ironically—by the private market at that time.

When Huong met the CEO of a global advertising agency active in the Asia Pacific region in 1995, who offered her an opportunity to be the Vietnamese representative of the firm—one of the premier global advertising firms—which was looking to get in on the "ground floor" of one of Asia's newly emerging markets, she found it difficult to justify staying in her foreign ministry job. She took the job and opened a representative office in Hanoi (it was easier, since it was in the capital and close to the central control of the Ministry of Culture and Information). In a time when advertising was considered a "social vice," the advertising firm's creating a Hanoi office close to the political center made the government feel more comfortable about granting the corporation a license to operate in Vietnam. But since it made more business sense to be in Saigon, the economic center of the country, after one year, Huong moved to Saigon and opened the company's first office on a quiet corner of Hai Ba Trung Street. Although many Saigonese at the time spoke excellent English and were skilled in management, few could combine the unique mix of personal creativity and extensive education in both market economics *and* Socialist politics. This mix enabled Huong to manage artistic staff, negotiate with Vietnamese and foreign clients, and shepherd the final television, magazine, and billboard products through the ever-present Vietnamese government censors vigilantly on the lookout for disruptive political messages.

Today, Huong manages an office of more than one hundred staff, several million dollars in annual revenues, and a few dozen clients of large Vietnamese corporations as well as multinational brands, occupying a whole nine-floor building in the affluent District 3. These daily circles are a far—and unexpected—cry from the trajectory she began back in 1995.

Huong's professional success at navigating both the local and global environments present in Saigon rewarded her with the honor of being selected as one of five young Vietnamese businesspeople to spend an hour discussing contemporary Vietnam and the globalization age with U.S. president Bill Clinton in 2000 during the first-ever visit of a U.S. president to a victorious former enemy.

Along this professional pathway, Huong—a true Hanoian—transplanted her home south. In 1995, she married a foreigner. That marriage ended amicably seven years later but not before resulting in a beautiful daughter. To provide a stable home for her family, she bought land in Saigon's District 2, just across the river from downtown, a newly developing area of town popular among Viet Kieu—as overseas Vietnamese are known—returning to Vietnam and expatriate executives. In 2001, the choice to settle here was no urban escapist dream of escaping the grit of city life. Rather, it was the mix of global and local that made the area such a perfect fit. On the way home from a long day's work downtown, Huong could stop off at the international grocery, about five blocks from her house, to buy some French pate before stopping off two blocks down for an open-air massage and freshly cut coconut provided by one of the girls who had come in to Saigon from the Mekong Delta.

The seamless melding of her modern, global life with the amenities of a timeless Vietnam is what makes Huong's Saigon a global city. More than the mega size of a Mumbai or a Beijing, Saigon's approximation of the globe's 50 percent urban residents and 50 percent agrarian folk make it the true crossroads of humanity, and part of the global urban ecosystem.

Not all professionals who migrate south to Saigon come from such fortuitous positions as Huong, however. While in the early years of Doi Moi, foreign ministry and family connections might have been a prerequisite for success in the South, by the mid-2000s, a move south held opportunities for many more. Thao was born in the small province of Tuyen Quang north of Hanoi in 1981. As the eldest of three children, Thao was part of a working-class family with limited financial or political means. In high school, Thao excelled at English and literature and earned third national honors in the national exams for English as well as a coveted place at the prestigious Institute for International Relations (now known as the "Diplomatic Academy of Vietnam") in Hanoi.

Being the first in her family to attend university, upon graduation in 2003, Thao was motivated to use her education to help improve the living conditions of farming and natural-resource-based communities in the remote region of Dien Bien Phu, working as an interpreter. After working one and one-half years for an EU-funded development project, the physical isolation of rural life led her to successfully apply for a similar position in Saigon with another EU-funded project focused on urban planning education and environmental issues.

For three years, Thao translated documents, interpreted for foreign guests, and organized study tours for a constant flow of guests from Europe, North America, and East Asia. As a young, single woman away from her family in the North, Thao cultivated a network of young professionals from Saigon, Hong Kong, England, Germany, and the United States, getting a crash course in international norms through these professional and personal connections. It was through these connections that Thao secured a position with a foreign consulate in Saigon, where she met her future husband (an expat residing in Saigon), and eventually earned a law degree in the United Kingdom. By 2010, Thao had gotten married and relocated back to Saigon with her husband, becoming a staff lawyer at one of the international law firms advising on foreign investment and real estate development.

Like Huong, Thao found a home in one of the newly developing neighborhoods on Saigon's outskirts (at that time) in an area frequented by local Vietnamese and foreigners. Unlike Huong, Thao lived in a modest house next to a new high-rise condominium tower. Also unlike Huong, Thao's small rented house served as a home base for her younger brother who had also moved south from Tuyen Quang to attend school (HCMC University of Technology). Talking with her mother daily, Thao negotiated the professional and personal worlds of twenty-first-century Saigon as an ambitious woman of modest background. The first in her family to attend university, Thao's professional and personal trajectory is a kind of emigration to a new physical and social world unknown to her parents. For them, she may as well have moved overseas, given the difficulty they have comprehending her new environment. In one generation, she has skipped from being a rural girl to being an educated urban professional working with colleagues from around the world. It is the dynamism and vertical integration of Saigon that makes this jump seem the most natural thing in the world.

From a similar background as Thao, but without a similar education, Dao and Hoang[32] were a typical brother-sister pair of teenagers, from the remote Mekong Delta province of An Giang, who followed a similar pathway. While they were very poor and grew up without much support from their family, Dao and Hoang were blessed with politically connected and financially stable relatives in Saigon who took them in and sheltered them in exchange for housework, babysitting, gardening, and other kinds of odd jobs. A common story during the early period of Vietnam's reconstruction, and a time-old one dating back to the earliest days of the city's existence, Dao and Hoang's choice to move to Saigon enabled them to attend economics and engineering classes at night, and by 2002, they had found entry-level jobs with good career trajectories in tourism and construction; positions they would have never been able to secure had they remained on the farm in An Giang.

PERSONAL SERVICE FREELANCERS: THE WORKFORCE OF URBAN LIVABILITY (THE LOW-WAGE SERVICE WORKERS THAT MAKE IT ALL GOOD)

One of the unique characteristics of Saigon is that everything is available and for sale—and usually with a smile. For those who have ever visited, this may be a familiar story: You are sitting at a roadside restaurant that sells only noodle soup, because that is what a friend wants. But you want a pork chop. Rarely is this a problem because the proprietor will usually just run next door to get you a delicious chop and serve it at the same time as your friend gets her equally delicious soup—if you want a pork chop, you want a pork chop! One can buy a soup, order a coffee from a vendor across the street, or purchase a homemade hookah from the central market without ever leaving your seat in Saigon: it is a city full of residents with a service mentality. While convenient and uniquely endeared in Saigon even among locals, the service mentality lies atop the gritty reality of this do-your-timer city's desperately ambitious labor market.

Migration to Saigon is an equal-opportunity affair in the twenty-first century. Corporate manufacturing firms trolled the Mekong Delta's villages for the best workers and set them up in jobs and dorms in Saigon during the late 1990s and early 2000s. Huong and Thao made professional choices based on educational excellence and their professional networks, and moved to Saigon supported by employers that wanted them there. Others, like Dao and Hoang, made the move on a wing and a prayer supported by relatives. Industrial contract workers, laborers, and other formal low-level workers staff the globalization of Saigon's economy, and the service and management professionals manage and diversify this global connection. But it is the Vietnamese freelancer that makes Saigon a fun place to live, work, and play; they are what I call the "workforce of livability," because it is they who make the daily trials and stresses of Saigon tolerable . . . for those who can afford it. Being able to get a US$5 massage at a moment's notice, a US$1 motorbike trip across town, or a US$20 hotel room on a walk-in basis makes life on an average salary of about $2,500 per month—the average expat Saigon salary—an amenity-filled playground. For the average Vietnamese, subsisting on about $100 per month, these amenities are just out of reach.

Between 1998 and 2007, about 750 foreign real estate, rental, and business projects invested over US$4 billion in the city, while 78 projects in hotels and restaurants invested about US$2 billion.[33] Today, Saigon offers hundreds of high-end restaurants and accommodations, ranging from hostels to five-star hotels. Several major taxi companies have established themselves in the city and transport everyone, from foreign executives to middle-class Vietnamese families, around town. For those less wealthy, hundreds of motorcycle taxis known as "*xe oms*" convey everything from people to pigs around town—a number that can swell to thousands if counting those opportunistic motorbike owners willing to be a xe om—for a few minutes, at least—to earn an extra dong or two. These service industries rely on the workforce of livability in which a full-time housekeeper/maid could be secured by offering a room and board, and a full-time driver can be employed for a salary of about US$150 per month. US$20 per night hotels in 2005 would even do your laundry—including fully ironed socks and underwear—for a pittance.

This post-1990 growth, built upon a pre-1975 foundation of service mentality, is based partly on cooperative social capital, partly on aggressive market initiative, and partly on that great "mother of invention": need. In reality, the three may be inseparable. As Saigon began to develop in the late 1990s, growing economic inequality reinvigorated a preexisting market in personal services that underlies what has become a relatively high quality of life in contemporary Saigon for professionals. As wealthier city residents earned more and migrants arrived with professional skills and jobs and obtained employment, they found themselves able to pay for all the inconvenient and bothersome tasks such as cooking, driving (motorbikes and cars), and cleaning.

Unlike the goods produced by Saigon's factory workers, these personal services are almost all things that Vietnamese people—no matter what their education level—have done at home. Folding sheets, driving a motorbike or car, and giving a foot massage are all things that young boys and girls in the Mekong Delta and elsewhere throughout rural Vietnam know how to do, and with the newly acquired disposable income present in the city, virtually every boy and girl and young man and woman in the region formed a new labor market for personal services. This population of roughly fifteen million latent workers formed a huge reservoir that naturally drove down the prices of these amenities, thereby increasing further demand. Thus, ever more Saigonese could partake of these services as their prices dipped further and further into affordable levels based on the sufficiently skilled and low-wage latent labor force lurking just outside the city's boundaries. While perhaps somewhat less financially stable, the mid-level professional in Saigon probably lived a more luxurious daily life than did his or her counterpart in New York City or Paris. Saigon is a great place for these professionals to live it up.

While the workforce of livability serves the growing middle class of the city in a very competitive market for services, they themselves generally fare better than do their counterparts in the countryside. Hung, for example, came from the countryside around Hanoi and drives a taxi at night in Saigon, but he owns a house in his native village. His income in Saigon is sufficient, so he doesn't need to rent it out or let family use it, but he rarely visits because his heart is not there. His future lies in Saigon, and he's not going back.

THE EUROPEAN AND NORTH AMERICAN EXPATS

As the crucible for migrant workers from the Mekong Delta and other regions of Vietnam and ambitious professionals at both the high and low end of the service industries, and being the site where engineers, architects, and planners are shaping the physical landscape of a city of six million, Saigon is a dynamic and globally connected city. It is the presence of a complex international community, however, that makes the fabric of the city part of the global urban ecosystem.

Saigon is home to young, old, European, American, Asian, and African migrants piggybacking on the city's dynamic export economy and on the workforce of livability, who are also carving out a new pathway of contemporary globalization. Some of the city's global pioneers are the overseas Vietnamese, or "Viet Kieu," who left Vietnam before the takeover of Saigon by the Socialist Republic of Vietnam forces on April 30, 1975, or fled in creaky boats in the following decades, negotiating pirates, refugee camps, and new cultures along the way. The first act of their painful, traumatic, and frequently inspiring story has been memorialized in historical, poetic, and dramatic work,[34] but the second act of their drama has yet to be written. Some of the more interesting parts of this second act are playing themselves out on the streets of Saigon.

Beginning in 1985, Viet Kieu began returning to Vietnam as the country's Doi Moi political and economic reforms opened the door for collaboration with citizen groups outside of the Soviet Bloc countries. While there had always been groups, such as the Vietnam-U.S. Friendship Association, to connect Vietnamese with nongovernment entities abroad, it was only after the passage of Doi Moi that these associations were able to develop long-term relationships with the countries where most Viet Kieu now resided. Working with the other official government agency, the Committee on Overseas Vietnamese, these friendship associations allowed Viet Kieu an early entrée into the country.

The first of these intrepid voyagers focused on humanitarian work and small-scale business investment; and the vast majority of returning Viet Kieu were from greater Saigon and sought opportunities there.[35] In *Saigon's Edge*, for example, Erik Harms articulates well the powerful forces that Viet Kieu represent in contemporary Saigon. In describing the story of Hoan and Hung, two friends in Hoc Mon with visions of investing in all the social and physical change they see around them, Harms illustrates the importance of residents' ability to negotiate the old and new categories. While Hung struggles to find work and escape from what he sees as the dysfunction of Hoc Mon, Hoan sees only opportunity and possibilities for business and real estate advancement in Hoc Mon. While both share a similar upbringing, Harms astutely points out that beyond their personality differences lies the key factor that Hoan—because of his experience as a refugee to the United States—has access to outside capital and other resources that not only allow him to realize his business ventures but, indeed, enable him to even imagine them. It is the powerful combination of English-language skills, local Saigonese connections, American education, and the ability to access financial capital that make Hoan's position so enviable. And he is by no means the only one to see this opportunity.[36]

In 2010, over five hundred thousand[37] Viet Kieu returned to their birthplaces, most of them spending at least a part of their time in Saigon. According to the World Bank and the International Monetary Fund, the amount of remittances to Vietnam tripled from 2001 to 2008, to US$7.2 billion, 8 percent of the country's GDP,[38] much of which went to residents in and around Saigon not just for general support but also to start businesses and take advantage of the rapidly growing economy.

Finally, the dynamism, cheap services, and economic opportunity work well for older Viet Kieu who never fully adapted to their lives in the United States, France, Australia, and elsewhere. According to Wikipedia, in November 2012, over three million Vietnamese lived outside of Vietnam, and many were over the age of sixty-five, entering the latter phases of their lives. The warm climate, affordable workforce of livability, and cultural familiarity make Saigon an attractive place indeed.

While these qualities are especially attractive to Viet Kieu retirees, they have broad global appeal. A downtown Saigon bar will sit Viet Kieu artists together with young American entrepreneurs, European adventurers and bohemians, and international NGO staff on any given evening. At the end of the night, they each return home to their newly constructed condos, restored villas, and run-down apartments, secure in the knowledge that when they wake up, the city's churning dynamism will greet them with something new. Few of them, however, know anything at all about the city's newest residents.

Technical Experts in the Sports Economy: The African Journeymen

Viet Kieu were the first, and in many ways the most predictable, foreign migrants to Saigon, but it is Saigon's most recent migrants that truly make the city part of the global urban ecosystem. As Vietnam and its primary economic center, Saigon, have opened up to the world, ever-expanding networks have tied its neighborhoods into not just the industrialized world of North America, Europe, and East Asia further up the development ladder, and not just to those regional neighborhood peers of Indonesia, Thailand, and Cambodia, who provide convenient trading partners, but also to unexpected countries both distant in geography and seemingly far-fetched in terms of economic complementarity.

In 2009, the Saigon police raided a number of houses in District 7 in a nighttime operation to net dozens of supposedly illegal African men who had overstayed their tourist visas. According to blogger Trung Phan,[39] the authorities were attempting to limit a wave of crime by "foreigners," but in doing so, they revealed an unknown pocket of globalization that says a lot about the contemporary political economy of globalization. This operation was in response to several confirmed and unconfirmed cases of drug dealing among the Nigerian community that sparked broader concerns about illegal immigration from Africa among the local authorities. During that year, the best count of Nigerians in Vietnam was about two thousand, most of whom were based in and around Saigon. After the city's raids, that number was down to about two hundred, and several prominent members of the Nigerian community in Saigon decided that they needed to take a more prominent role in presenting a positive face for the Nigerian residents in the city and a conduit for the local authorities to engage a growing African presence in the city. Thus was born the Nigerian Union of Vietnam (NUV).

According to Solomon Bamidele Junior, president of the NUV, the great majority of Nigerians living in Vietnam are "successful in their profession, well mannered and of high integrity, such as 1) teachers in some Vietnamese universities, colleges, primary, nursery schools, and English centers, 2) textile business, 3) football players mostly in the Vietnam football league, and 4) exportation of goods from Vietnam to Nigeria e.g. Rice and Cosmetics."[40]

This valiant defense of the reputation of Nigerians in Saigon, and implicitly of all of the city's residents from Sub-Saharan Africa, was in response to an article run by the popular *Thanh Nien* newspaper documenting the spread of Nigerians in Saigon and the problems it presented. This largely negative portrayal of the African community focused on the less interesting issue of how to control their presence rather than on the much more interesting fact that so many of them were there in the first place. As with other cosmopolitan cities, Saigon has come to represent opportunity to a far-flung labor market and pool of entrepreneurs. In particular, in cities such as Lagos, Nigeria, where poor urban services, unemployment, and crime limit opportunities and undermine the quality of life, young and educated graduates have begun to look ever further afield, including Ghana, Ethiopia, and Vietnam.[41] While a necessary local response, the paper's choice to focus on the crackdown obscured the more relevant story of how Saigon has globally integrated itself through an economic complementarity with Sub-Saharan Africa.

As is often the case, the vast majority of Nigerians appeared to be law-abiding and contributing positively to the city's growth. Kevin and Don, for example, are two young brothers who have become successful Saigonese entrepreneurs. They not only happen to be from Nigeria, but, indeed, it is their national origin that makes what they have to offer a particularly astute business venture. Their story illustrates one of the new global markets that the city represents and its growing global niche. Kevin left Nigeria in 2005 to work in a Vietnamese garment factory, but after one year there, he discovered a passion for business that seemed more lucrative than the 9–5 drudgery of factory work. In 2006, Kevin's former Vietnamese boss and colleagues helped him apply for a business license and introduced him to local suppliers so that he was able to open a small shop in Tan Phu District selling fashionable clothing and other accessories. He brought his brother Don in later, and now Kevin and Don's Thanh Le shop does a brisk business selling the latest clothing and accessories to local Vietnamese women. Initially, customers seemed to just be curious about a black African–owned shop in a nondescript suburban neighborhood of Saigon and about the items for sale there, which were original in the context of Saigon. Now that this initial introduction has worn off, Kevin and Don's Thanh Le shop has found that it has a loyal following. They maintain this loyalty—and their comparative advantage—in part because they source most of their products globally, including Nigeria, but keep prices very affordable at about US$1.80–$5.90 apiece. In fact, their shop began a mini-cluster of economic activity in which the Tan Phu neighborhood, with its relatively affordable rents ranging from about $236/month, came to be home for a number of Nigerian-owned and -run shops selling shoes and other fashionable goods. In the early years, Vietnamese suppliers were not comfortable selling to them, but over time, the Nigerian business owners have gained their confidence and proven their business acumen such that they now have an established neighborhood business offering a global connection at extremely competitive prices.[42] Even more surprising than the simple fact that these businesses exist is the fact that their marketing extends beyond Nigeria, to Africa as a whole, and to the United States, where, through the Port of Los Angeles, Vietnamese and African products get to American consumers.

The niche established through Kevin and Don, however, soon wore out its welcome, as the number of Nigerians arriving in Saigon spiked, and in 2009, the community began to unravel. On July 21, 2009, Vietnamese authorities arrested a group of three Nigerian men and one Vietnamese woman—a spouse of one of the men—for heroin trafficking, and again in December 2009, another Nigerian man and his Vietnamese wife were arrested for the same crime. In the latter case, the man was executed by firing squad, while his wife was spared because she was the mother of an infant child, and given a life imprisonment sentence. These events sparked a public debate on the dangers presented by immigration from Nigeria and, more broadly, from Africa, since many assert that the "Nigerians" in Saigon are also Ghanaians and other English-speaking Africans. The Vietnamese government banned all migration from Nigeria, including business owners and other apparently legitimate migrants. According to the NUV, about 250 Nigerians returned to Nigeria on tickets purchased by the local Vietnamese authorities, and another 200 left under their own means.

This decimation of the Nigerian community of Saigon led to the formation of the NUV. At latest count, the number of Nigerians in Saigon is estimated to be about two hundred, and Kevin and Don's Thanh Le neighborhood has taken a hit. On the other hand, the NUV has, according to its website, worked closely with the Vietnamese authorities to ensure that Nigerians entering Vietnam since 2009 are legitimate businesspeople, and it states that most Nigerians in Vietnam are playing with local football (soccer) clubs, work as teachers (mostly of English), and are involved in the purchase of excess stock from Saigon's textile manufacturers for export back to a vibrant consumer market in Africa. If the NUV's efforts are successful, they will be able to ensure legal rights for Nigerians doing business in Vietnam similar to other national chambers of commerce currently active in Vietnam such as the American Chamber of Commerce, the Canadian Chamber of Commerce, and the European Chamber of Commerce.[43]

The African presence in Saigon is on the rebound, however, being led by Vietnam's love of the "beautiful game": soccer/global football. With the availability of social media, such as Facebook—and their ability to link globally disparate Internet users—talented players, brokers, and forward-thinking coaches have found one another. Vietnam's V-League soccer has become hugely popular, keeping in step with the country's overall development, however, its teams' talents cannot live up to these expectations. With domestic football skills developing but in need of support, coaches have gone international, recruiting players from Brazil and Africa, where their precious salaries go furthest.

Adeyami Michel came to Saigon from Nigeria in 2004 to play for the V-League's Da My Nghe-HCM City. *Viet Nam News'* reporting of his team's holding on to the Division I V-League spot in its race for the championship is a typical report about the kind of diverse environment he entered:

> HCM CITY—Striker Van Hung's goal was enough help Da My Nghe-HCM City to secure a 1-0 win over Thanh Hoa at HCM City's Cu Chi Stadium last weekend. The HCM City team continued their unbeaten run in the First Division, and lead the division with 10 points after four matches.
>
> From a throw-in by Uganda's Kyambade Willy, Nigerian Adeyemi Michel sent a header into 18-yard box area onto an oncoming Van Hung, who smashed the ball home. Thanh Hoa responded to the goal with a flurry of attacks, but were blocked by the hosts packed defence and some superb goal keeping by Thailand's Kittisak Rawaangpa.
>
> The win will boost the Saigonese ahead of their clash with The Cong-Viettel, the Army team this weekend.
>
> Meanwhile, The Cong, who officially transferred to the Army's Telecommunications Company (Viettel) last week with hope of returning to the V-League next year, drew 1-1 to Dong A-Pomina Steel (Dong A-Pomina) at HCM City's Thong Nhat Stadium. Striker Nguyen Duc Manh took The Cong into the lead on 11 minutes, but Dong A-Pomina stunned The Cong two minutes later.
>
> Ivory Coast's Camara Souley Mane turned a long pass from the centre to the back of net with powerful volley. The draw took Dong

A-Pomina to fourth place with six points, while The Cong dropped to seventh place.

— VNS

Clearly, Michel joined Africans and other foreigners who also became established in Vietnamese soccer. After earning the V-League's top goal-scoring honors in the 2004/2005 season, Michel moved to the An Giang club and others over the next seven years. His immediate impact on the Vietnamese game garnered him $2,000 per month, roughly ten times the amount of the average Vietnamese player on his teams, before a ligament tear in 2011 ended his playing career.

During his playing years, Michel fell in love with and married a Vietnamese woman with whom he had a beautiful daughter. Although currently split from her mother, Michel cannot imagine leaving Saigon and missing out on his daughter's childhood, and he has settled into a role as a professional manager for African players in Vietnam. Unlike the Brazilians, he argues, Africans are strong and aggressive players, like the Vietnamese. Their willingness to play through injuries, he believes, mirrors the Vietnamese psyche, which enables the endurance of pain for future benefits, and makes African players in Vietnam popular. From the Africans' side, Saigon is a great place to be, even if it is far from home. The 2011 V-League Best Foreign Footballer of the year, Samson Kayode, for example, was offered a position on the Athletico Madrid squad in Spain's prestigious La Liga. According to Michel, signed at $25,000 per month, Kayode left for Spain and was placed on loan to a Portuguese club as a long-term "tryout" on a European club. After several months and contract negotiations with his Vietnamese club, Kayode chose to return to Vietnam from Europe when one of the teams matched his salary. With no taxes, an affordable cost of living, and a great quality of life, what other choice could there have been? In addition to staying for his daughter, for these very same reasons, Michel does not see leaving Saigon anytime soon.

Overall, the road for Nigerians' and other Africans' entries into Saigon is a bumpy one. The difficulties they have faced have to do with the presence of the lucrative illegal opportunities presented by Saigon, as well as local unfamiliarity with African cultures and a latent racial bias toward Africans. Nevertheless, the complementarities between Saigon and traders, technical experts (including footballers), and adventurers from Sub-Saharan Africa are powerful. As with other cities possessing globally attractive power, local crackdowns and policies can only shift the nature of that complementarity, not stop it. In fact, it is the presence of the NUV—with all that it represents about the latent global connection between workers, traders, business owners, and consumers from developing Asia and Africa—that marks Saigon as a sharpening edge of the global urban ecosystem.

"REAL" ESTATE AND IMAGINED ASSETS: THE POST-2000 BOOM IN CONSTRUCTION

The story of contemporary Saigon began with rural land rights and may end with an urban real estate bubble; its livability, if not managed carefully, may ultimately mark its demise. At the end of the first decade of the twenty-first century, the time-old plague of urban real estate speculation had begun to raise its ugly head in the city, potentially marking the turning point of a city in which everything had seemed affordable and anything possible. Like a party winding down at 2 a.m., the city's exuberance began to exhaust itself as the consumer price index grew by 26 percent from 2000 to 2005 and annual inflation skyrocketed by 25 percent as late as 2012;[44] and these became the primary coffeehouse topics of conversation.

It is remarkable that in a Socialist country with no private property, one can observe one of the freest markets in land and construction. From 1990 to 2000, the population of Saigon grew by 27 percent,[45] and then another 46 percent from 2000 to 2010.[46] Migrating from rural regions, finding industrial work, and starting businesses were only the sparks that lit the fire of urban development in Saigon.

At the end of the first decade of the twenty-first century, Saigon's real estate market boomed. Office rents at $61 per square foot rivaled downtown New York City's $65 per square foot and beat out Shanghai's $40 per square foot,[47] even though incomes and business activities were much less comparable. This mismatch was in large part due to the fact that land in the city is valued speculatively, and entrepreneurs of all kinds are willing to pay inflated prices as they seek to cash in on the city's process of what author Annette Kim calls "learning to be capitalists."[48]

As in so many other growing cities, most of the residents are focused on the future rather than on enjoying the present; speculation about what they might become tomorrow dominates their ability to focus on who they are today. Real estate in Saigon is certainly not as valuable as in Manhattan, but the gains to be had may be. With ninety million people and years of double-digit growth, Vietnam and its economic center, Saigon, are all about investment in the future. Work hard today and reap the rewards during the next generation. For Vietnamese professionals and laborers alike, this truly means invest today so that your children's lives will be better. For Western expats, this means become an "early mover," investing your time and energy in an emerging market so you can reap long-term business benefits. And for African migrants, it means if you venture out across a vast geographic and cultural ocean, you may be rewarded both economically and personally. It is the fact that each of these communities is investing their time in the future that makes the small niceties provided by the workforce of livability so important.

Each of these communities comprise a group that is "doing their time"—risking separation from their homelands in search of a better life. Along with this status comes a deep unease. For Hanoians, the traditional pull of Que Huong,[49] a homeland, comes into conflict with the excitement and liberation from Hanoi's constraints. For foreigners, who know they are clearly transients and unable to overcome the barriers of nationalities, the anxiety of securing a sufficient financial cushion of success is ever present. Migrants from the Mekong Delta work hard, and the money they make goes home, back to the Delta, to support their families and the futures of their children. However, like the Western foreigners—even those who marry local Vietnamese residents—the true enjoyment and participation in the life of the city must wait for their children. For the African businesspeople and players, Saigon represents a migration into a more dynamic economic environment, which makes their temporary and marginal status tolerable. As they more explicitly look to ramp up to greener pastures (better leagues and bigger markets), their focus is sometimes temporary. The twin phenomenon of prejudice and fetishism—both of which lead to unease—is balanced out by the comparative advantage they have in this market compared to the ones they left.

For the fast-diluted community of "old-timers"—those whose families have settled Saigon for generations—migrants are welcomed because they enable the kind of growth that locals seek. At the same time, they threaten to overrun the local culture, family, and community relationships of the agrarian Mekong Delta to the point of extinction. As Erik Harms[50] describes, many await to see how Doi Moi will evolve before determining their ultimate position in the new and revamped city. Like the others, though perhaps with a greater investment in and fewer levers of control on the city, they "do their time" during a transitional phase to see how it all works out. And for them it is most important because there is no alternative home for them to go to.

There is no going back to the same agrarian society of the 1950s. As the ecosystem of Saigon's daily life evolves, it will be influenced and transformed by the communities of visitors and residents described above; and because of this, it has already begun to develop the kind of urbanity seen in some of the most cosmopolitan of global cities.

Chapter 4

"Do-Your-Timers" African Style: Addis Ababa, the Unlikely Capital of Africa

In 2004, I spent a couple of months in Addis Ababa working with an NGO and got to know a bit of the demographics, sounds, and rhythms of the city. On my last night in town, my hosts graciously invited me to a traditional dinner and show at the Crown Hotel, a famous, but slightly out-of-the-way club on the southern outskirts of town across from the city's prison. After a sumptuous meal of spicy stews, grilled meats, lentils, and the ubiquitous *injera*, I settled in to watch a singing and dance show illustrating all the various cultural and regional traditions of Ethiopia. Out of the corner of my eye, I noticed a group of a dozen or so Asian men slip into the back of the sitting area and order up a few beers.

The next hour or so, I was treated to Oromo head twirling, Amhara shoulder flexing, and Gurage feet stomping set to infectious music and booming lyrics sung by a middle-aged diva steeped in the diverse cultures of all nine Ethiopian regions. The next number changed my perception of Addis Ababa, with its rickety cars, jerry can water supplies, and muddy alleyways forever. Following a brief Amharic introduction, our diva launched into a melodic and warbling voice of Mandarin lyrics as she strode onstage with the colorful and flowing gowns of someone equally comfortable in the Peking Opera and a deteriorating old hotel in Addis. One verse into the song, our diva was joined onstage first by one, then a couple more, and finally the whole group of—apparently—Chinese residents belting out an old Chinese favorite. China is the tenth region of Ethiopia, it seems. To me, the encounter was a wake-up call about contemporary globalization; to others, it was the most natural thing in the world. Something important is going on in Addis, under the radar, that we need to recognize.

The city's dusty exterior belies a deep and growing urbanity that characterizes the philosophical outlook of its residents. Everyday life in Addis brings some of the most geographically, economically, and socially disparate individuals together in a way that—like Saigon—lies atop a persistent local culture that has grand plans for the future. Beyond economic growth, however, Addis' political aspirations and its fierce ambitions to improve its material well-being while simultaneously highlighting its unique culture creates an underlying tension similar to Saigon's. No one questions change and transformation, though the directions the city can take are numerous. Seen through the lens of the global urban ecosystem, Addis is, remarkably, a global connector. The rural migrants to Addis, even more so than those to Saigon, encounter not just diplomats but also everyday workers from halfway around the world. These encounters have forged a particular brand of urbanism recognizable to even the most naïve of visitors.

As with Saigon, Addis Ababa is not the biggest fish in the regional or global pond. It is only the seventeenth largest city in Africa, but its connectivity, as both a regional and global hub, is remarkable, given its size and level of development. Similar to its counterpart in Vietnam regarding its rate of growth and stage of development, the forces driving change here are different; similar in type but of a different flavor.

As the capital city of a culturally diverse and sprawling nation, Addis Ababa is the cultural and geographic center of Ethiopia, and like Saigon, Addis connects its host country to the world both physically and symbolically. Also similar to Saigon, Addis Ababa is emerging as a trading center, funneling the produce of a vast agricultural hinterland into global markets. Where Saigon excels at rice, fish, and fruit, Addis Ababa is the trading center for Ethiopia's global brand in coffee, seeds, and flowers. Beyond these similarities, however, today's Saigon and Addis do actually look continents apart. And that is the reason why understanding the shared roots of "do your timer" cities can help us better understand the global urban ecosystem.

The scale of Ethiopia's export is dwarfed by even Vietnam, so the attractions of being at the center of a global economy—while growing—have yet to evolve into the widespread opportunities seen in Saigon. Following the agricultural products funneling through Addis, migrant workers and traders have tried their luck in the city. However, Addis' nascent workforce of livability has yet to even conceive of the material gains to be had by sticking it out through all the hardships that the city represents. While most of the city's inhabitants have access to clean water, over 26 percent of households must use open spaces for basic sanitation. Unemployment hovering around 30 percent and some of the worst urban roadways in the world round out the basic challenges that Addis represents to migrants.[1] In recent decades, however, the city's pull, and growing promise of economic improvement, has been nudged along by a significant push toward the relative security of the city, and even today, Addis Ababa functions as a safe haven for the country. Given its very recent history of military conflict within its borders as well as its conflict with Eritrea, which continues to show low-level tensions, the city represents a physical shelter for all Habesha—the affectionately used local term for Ethiopians—from the dangers of life in the countryside.

Amidst this dance of push and pull factors, to an even greater degree than Saigon, Addis Ababa is a center of globalization at the human scale like few others. International diplomats, Ethiopian expatriates, Somali refugees, and Chinese workers all rub shoulders along the city's crowded boulevards and engage with the city's almost five million Ethiopian residents who, themselves, come from a country of roughly seventy-five languages and ethnicities. At the same time that twenty-first-century Addis Ababa is the economic center of one of the world's poorest countries, being home to the African Union administrative offices, it is also the "capital of the African continent." It is a global city where none should exist. It is one of Mumford's meeting places in a global world, with physical monuments representing the globe, and priority placed on connecting diverse peoples and cultures over the day-to-day efficient functioning of the city. It is the modern city as a gathering place before it is the place of permanent residence.

Seeming to defy conventional perceptions, as Mumford's "meeting place" this modest city on the edge of a largely overlooked continent may be unrivaled in the depth of its spontaneous and planned human encounters. It is very much a globally and vertically integrated city. Encounters across vast distances infuse the streets, shops, and spirit of Addis with a rich and adaptable culture that holds symbolic, historic, and ideological realities and aspirations. It is these attractions that Addis Ababans hold dear to their hearts. Like Saigon, Addis Ababa does serve as a tractor beam pulling in rural migrants in search of greater economic opportunities and markets. Unlike its Southeast Asian counterpart, however, the city struggles to provide even the most basic services and amenities to these migrants, who are unable to pay for them on the private market. What the city boasts as symbolic, cultural, and artistic success is equally matched with material and economic troubles that undermine the quality of life. And without that workforce of livability, life in Addis is a constant struggle, and many who have the chance, reluctantly leave for greener—and easier—pastures.

It is no surprise, then, that urban share growth rates in Addis Ababa decelerated from 15.7 percent between 1995 and 2000, to 12.2 percent between 2000 and 2005.[2] The city's problem is one of retention as the initial spurt of urban growth is tempered by the realities of a very "gritty" urban life without basic services and amenities such as water, sanitation, parks, and sometimes even basic security from street crimes, even though it is still the safest big city on the continent. Even more so than Saigon, Addis Ababa is the meeting place as yet to become the vessel, as people come and go according to the fast-changing opportunities and challenges that ebb and flow.

Today, the city is caught in the vacuum of a bimodal "brain-drain" keeping it from emerging into its fully formed crucible of long-term residence and a stable identity. The rural migrants understand the significant sacrifices and modest economic payoff of urban life, and some do return home—the safety of family and social networks outweighing the opportunities of the nascent urban economy. Some of the more well-heeled residents see Addis Ababa as a launching pad or stopover on their way to Bahrain, Europe, North America or even just south to

Kenya. The "do-your-timers," those able to envision urban transformation, side by side with those with no alternatives, stick it out to see what the city will become and prepare for how they might make its future incarnation work out for themselves.

While currently struggling in its ability to retain these residents en masse, Addis Ababa's time will come. Fixing its housing, water, sanitation, and pollution problems is relatively easy and sure to have disproportionate positive effects on the city's viability as a vessel for residents beyond the "do-your-timers." Solving the relatively straightforward problems of urban amenities will remove the centripetal pressures for residents of all kinds to flee. And from that point on, the new global political economy will surely drive the city's development into one of the continent's great nodes on the global urban ecosystem.

To understand why contemporary Addis is part of the global urban ecosystem, one must understand both its history and how its historical identity positions itself with respect to other, similar cities. While Saigon has positioned itself as its region's economic firecracker, Addis Ababa positions itself as a regional and global icon based on its symbolic importance for a continent defined—willingly or not—by its subjugation to colonial outsiders. As the capital of the only black-African nation never fully colonized, Addis Ababa has come to play a symbolic role as the pride of Africa—and through the Rastafarian movement, it has become one of the shining jewels of black culture globally. It is this pride that is recounted through history lessons and tourist brochures, cemented in place by monuments and roads, and performed in song and dance. The human and built environment ooze this identity just around every corner of the city.

How did a city seemingly so far off the global radar come to embody such an important symbolic crossroads? To understand, one must review the complicated, but steadily growing and deep, relationships between Sub-Saharan Africa and its new geopolitical partners—in particular, China.

AFRICAN DEMAND AND CHINESE SUPPLY: AFRICAN SUPPLY AND CHINESE DEMAND

China's meteoric surge from revolutionary kingdom to the world's factory is well documented and discussed. Part of this rise is an aggressive exploitation of its own natural resources that—at the beginning of the twenty-first century—have begun to run dry. Because of this exhausted resource base, China has had to search for energy to fuel its continued position as the world's primary manufacturer. Moreover, as the capital of the future's largest national market for consumption, Beijing has had to build extensive inroads into natural-resource-rich parts of the world. The most important of these ventures has been into Sub-Saharan Africa; although China's activity in SEA is extensive, it is more fraught with historical tensions and stronger local states possessing the local interest and capacity to exploit their own resources. Through strategic partnerships in Africa, China can position itself to grow extensively in the coming decades and make the unlikely contact between African farmers, politicians, and professionals and Chinese technical experts ever more common.

Much less documented, but no less dynamic than China itself, is the economic rise of Africa below the radar. Excluding Afghanistan, SSA has almost as many economies growing at 7 percent or higher as does Asia.[3] Despite the negative images of corruption, poverty, and health crises, the continent has created market quid pro quos that have bolstered its banking systems, begun to overcome major infrastructure gaps, and opened its doors for foreign investment. In part due to the rise of South Africa beyond apartheid, in part due to the growth of an educated generation, and in part due to the global search for ever-cheaper labor and products, many African countries have posted very high growth rates and foreign-investment statistics.[4]

This growth in the capacity of SSA countries has positioned China well to build vertically integrated connections of mutual dependence with the region; a position not due to chance. The relationship between China and Africa is not new; rather, it has merely accelerated and focused since the turn of the twenty-first century. Many scholars and analysts attribute this relationship to the rapid, extended economic growth trajectory of China since it began to implement its structural reforms and move to a market economy under Deng Xiaoping in 1979.[5] With over twenty years of double-digit economic growth behind it and potentially another twenty years projected into the future, China has begun to focus on securing the needed resources for future development. Popular stories have pointed out that without needed energy resources the country will grind to a halt, placing the impressive achievements of lifting hundreds of millions of peasants out of poverty in the matter of a few short decades at risk. With this kind of demand, Africa's relative underdevelopment and its rich natural resources loom large as untapped opportunities for Beijing. Accounting for roughly 13 percent of world demand for oil, China is expected to double its petroleum consumption within the next two decades to sixteen billion bbl/d,[6] a figure necessitating a long hard look at how to secure long-term arrangements for African petroleum. While oil is the top African commodity imported by China at 64 percent of the total, other notable resources shipped from Africa to China include iron ore (5 percent), cotton (4 percent), iron and steel (3 percent), and lumber (3 percent),[7] following a conventional H-O model of factor endowment complementarity: Africa trades in raw materials to China, while China provides African countries with finished products.

Contrary to them sometimes being considered a twenty-first-century version of the pillaging of Africa's resources,[8] the emerging relationships seem to be more balanced. In 2008, trade between Africa and China was growing at 50 percent annually, while in some countries, such as Kenya, it has doubled over the course of a single year.[9] In 2000, imports to China from Africa totaled $5.5 billion, while African imports from China were $5.04 billion, a deficit of only about 8 percent,[10] indicating that the relationship is not simply extractive, but mutual in its benefits. As with other areas of the world, Africa is a growing market for affordable Chinese products ranging from cheap dishware to mobile phones to major infrastructure projects such as dams and highways. From a Chinese perspective, African consumers are perhaps the greatest untapped opportunity out there, and this market depends on steadily increasing African incomes and consumer purchasing power.

Unlike anywhere else in the world, the Chinese in Africa can play a full service supplier up and down the value chain. Take telecommunications, for example. In many countries, the Chinese provide cheap and reasonable quality mobile phone units for African customers to connect with their family and friends, make domestic and international business connections, and—in some cases—do their personal banking. Unlike in other parts of the world, the Chinese also have built the system of mobile towers, provide the satellite connection, and manage the network—sometimes in direct interface with customers. It is not uncommon, when calling in Ethiopia, for example, to hear an

English-speaking Chinese voice notify you that your call cannot be completed due to heavy use of the network.

In this way, the Chinese role in Africa is more than just selling its wares in a new market; rather, it involves a process of negotiating long-term and deep relationships with African governments and private companies, commonly in public-private partnerships for infrastructure provision. In many ways, China's role approximates that of corporate Western providers of water supply, transportation, and telecommunications who partner with local governments worldwide. However, in the context of developing countries like those in Sub-Saharan Africa, because of relatively underdeveloped local technical capacities, foreign firms must take a more active role in advising and managing local partners in order to meet timing and quality criteria. Because the Chinese firms are willing to take on these roles and endure lower profit margins than are their Japanese, European, and North American counterparts, they are the foreigners positioned to dominate the markets in Africa.

This kind of relationship is no charitable form of development assistance. Backed by low-interest multilateral and bilateral loans, many African governments let out bids for such complex infrastructure projects for which Chinese firms aggressively compete. In some cases, Chinese firms will reduce their profit margins to less than 3 percent, and even take a loss on a project in order to secure a greater share of the African market.[11] This kind of commitment to the future growth of the African market forces Western firms out of the more lucrative portions of trade with SSA.

China's engagement in Africa is not only at the corporate level. Small traders have come to dominate niche markets in southern Africa and elsewhere, plying goods generally unavailable locally.[12] This kind of grassroots engagement is something different and signals a deeper relationship sure to persist in the long term. However, as both Africans and Chinese have discovered over the past decade, business relationships are rarely limited to financial transactions. This long-term relationship is not without social, economic, and cultural challenges, as increasing resentment of Chinese firms has risen to the surface.[13] Resentment of Chinese in Nigeria, for example, has grown in recent years due to claims that Chinese businesses are putting local manufacturers out of work. And there may be some truth, for example, to the allegation that cheap imports of textiles from China have put the Nigerian industry out of business. In decline since its heyday in the 1980s when about 175 textile plants employed 250,000 workers, it was estimated that only about 6 plants remained in 2008. Although Chinese competition simply hastened an underlying decline, the fact that claims of unfair trading practices, such as circumventing import and export regulations, underlay the perception of local Chinese traders only magnified the tensions inherent in competition from afar.[14]

Even within the large-scale projects for which there are no local competitors, the Chinese presence in Africa has led to some emerging tensions between immigrants and locals. While difficult to get a clear account of precise numbers, estimates suggest that approximately fifty thousand Chinese live in Nigeria, many of whom work for foreign contractors building infrastructure, working in the oil industry, and providing essential services.

In part, because of these kinds of tensions inherent in the growing relationships between African countries and the Chinese, Beijing has an active engagement in many countries on improving diplomatic, social, and cultural exchange. As of 2008, there were Confucius institutes in Kenya, Nigeria, Zimbabwe, and South Africa. Likewise, the Chinese Ministry of Education helped to establish the Center for African Educational Studies in 2003, which runs seminars for African teachers and administrators and hosts high-level discussions on the future of education and exchanges between the country and the continent.[15] Such formal educational exchanges are only the tip of the iceberg on a much broader strategy for engagement intended to provide a long-term relationship of mutual interest and benefit based—at least in theory—on the principle of equality.

While the scale of engagement has accelerated in recent years, China has always seen itself as a friend of Africa—even since the days before it embarked on its own dramatic development trajectory and the consequent demand for Africa's abundant resources. From his very first visit in 1963, Zhou Enlai outlined "Eight Principles of Economic and Technical Aid" that established a long-term interest on the part of China in the continent's development. These principles were extended in 1982 by Chinese premier Zhao Ziyang, who announced "Four Principles on Sino-African Economic and Technical Cooperation" that included equality, bilateralism, effectiveness, and codevelopment.[16] These principles are unique for China—in no other diplomatic relationship does Beijing explicitly specify a strategy and form for engaging with another country or region on such terms.[17] These principles seem more than mere aspirations, as the number of tariff-free products exported to China from the twenty-six least-developed countries in Africa has expanded from 199 to 454 in recent years. It is not just African products, however, welcomed to China's ports but its business men and women too. In 2005, roughly 12,400 African businesspeople attended the ninety-seventh Guangzhou Trade Fair, looking to take advantage of the growing ties.[18]

Overall, the contemporary engagement of China with Africa, and in particular Sub-Saharan Africa, rests upon groundwork laid down during the Cold War, before China's rise to economic prominence. The political role that African countries played in helping China establish its legitimacy on the global stage cannot be understated, and in a certain way, Chinese leadership at the highest levels seems to hold many African countries and peoples in an exalted ideological position for undergoing brutal European and Western colonialism and dominance to reach their current state of independence. Likewise, many African leaders appear to respect the astonishing economic progress that China has engineered over the past twenty years. In particular, China's ability to lift over four hundred million peasants out of poverty is seen by some leaders as—what Niall Ferguson[19] has used to describe the global dominance of the West for five hundred years—"the Secret Sauce" for economic development and prosperity.[20] Through this growing relationship, China secures not only African resources and markets for its rise to prominence in the twenty-first century. Additionally, it gains a globally symbolic and moral position commanding respect abroad, whatever human rights and other problems beleaguer it at home, as it reaches middle age in its economic development trajectory.

From an African perspective, besides securing infrastructure, technical expertise, and trade relationships with the world's second largest economy, African leaders recognize that China's interest in Africa has brought what has at times been seen in the West as an irrelevant continent to center stage.[21] Such attention hearkens back to the multipolar world of the Cold War, during which small countries and economies such as those in Africa were able to play the Soviet Union off the United States and others. As any student of politics will recognize, such a position greatly enhances the bargaining power of small African "swing voters" on a global diplomatic stage.

While Chinese leaders are able to relate the continent's history to their own country's history of humiliation and dominance during European colonialism, the Chinese migrants seem to look upon African societies with less affection. And everyday Africans feel no natural affection for the Chinese traders, technical experts, and professionals increasingly appearing at African ports. In part due to the lack of contemporary familiarity between two very locally rooted cultures, and in part because of the structural economic changes that the partnership requires, scholars and others have increasingly called for greater civil society connections that are able to manage the future tensions sure to arise as the partnership develops.[22]

In sum, China's search for resources and legitimacy and Africa's quest for an understanding sponsor begin in the port cities of Africa and Asia; it is the cities of the two continents where the economic, cultural, and physical contact begins. Our story of contemporary globalization and urbanization here begins when the first Chinese experts check into the local hotel for a six-month stay, or when the Nigerian businessperson lands in Guangzhou and heads straight for the Sanyuanli Market,[23] where compatriots and other Africans have carved out a small foothold in the most dynamic economy in the world.

It is within this larger global political economy that residents of African capitals such as Addis Ababa hobnob with Chinese technical experts and educators. As long as China remains focused on Africa and the Second Green Revolution marches on, Ethiopia and its Addis Ababa will only rise in prominence on itineraries as a stopover from Chicago to Shanghai.

ETHIOPIA: AFRICAN SOVEREIGNTY IN A GLOBAL WORLD

Ethiopia is the only large nation on the African continent never to have been significantly colonized by a European power. Although Mussolini's Italian army briefly occupied the country, sometimes known by its other name "Abyssinia," from 1936 to 1941, it was roundly defeated by a combined Ethiopian/British military force in World War II. This ended European intervention in Ethiopia, which had begun in 1896 when Italian forces overstepped their small concessions in the northern part of the country to encroach on Ethiopian territory. This venture resulted in a resounding defeat of the Italian army at the Battle of Adwa, and, significantly, this is said to be the only battle in which a European army was defeated by an African one.

It is this history that Ethiopian emperor Haile Selassie inherited when he assumed the monarchy's throne in 1930 as—it is convincingly argued—one of the direct descendents of the union of Ethiopia's legendary Queen of Sheba and Israel's King Solomon. Selassie's global image among wealthier countries as a respected monarch cannot be understated. His eloquent pleas at the League of Nations in 1935—as the Italian army was encroaching on Ethiopian territory—earned him the designation of *Time* magazine's Man of the Year, and his early adoption of technologies, such as the telephone and the automobile, earned him recognition far beyond his country's borders.

At the same time, Selassie unwittingly became the champion of black, African-origin countries worldwide, in part, through his engagement with Jamaicans struggling for justice in their postcolonial politics. While Jamaican Rastafarians had seen Selassie as "God incarnate" since their emergence as a social and liberation movement in the 1930s, their allegiance to the monarch—it is said—grew in 1966, when he visited the island state for a diplomatic visit to its capital, Kingston. His descent from the plane onto the tarmac amidst a rainstorm, some observers say, coincided with the end of a long drought that had been plaguing the small nation, and locals instantly took this as confirmation of his divine presence. It was also in this year that world-famous reggae superstar Bob Marley converted to Rastafarianism. An Orthodox Christian with deeply held values of justice, humanity, and rebirth, Haile Selassie represented a positive future to a global Rastafarian movement believing in radical Christian liberation of oppressed black people around the world. Selassie's influence on this movement was so deep that they took on his name, calling themselves Rastafarians—quite literally meaning the followers of King Tafari—referring to Selassie's birth name, Tafari Makonnen.

The popularity of reggae music and culture associated with the Rastafarians spread this history through committed communities across the globe from Jamaica to across Africa, New York, London, Honolulu, and even Tokyo. Musicians such as Marley and Jimmy Cliff popularized the Rastafarian philosophy even further through their music with linguistic and historical references to Ethiopia peppered throughout their lyrics. Not one to disrespect adoration, Haile Selassie reciprocated this love with an offer to some Jamaican Rastafarians to return to the continent of their forefathers, where they could build independent communities shaped to their values. Backed up with a 1963 land grant of five hundred hectares in a town south of Addis called Shashamene, this community houses a truly global village of about two hundred Jamaican families coexisting with their Ethiopian neighbors.[24] It is also this kind of symbolism that defines Shashamene's big neighbor to the north: Addis Ababa.

Immediately after this period of Ethiopia's global reach, the country and its capital city underwent a convulsive period of violence and political turmoil that shaped the physical and psychological character of the city.[25]

THE SOCIALIST PERIOD

In 1975, Mengistu Haile Mariam and a small group of military officers overthrew Emperor Haile Selassie, the longtime ruler of Ethiopia and the last of a royal lineage said to date back to King Solomon of Israel's affair with the Ethiopian queen Saaba (known in the West as "the Queen of Sheba"). After consolidating national power, "the Derg," as this small group of generals was called, instituted a Soviet-style Socialist government and nationalized land, industry, and other key assets. Building on its close ties to the Soviet Union, the Derg imposed on the country an industrial and physical development strategy consistent with the Communist ideology of the time. As the national capital, Addis Ababa became an ideological center, with the construction of wide ceremonial plazas and Social Realist buildings that mirrored a global Soviet Bloc style found from Havana to Hanoi.

In the countryside, the new Socialist government built schools, subsidized farmers, and grew a cadre of local leaders who would lead the new Ethiopia into an industrial and prosperous future. Although the country remained primarily a rural one, the Derg's military-like national efforts led to the rapid growth of Addis Ababa's population and infrastructure, and established the city as the symbolic and economic capital of an independent, rural, and truly postcolonial nation.

This period of rapid Socialist growth was interrupted in the mid-1980s, however, by political discontent and rebellions in remote rural areas of the country that diverted domestic and Soviet attention from development investments to fighting organized opposition to the regime. After roughly a decade of civil war, the Tigray People's Liberation Front (TPLF) came to power in 1991, overthrowing the Derg and initiating a gradual transition to a market economy. Under Meles Zenawi,[26] the TPLF's leader who became the longtime prime minister, Addis Ababa once again underwent an urban growth spurt, which continues today as the national government attempts to attract foreign investment and the private sector learns to improve its management capacity to exploit the significant labor and natural resources of the country.

With the end of the civil war and other major armed conflicts, the TPLF's victory in 1991 provided the stability necessary for the investments in Addis Ababa that have shaped its contemporary identity.

POLITICIZING AND CONNECTING ADDIS: THE AFRICAN UNION AND BOLE AIRPORT

The combination of African Union (AU) designation and the construction of a modern, international airport in the Bole neighborhood of the city cannot be underestimated in shaping the contemporary character of Addis. Both completed within the first decade of the twenty-first—and urban—century, their convergence provided the reasons and lay the infrastructural groundwork for global diplomats, investors, and expatriates to join rural migrants to the city in carving out a node on the global urban ecosystem.

Amidst the rush to create the building blocks for rapid economic growth in the post-Mengistu era, Addis Ababa became the home to the AU, which marked the modern emergence of Addis Ababa as a global center at the crossroads of Sub-Saharan Africa and the international community. Newly established in 2002 as an international governance institution, the AU was created as the regional organization for African states to manage their international affairs.

Although the African Union had been an idea in the works since the Mengistu era under the continent-wide Organization for African Unity, it was not until the relative peace on the African continent began to prevail in the post–Cold War era that a regional organization shifted from a good idea to a necessity. By the late 1990s, with an African secretary-general of the United Nations and the end of major civil wars in Rwanda, Mozambique, and elsewhere, it was clear that the continent was ready for change and greater stability. At the beginning of the twenty-first century, the future of Sub-Saharan Africa looked brighter than it had ever before in modern history, and it was time to invest in the continent's collective future through the creation of a regional organization. As with similar efforts, such as the United Nations and the Bretton Woods organizations, a physical location would have to be found.

In 1999, the push for formalizing the AU came to a head in Sirte, Libya. During its annual meeting, the former Organization for African Unity voted to create a more robust regional economic, social, and diplomatic development organization. While representing the African continent as a whole, the AU decided to house its secretariat, the African Union Commission, in Addis Ababa. At first glance, it seems strange to choose a country like Ethiopia as the home for a twenty-first-century regional organization tasked with managing global problems, given its Socialist history, ongoing low-level conflicts, and distinctive but difficult-to-learn language and culture presenting numerous challenges.

For example, Ethiopia has a unique script, called "Amharic," that is based on an ancient language called "Ge'ez." Modern Amharic belongs to the Semitic family and is closer to the modern languages found in Israel and Armenia than it is to either the European colonial languages of Africa or the indigenous Bantu and other Niger-Congo languages still spoken today throughout the continent. While Addis Ababa's language has been spoken on the continent for over three thousand years, Ge'ez and its modern Amharic form is as foreign to other Africans as it is to Europeans.

Beyond the written and spoken vernacular, Ethiopia *does* appear to reflect much of Sub-Saharan Africa in the tense balance of Christianity and Islam. However, its Christian roots lie some distance from the modern Catholic and Evangelical versions that came to the continent directly from Europe along with the colonial powers and that are practiced widely throughout the AU region. The country is 43.5 percent Orthodox Christian—and less than 20 percent other denominations of Christianity—and Addis, at 82 percent and home to hundreds of major Orthodox Christian churches, is even more so.[27] This Ethiopian

Orthodox religious history traces back to the first century AD, but its Semitic religious roots go back further than that.[28] It is a far cry from the King James Bible and that of the Catholic churches found across the continent.

At the ground level, these religio-cultural traditions mean that the country (and even Addis Ababa, its link to the global urban ecosystem) follows a unique system, based on the Coptic calendar, for keeping the time of year in order to keep track of important historical dates, administrative functions, and personal birthdays. Beyond being simply an interesting cultural artifact, this history has practical implications. The Ethiopian calendar, for example, is fully seven years behind the Gregorian calendar, used almost universally for keeping track of local and global business transactions around the world, and has thirteen months rather than twelve. For followers of the Ethiopian calendar, World War II ended in 1938, and the Soviet collapse came in 1984; for that matter, according to Ethiopians, the African Union itself was created in 1992. Moreover, many of Addis' residents' pocketbooks are full around the end of August, because the thirteenth month—falling in the seven days between Ethiopian August and September—is rent-free! Whatever the soundness of the logic underlying it, the Ethiopian calendar's design does not integrate well with a global society.

To compound these challenges of global and even regional business and diplomatic "interoperability," the country keeps daily time on a different scale than almost everywhere else in the world. What is 8:00 in the morning for a foreigner in Addis, be they Kenyan, American, or Japanese, is considered 2:00 a.m. for locals, and 8:00 in the evening as 2:00 p.m. respectively. Regardless of the fact that most Ethiopians—quite reasonably—argue that waking up around 1:00 in the morning makes more intuitive sense than waking up at 7:00, the potential for missed appointments, late arrivals at important meetings, and uncoordinated and confusing flight schedules in the daily lives of African Union diplomats and international visitors and residents could not be higher.

Nevertheless, Ethiopia was chosen to host the African Union Secretariat, and the city functions well as a regional and global crossroads. It functions well, not because it is a model of efficiency or because it represents the shared experiences of the African continent. Rather, it functions well because the African Union's diplomats and constituents value its symbolic and spiritual identity. It functions well because Addis represents aspirations of independence, self-reliance, and cultural identity in a neo- and postcolonial world. In that, Addis is a city of aspirations.

The fact that the city was chosen for the distinction of hosting Africa's leadership in spite of the challenges it presents to efficiency and convenience illustrates the unique niche that Addis Ababa occupies in the global urban ecosystem. Since Ethiopia is only the second-most-populous country on the continent and since the post-1975 market reforms begun under the Zenawi regime only recently brought it more closely in line with global norms, it is the distinctiveness of Ethiopian history that actually lies at the heart of its selection. Rumor has it that, in the early 2000s, when the AU was deciding where to locate its secretariat, Col. Muammar Gadhafi, even then the longest-reigning head of any African country, had delusions of leading a Pan-African movement in defiance of the perceived hegemony of the West. Pumped up by such grandiose visions of his legacy, Gadhafi presented a strong argument—backed up by over US$150 billion[29] in foreign aid to African countries—for locating the African Union headquarters in Tripoli. With the competition winnowed down to the final two candidates, it came down to the alternatives of Tripoli and Addis Ababa. Gadhafi publicly dismissed Ethiopia's bid for the secretariat, saying, "How can you have international meetings in Addis Ababa when the streets are so dirty and the infrastructure so rundown?" President Meles Zenawi's reply, paraphrased here, was concise and compelling, temporarily earning him the good universal graces of the Ethiopian population: "We can clean up our streets and make them more pleasant; you cannot clean up your history."

Saigon is a regional and increasingly global city because its commitment to material improvements and efficiency has drawn a wide range of migrants to a gathering place representative of the human diversity of the planet. As the southern pre-1975 capital of the Republic of Vietnam, it retains some symbolic political characteristics, but its development hinges on economic fortunes. On the other hand, Addis Ababa is developing slowly economically, but it is becoming a global city because of its commitment to independence and sovereignty in the face of economic, political, and social globalization. While both cities move in the same direction—into the global urban ecosystem—they have carved out distinct pathways as "do-your-timer" cities.

It is not just the symbolic designation of Addis as a diplomatic capital that makes it a city in the global urban ecosystem. Despite the fact that Geneva is the center of the United Nations system, for example, it is hard to make the case that Geneva is a truly global city. Without the seamless integration of global characteristics into the fabric of everyday urban life, global political capitals cannot become global cities. The designation of Addis as the AU's home initiated a major push for infrastructure development of the city that has led to major public investments. On the positive side, such greater regional prominence has spurred the construction of a major international airport in the Bole neighborhood of Addis. Finished in 2003, this infrastructure enables diplomats and other global travelers to fly comfortably in and out of Addis directly from Lagos, Bangkok, Washington, D.C., Milan, and dozens of other international destinations offered on a daily schedule by Ethiopian Airlines out of its hub at Bole Airport. The global connections that Bole offers, however, exacerbate major challenges that leaders currently confront.

Although the idea of a major air hub in Ethiopia has been in existence since at least the overthrow of Emperor Haile Selassie, Bole Airport has been more recently planned to be a "superhub for the African continent." In 2003, completion of the work on a major renovation of its international passenger terminal, control tower, and a new 3,800-meter runway[30] greatly expanded its capacity to host long-haul international flights and manage the greater complexity and sophistication required to accommodate both the passengers and cargo that accompany such long trips. A 2010 plan to invest an additional $30 million in expansion shows that this expanded capacity is no one-off investment. According to Ethiopian Airlines' chief operating officer, Tewolde Gebremariam, as recounted by John Kasarda and Greg Lindsay in their description of Addis as a major "Aerotropolis," the national carrier planned to purchase several new Boeing 787s. Gebremariam says, "We know the 787 can fly ten hours nonstop. Within that ten-hour radius are five billion people. This is tremendous! Although we've always developed Addis as the best hub in Africa, we have an opportunity to make it even bigger by moving these five billion through it. Being a landlocked nation, airfreight plays a major role, but connecting Africa to the forces of globalization is ultimately about connecting people. The 787 is globalization in action."[31]

In their interesting book on the Aerotropolis, Kasarda and Lindsay describe the evolution of Bole Airport as beginning with the export of raw, natural-resource-based goods from East Africa to markets in Europe, Asia, and North America. Flowers running through what they call the "cold chain" from Kenya and Ethiopia are exported overnight in refrigerated cargo planes to Holland where they are rerouted to the Safeway and Casino chains of the United States and Europe. While this export gateway was profitable, the problem was that flights returning—initially—had nothing to take back. As Kasarda and Lindsay describe it, a Ugandan émigré in Dubai had the brilliant idea of filling that open airliner space with finished goods for the upwardly mobile class of Africa through the development of the Sea-Air-Model (SAM) of global shipment. By combining bulk container shipments from Asia to Dubai and then packing goods into the empty cargo planes returning to Africa, Issa Baluch both served and encouraged an army of small traders from African capitals to purchase top-, mid-, and bottom-notch quality, rock-bottom-priced goods in Asia. He knew that simply by paying a premium for the air cargo final portion of the journey, their goods could be delivered within a reasonable time frame and at a reasonable cost to even the most inaccessible corners of the continent that were formerly isolated, by grueling overland or river connections, from its seaports. Negotiating these routes often took longer than the transoceanic journey itself. It is said that these small-scale African traders are even beating Chinese traders at their own game, since they have deeper knowledge of the African market and the Chinese suppliers are increasingly accepting of African traders as good partners.[32]

Everyone is always on the lookout for quality and affordable goods. The tiny, but growing middle class of Africa is no different and needs everything from DVD players to handbags to printers to furniture; almost none of these items are made in Africa, so the only option is to import, and in a largely landlocked continent, air freight is the way to go; and much of it does go through Addis. In the form of bundles of finished goods bought up in the markets of China, Thailand, Vietnam, and other manufacturing countries, cargo moving through Addis has the luxury of bypassing the notoriously slow ground transportation network of Sub-Saharan Africa, for a price, arriving in the continent's capitals of Kinshasa, Lagos, Kampala, and Harare. Many of Baluch's clients, presumably, were Nigerian traders operating in Saigon, and the

SAM helped the emerging middle class of Sub-Saharan Africa keep up with the latest fashions, movies, and technologies. And, of course, this kind of sophistication allows them to keep up with their urban counterparts oceans away.

On the flip side, such major public infrastructure projects as the Bole Airport have led to strong-armed land grabs and the contentious relocation of poor communities in the city. Originally, the evictions from Bole land were poor, agricultural households with nowhere else to go.[33] Faced with the bulldozers of "progress," these families adapted by shifting from farming to temporary and migrant labor within the metropolis, and the community was largely disbanded. Following the upgrading of the airport in 2003, the Bole neighborhood became one of the tonier spots in Addis, hosting much of the residential real estate capital investments of the 2000s as well as commercial investments in shopping centers and middle- to upper-end restaurants. Because of this, upwardly mobile Ethiopians moved in and started the process of gentrification.

Private capital investment, however, outpaced the city's ability to provide the necessary infrastructure and services, and by 2005, the Bole neighborhood evolved into a strange mix of modern conveniences and rustic living. Even stranger was the resulting built environment of rapidly produced private structures without adequate public infrastructure. By 2004, Bole had turned rubble-strewn former "war-zones" into mini-hotels (given such aspirational names as the "Mariot Hotel"—no, not "Marriott"), fancy villa compounds without running water, and mini-malls with no parking lots. More recently, as the airport continues to grow, the Addis Ababa city administration has faced the challenge of displacement of a newly minted middle class, as it plans to expand its airport's global capacity. Thousands of neighborhood residents watch carefully as development plans for the airport progress. Even though the city master plan had forbidden development within three kilometers of the Bole runways to preclude the eventuality of relocation, the neighborhood has crept ever closer. Nevertheless, residents currently hold out hope that the neighborhood will not be disrupted by future plans. This is not such an unreasonable stance, since the new residents have greater resources, both political and economic, than did their farming predecessors, and the cost of relocation may ultimately prove too prohibitive.

Despite these questions about the future, the Bole neighborhood is the place to live in Addis. It has the highest percentage of access to clean water sources at 98 percent, and, of the measly 14 percent of Addis Ababa's households that use a flush- or pour-toilet sewage or septic system, fully 50 percent are in Bole. And residents are willing to pay to complement government services: 37 percent of households hire private or community waste management companies to dispose of solid waste to supplement the inefficient government service. It has the fewest number of residents per floor space, the highest-grade construction materials, the highest percentage of formally salaried residents, and the greatest percentage of residents who receive financial transfers, presumably from overseas family and friends. The list goes on and on and includes telecommunications, savings accounts, and expenditures.[34] This is the place to live in Addis.

This neighborhood, however, is no Beverly Hills or Upper East Side. It does have, by a factor of at least two, the highest percentage of non-slum households of all of Addis' ten subdistrict neighborhoods. This percentage, however, is less than 25 percent. That means that over 75 percent of the wealthiest and toniest neighborhood in Addis is considered a slum.[35] What it also means is that every diplomat, businessperson, technical consultant, or returning emigrant rides into the city through slums, shops in neighborhoods peppered with houses lacking running water, and fights for space on the ubiquitous taxi-minibuses with residents much less fortunate than he or she is.

The extreme inequality of Addis Ababa might best be seen as one of the growing pains Addis is sure to endure as it presses forward with a new development agenda. While some political tension remains because of this, economic development in Addis Ababa has rapidly progressed, with highly visible hotel and industrial investments as well as smaller expatriate investments in small businesses and housing. As with Saigon, a speculative real estate boom has engulfed the city, even as a very traditional and rural culture coexists side by side with a fast-growing political and economic global elite.

This dynamic has led to a city characterized by some scholars as rife with ethnic tensions,[36] chaotic, and lacking planning capacity.[37] With such dysfunctions, how has Addis become such an attractive place to be?

DOING THEIR TIME:
URBANIZATION WITHOUT DEVELOPMENT

Four unlikely communities have taken root in Addis Ababa over the past decade: an international diplomatic and NGO corps, drawn to the political- and development-aid infrastructure in the city; a small but growing expatriate community of investors from Europe, the United States, and elsewhere, doing their time by building up relationships for future opportunities as the city struggles to develop the infrastructure for a future period of sustained economic and physical growth; an extensive expatriate community of Chinese and other technical experts, facing vast language and cultural differences as they manage major public infrastructure projects on behalf of the Ethiopian government; and the ever-present rural migrants, escaping poverty in the rural areas of Ethiopia and violence in Somalia and Eritrea.

This constellation of Addis Ababa's communities is best seen through the physical imprint of its neighborhoods. With no major rivers, mountains, or other geographic constraints, the city has spread out more-or-less evenly along major arteries, foreshadowing the city's regional and even global ambitions. (See figure 4.1.)

For many years, the complexion of Africa has been cemented into the foundation of modern Addis Ababa. Upon arrival at Bole Airport, both visitors and residents alike exit the airport in a taxi onto Bole Road, also known as "Africa Avenue," and can ride directly, on one of the avenue's six lanes, into the heart of the city at the southeast corner of Meskel Square, where Africa Avenue meets equally impressive Jomo Kenyatta Street. This corner houses the Addis Ababa Museum and Saint Stephen's Orthodox Christian Church. The former, while less impressive than the National Museum on King George VI Street, is an homage to the city and lies on the former residence of Menelik II's former minister of war, while the latter is one of the major Orthodox sites in the city and is said to be home to several miracles in recent years.

Make a right at this intersection and the taxi climbs Menelik II Avenue, first past the new African Union Secretariat and then, a block later, past the Hilton Addis. The latter predates the former by almost fifty years and is tastefully designed in a style reminiscent of the architecture of fourth-century BCE Axum, the prior capital of Abyssinia. Across Menelik II Avenue lies the quaintly decrepit Ministry of Foreign

Figure 4.1.   A global crossroads mapped onto the city: the intersection of Angola, Algeria, Tewodros (an Ethiopian king), Russia, and King George VI (an English king) Streets in Addis Ababa. © 2013 Google

Affairs compound, with it colonial-era style mixed with Soviet-style realism. This compound hides a wide swath of single-story hovels and shacks housing hundreds, if not thousands, of very poor residents who could never hope to get past the guards at either the Hilton, the AU, or the Ministry of Foreign Affairs.

Once past this topographic depression, the stately, but almost gaudy, Addis Sheraton looms as a statement about Addis' future. Built by billionaire Mohammed Hussein Ali Al Amoudi, the son of a Yemeni father and an Ethiopian mother, the Sheraton has twice the luxuries of the Hilton and none of the historical charm and character. The Sheraton is the Mr. Hyde to the Dr. Jekyll of the Addis Hilton, as standardized global luxury competes with historical class in the architecture of this emerging city.

Continuing on through the center of town, Niger Street leads further uphill toward the outlying neighborhoods to the north, and eventually takes you up toward Unity University after connecting with Russia and Comoros Streets. Within about 750 meters of this intersection, one can turn onto Senegal Street, Botswana Street, Madagascar Street, or Angola Street—an area of the city representing over 7 percent of the African continent. The city's imprint of the world's nations is no concession to the efficiencies of a diplomatic quarter. Across town, over near the airport, one can cruise Ghana, Côte d'Ivoire, Democratic Republic of the Congo, and Cape Verde Streets, and over on the western side of town lie Guinea Bissau, Lesotho, and South Africa Streets, among others. Addis was planned to be an African regional city from the get-go, and the presence of Ethio-China, Queen Elizabeth, and Roosevelt Streets— even without a colonial history—suggest that its ambitions have long lain further afield than that. If ever a city's street signs were designed to stake out a global reach, those of Addis are the ones.

The physical imprints on Addis Ababa reflect the globe. The naming of streets is a symbolic identification of the world within the confines of a daily lived space for its residents. This global city was set in concrete before Dubai's Sheikh Mohammed bin Rashid Al Maktoum could even imagine similarly capturing the globe in an urban landscape by developing The World, an effort to encapsulate global geography in a fully man-made archipelago on the shores of the Persian Gulf. But what makes Addis such a better "map" of the world than The World itself ever could be is seen in the Sheraton's backyard of hovels, where a billionaire must look out at some of the poorest people in the world. Other cities surely have financial inequalities, but few—including even New York, with its Wall Street executives and poor immigrants—can match the span of social and economic divides in downtown Addis. The whole world of global inequality can be seen in Addis.

The physical contrasts of the built environment, even more so than in Saigon, reflect the social trend of development. It is a city where muddy tracks lead up to mansions and diplomatic compounds, where steel shipping container shops and houses nestle, unaltered from their original use, in the shadow of AU Secretariat buildings, and—to use a Gilded-Age American metaphor—where town meets country.

These differences seen within neighborhoods mark immense inequalities, and many rightly lament the ways in which these inequalities represent injustices, both past and present. Even as they do represent severe inequality, however, they also are the physical forms consistent with the basic demographic facts that make Addis such a global city. In fact, chaotic and inadequate as much of the housing and other physical forms are, they mostly *represent* existing inequality rather than *cause* it. Poor coffee sellers live and work in converted shipping containers because they are the most cost-effective structures available to them; they have no interest in building a stand-alone house on their small plots because they would never be able to afford the costs of construction and maintenance. Diplomats from Saudi Arabia are perfectly happy building an opulent villa next to them, because other areas of the city don't really present significantly better amenities such as water and sanitation, roads, or an exclusively gated community. Seeing the remarkable, socially vertical, contrasts within neighborhoods, one can immediately see that Addis Ababa is, perhaps, the world's largest "mixed-income" development. And this is not some planner's utopian vision transported from Portland, Oregon, or Atlanta, Georgia. The city displays a vastly mixed-income physical face because it has perhaps the widest mix of incomes and experiences anywhere in the world. Addis truly represents the globe—including in regard to the stark global inequalities of human society that we hear about and know exist but few have the opportunity to see and engage in the same place.

GRASSROOTS GLOBALIZATION IN URBAN PRACTICE

At the top of this mixed-income city, diplomats posted to the African Union and international staff of foreign NGOs haunt numerous watering holes run by expats, such as the Milk House, just abutting the Addis Hilton, a low-key watering hole and restaurant run by a Dutch proprietor that offers good traditional Ethiopian food, reasonable drinks, and a smattering of uncomplicated and generic "international" cuisine. As one of the few affordable spots targeted toward foreigners, the Milk House attracts regular European tourists, African diplomats, and upper-middle-class Ethiopians into a bridging space of interaction.

Notably, the lack of Chinese patrons of the Milk House is probably not the result of a lack of affinity between Ethiopian and Chinese cultures. Just as the Africans in Saigon have a relationship with local Vietnamese independent of the Europeans and North Americans, so do the Chinese have their own watering holes in Addis. While Chinese nationals may sometimes venture out into these spots, their socializing is more about building business relationships.

In the market for infrastructure construction in Ethiopia, for example, Chinese firms are engaged in stiff competition with their compatriots, not with Western or other firms. Western engineering companies from the UK, Holland, and Canada, for example, restrict themselves to design and engineering consultancy roles, while the Chinese firms compete for the implementation of projects. This role of primary contractor includes a very wide range of functional and professional roles as the overall supervisor of the project, including managing subcontracts with design and engineering firms, local partners, equipment lessors, suppliers, labor contractors, and insurers, as well as being the primary liaison with the national and municipal government agencies. Being at the center of such a complex project, Chinese firms must employ people with a range of capacities, from high-level technical experts to advisors to local teams of African laborers, and, therefore, they employ a much wider social and professional network of workers.[38] This comparative advantage of Chinese in Addis is no isolated phenomenon: spending time at the airport hotels in Addis will soon illustrate the extent to which Bole Airport is a transit point for Chinese working on similar projects across Africa.

For participants in this local labor market, little is gained by socializing with Westerners. Rather, this community of Chinese and other Asian technical experts is served by unobtrusive Chinese restaurants and local restaurants and clubs, where group events are the norm, that cater to the language and cultural habits of the Chinese residents. Beyond the Western "holes in the wall" where diplomatic and business elites rub shoulders with locals, several Chinese restaurants lie tucked in among single-story offices and houses, serving up home-style meals to the local Chinese community and occasional adventurous Ethiopians. Similar to the Milk House, the Concorde nightclub—in addition to the Crown Hotel—is a famous spot where a disproportionately Asian clientele mingles with locals and AU staff, listening to traditional Ethiopian music in the early evening that quickly becomes African, Middle Eastern, and "global" pop later on.

More prominent along Bole Road than the Chinese-serving establishments, the New York Café announces itself with the image of a Big Apple as a place welcoming an international clientele browsing through a new mini-mall next door. Just up the street, the Boston Day Spa and Massage announces a new kind of service more often associated with Thailand and Vietnam than with Africa, enticing travelers and locals alike into the kind of luxury abundant in Saigon but not yet common in Africa. According to journalist Tia Goldenberg, it is part of the peculiar increase in massage parlors and day spas in the city that has led to people calling Addis "the spa capital of Africa." When Tadiwos Belete opened the spa in his home country after living in Boston for twenty-six years, he tapped into a growing demand for the kind of services that would attract global visitors looking for affordably priced services for pampering with good quality, as well as a local market of Ethiopians accumulating wealth but unfamiliar with this kind of luxury. Tadiwos sees his work, however, as no simple moneymaking effort. Rather, he says, "As an Ethiopian, I have a responsibility to change the image of my country. We are known for starving people, but it is capable of really changing." While yet to develop a full workforce of livability on the scale of Saigon, all indicators are that Addis hosts a new kind of small entrepreneur "doing his time," investing in a city of the future.[39]

Of course, Addis Ababa's poorest residents cannot afford these luxuries and cannot even imagine working in the corporate Asian or Western firms. Nevertheless, in the backstreets, where rentals are cheaper and customers more easily accessed, small hair salons, Internet shops, groceries, and language schools offering everything from Chinese to local dialects, English, and French—in that order—announce their wares and services. In a city where almost no broadband backbone exists, where mid-level grocery stores are almost nonexistent, and where higher-end services such as the Boston Spa are limited by being a once-a-month luxury, the smaller backstreet shops fill essential daily needs for expats, middle-class Ethiopians, and struggling Somali refugees who have come to the city to flee conflict in their homeland.

THE HIGH COST OF LIVING AMONG THE POOR

As with Saigon, living among the poor can be quite expensive indeed. Although Mercer Consulting has recently ranked Addis Ababa as one of the cheapest cities in the world for an expat,[40] the cost of living is much more dire for those with longer-term aspirations. On the other hand, non-expat residents faced a 2011 inflation rate of 33 percent, the second highest globally.[41] Since 2000, real estate prices in Addis have skyrocketed by hundreds of percent. While a single-family residence cost ETHB500,000 in 2000, today it runs about 2 million to 3 million, even after adjusting for inflation. In part, these prices are driven up by the presence of expat renters and the lack of housing and office supply, but also compounding these prices is a tangible feeling that land and real estate values in Addis are poised to fly through the roof, and that anyone parting with real estate today had better charge an arm and a leg, whatever the current value.

In 2010, according to Access Capital's Real Estate Sector Report (May 2010), the rental prices of medium-sized and large-sized single-family homes in Bole/Japan, the most expensive part of Bole were ETHB45,000 (US$2,710) and ETHB70,000 (US$4,217) respectively. That there are some reports of over a 100 percent appreciation between 2003 and 2010 and of an appreciation of over 400 percent in other areas of the city over four years[42] suggests that speculation about the future is rampant. These sharp increases in home sale prices are not for just the upper crust. Struggling middle-class residents of Addis, during the mid-1990s, began building small homes in green pastures on the outskirts of town even before roads and services had been provided, rightly assuming that their expenditures on land and labor would be exceeded by the value of home appreciation. Percentage increases in value, however, are different from sales prices. While some real estate developments of middle-class Ethiopians surely led to accumulations of assets by the more perceptive of local residents, much of the baseline housing remains far out of reach for the majority of the city. In a city where the asking price for villas in Bole, its highest end neighborhood, can reach upwards of ETHB3 million, homeownership is far beyond the affordability of the majority of residents—even for professionals, such as university professors, making less than $300/month.

As with Vietnam, it is the residents of Addis Ababa with access to global investment capital sources that stand to benefit from the city's development. With inflation through the roof, the growth of the Addis Ababa economy gradual, and the distribution of that growth even slower, it is no surprise that the city looks outward. Certainly the overall economy has not kept pace with inflation; but then again, Addis is a city of "do your timers." The interest is not in today but in the promise of a long-term development trend that will reward future generations.

The edginess and surprises that Addis' particular version of globalization embodies have created a sense of excitement and potentiality—a sense of becoming—that helps all of its residents endure physical inconvenience and cultural misunderstandings. For longtime residents, visitors, and migrants alike, personal aspirations can easily find a comfortable space between complacency and excitement about the future. It is this promise of transformation that lies at the core of do-your-timer cities such as Addis and Saigon.

CHAPTER 5

THE INDIGENOUS CITY? RECONCILING AN OLD-TIMERS' HONOLULU WITH A GLOBAL SOCIETY

Unlike most in the United States, the Aloha State of pristine beaches and lush mountains is a state that is mostly a big city. What makes Honolulu so remarkable is that there is such a cosmopolitan place in a pristinely natural environment rather than vice versa; with beautiful and lush beaches and mountains endemic to the isolated Pacific islands, it is the city, rather than the lush green and brown natural beauty of Honolulu that catches the eye after a five-hour flight traversing the blue Pacific waters. Honolulu is the tenth-largest municipality in one of the world's most urbanized countries, in fact, and as goes the city, so goes the state.

Drive around the island of Oʻahu long enough and you will soon realize that the city and county of Honolulu—which is coterminous with the island—is a city of pack rats. For better or worse, its residents are accumulating and storing both material goods and garbage, as well as experiences, ideas, and aspirations, faster than the pristine and isolated island can cope with them.

Touring even the toniest neighborhoods in Honolulu, one can spy moldy and flaccid cardboard boxes filled with books, Pokemon dolls, and children's sports trophies stacked high in open garages, pushed up next to washers and dryers. Oftentimes, the same garage is home to a rusting 1980s-era Ford pickup used to cart these boxes around from storage to yard sale and back again. Mirroring a broader dissonance between appearance and reality, these impromptu storage spaces often front the streets in million-dollar-home neighborhoods and house some of the most influential residents of the state.

Unlike Addis Ababa, these neighborhoods are no social flotsam; these people just value old things. They have consistently elected the United States' most senior Senate delegation, for example—Senators Daniel Inouye and Daniel Akaka[1]—with a combined age of over 170 years between the two of them. The housing stock they live in dates— in large part—to a plantation era mostly characterized by an early-to-mid-twentieth-century style of single-wall-construction housing popular when the islands first became the Territory of Hawai'i under U.S. control (1900); this small island outpost of the United States would not see statehood for fifty-nine years. According to the 2010 U.S. Census of Population and Housing,[2] 14.5 percent of the state's residents were over the age of sixty-five, compared to the national average of 13 percent. This figure was mirrored for the city of Honolulu at 14.5 percent. While not remarkable at first glance, the sixty-five-and-up group grew by almost 18 percent over 2000 levels, while the eighteen-to-sixty-four group grew by only 10 percent over an admittedly larger baseline from 2000, but most important, the under-eighteen group actually decreased by 2 percent. To say that the state and its capital city, Honolulu, are places that hang on to the past—potentially at the expense of their future—is an understatement. The more relevant question is how this characteristic shapes the contemporary city's identity.

Honolulu is an aging city stranded in an ocean and is five thousand miles from the nearest major landmass; these are not qualities that city leaders like to highlight. Honolulu's days as a convenient stopover on a trans-Pacific flight or sail are long gone, and the city searches for a new identity that can be the leading edge for both maintaining a relatively high standard of living and sustaining the injection of new blood and ideas without compromising its past. Similar to what occurs in Addis and Saigon, forces for development and for historic preservation pull the local leaders and residents in very different directions. However, unlike the people of Addis and Saigon, few Honolulans agree that change and transformation are inevitable, let alone on what that change will look like. What Honolulu shares with these other cities is an underlying ecosystem of everyday life in which surprisingly global encounters permeate mundane routines. In some places, these encounters span vast socioeconomic divides, while in Honolulu, they cross daunting philosophical outlooks; the difference in outlook might best be characterized as a reluctant urbanism.

In part, Honolulu's brand of urbanism results from good publicity. The city and county of Honolulu comprises 70 percent of the state of Hawai'i population, and is the public face of the Aloha State, with an imagery and "imaginary" that has reached a global audience through popular shows such as *Hawaii Five-0* and *Magnum P.I.* since the 1970s. Few, however, realize that with a population of over nine hundred thousand, the municipality is slightly more populated than Detroit and slightly less than San Jose, California. Counting full-time U.S. military personnel and the average number of tourists in the city at any given time, the figure is well over one million. The downplaying of Honolulu's big-city character is not surprising, given the fact that Honolulu is essentially a city of "old-timers."

As a city built on the edges of pineapple and sugarcane plantations, Honolulu, it should not be surprising to note, retains the small-town, intergenerational character of plantation life and the gradual rhythms of a laid-back surf culture. Since the city has a significant percentage of residents who grew up during a previous era of global integration but geographic isolation, agricultural cycles, and segregated ethnic circles (a result of Hawai'i's history of importing Asian laborers from 1850 to about 1930), it should not be surprising that the social forces of conformity and historical continuity remain even as the city globalizes its economy, physical stock, and aspirations.

More surprising is the contemporary reality that Honolulu has become a center of what I call a "new communalism," which is emerging throughout the United States and cities in other tropical climates with old-world values and habits. Ironically, it is not just the aging plantation-era generation that is the driving force for "old-timers," but it is also the newcomers. For generations, Hawai'i has been a destination for American and Japanese tourists seeking tropical experiences with the convenience of modern American infrastructure and services. This exposure to the larger U.S. continental and Asian societies has generated a new kind of "settler" in the islands looking to find a simpler life that is more connected to nature, and a human-scale community. It is these settlers that perpetuate an identity of "old-timers" even when actual local old-timers are ever harder to find.

Even among those who are quite young, the search for traditional community life that Honolulu retains, in contrast to the chaos of "mainland" cities, provides not only a respite but also a chance to create the traditional social bonds of community that Jane Jacobs celebrated long ago with respect to the neighborhoods of New York and Boston. On the one hand, these well-educated and sophisticated new settlers rarely forgo the essentials of twenty-first-century cosmopolitan life. On the surface, a local coffeehouse, grocer, and friendly neighbor provide a traditional community-level experience. Deeper down, however, they also appreciate an integrated banking system, abundant and exciting culinary options, and a Costco that keeps the high costs of amenities mitigated by offering daily savings on mundane items. In Honolulu, global settlers join others aspiring to create those human-scale communities that simultaneously have all the amenities of a cosmopolitan urban life. Where else can they go surfing at a popular local spot and then drop in to see a world-renowned orchestra at the Honolulu Symphony on their way home?

On the other hand, the less-educated and the less-professional become entrapped in a dynamic of low wages despite their ability to reduce expenses by moving to the urban fringe. While global settlers enjoy the proximity of amenities such as the beach and symphony, others with low-end service, construction, and other jobs find themselves priced ever-farther out to less- but still-expensive housing on the urban fringe, where lack of transportation infrastructure prevents access to urban amenities; or, they find themselves crowded into more-central but cramped studios so these amenities are accessible. For them, quality of life remains an oft-repeated, but increasingly unattainable, mantra; there is no workforce of livability here.

Adding to this layering of old plantation families and new community-seekers is a recognition and tense commitment to the "proto-"

old-timers who predate the plantation society by several hundred years: Native Hawai'ians. Unlike other native peoples in many parts of North America, Hawai'ian culture has been weakened, but not decimated, by a history of disease and warfare. In fact, Native Hawai'ians have made strategic accommodations with European and Asian settlers, carving out a materially "disadvantaged," but symbolically triumphant, position within the racial and ethnic dynamics of the state. It is these indigenous "old-timers" who raise the bar of tradition beyond families and individuals to culture and community. The resurgent success and achievements of Native Hawai'ian culture, values, and people—while nascent—suggest an urban identity that cements the old-timer into a unique and historical local context, but with a vision toward how this historical uniqueness presents an alternative image of urban and cosmopolitan development. In this way, Honolulu is perhaps the most cosmopolitan and urban case exemplifying Frank Hirtz's[3] recognition that indigenous culture is the counterpoint to modernization.

Noted author Sherman Alexie is one of the leading contemporary thinkers in Native America and has made a name for himself busting up stereotypes of Indians on the continent. Although he may not be fully aware of it, urbanization appears to be one of his themes. Fully "seventy percent of Natives live in urban areas now," he says. "We might have better jobs or be college educated [now,] but the struggle to maintain your Native identity in a city is the primary struggle today."[4] Rather than a unique aspect of Indian culture, however, I argue that the struggle Alexie identifies is the central struggle of many city residents and that it defines an old-timer city. Native Americans and other indigenous peoples struggle most actively with this tension, but conflicting identities, more broadly speaking, lie at the true heart of an old-timer city and its identity in a globalizing world.

Honolulu is the shining case in point of how the tension between indigenous and nonindigenous—as both honor to, and co-optation of, indigenous identities—has become a marker of global sophistication. Because it is through the formation of an indigenous identity that Honolulu has become not just a modern, but also a cosmopolitan, urban center, it is ironically the case that the city's old-timers are some of the most forward-thinking globalists out there.

Honolulu has always punched above its weight class. At the time when the Hawai'ian island chain became a territory of the United

States, I'olani Palace and the downtown surrounding this seat of the Hawai'ian Monarchy had city streetlights, a public infrastructure not even seen at the time in Washington, D.C., the capital of its colonizer. Up until this time, the tiny settlement poking out of the vast Pacific Ocean had been a global export center for whaling through the mid-1800s and sugar through the 1970s.[5] By the middle of the twentieth century, it was the center of military operations for the world's largest military force, and by the late twentieth century, it had become the gold standard for a nascent cult of global tropical vacations.

Even Lewis Mumford himself saw the promise of this small and isolated city blazing an urban identity going far beyond the sleepy island shores and becoming much more than simply the largest settlement in a beautiful resort island chain. At the request of the Park Board of the city and county of Honolulu, Mumford provided his thoughts on the potential and planning of Honolulu, and they were disseminated via a brief booklet published in 1938 titled *Whither Honolulu*.

Ever the poet, Mumford describes the city of Honolulu as "a little like a beautiful woman, so well assured of her natural gifts that she is not always careful of her toilet: she relies upon her splendid face and body to distract attention from her disheveled hair, her dirty fingernails, or her torn skirt." With language a bit sexist by twenty-first-century norms, Mumford described and sought to conserve those unrivaled assets that remain compelling even today. First was the plentiful, calm, warm, and shallow ocean beaches that served as the economic, recreational, and symbolic spaces since the time the Native Hawai'ians first came to the shores of O'ahu. The second was the city's unrivaled tropical, yet cool, climate in which reliable trade winds sweep across the baking city, forming the "most admirable air-cooling apparatus that a community could boast," a characteristic complemented by frequent rains that keep high temperatures and humidity in check. Its "equable climate" was—and is—inseparable from the third asset Mumford praised: universal verdure. The ability to grow lush, tropical trees, plants, flowers, and bushes creates a Garden-of-Eden quality to the city but also—he argued—gave it license to neglect its insufficient physical infrastructure and "architectural misdemeanors," which would always be overshadowed by a leafy organic ceiling hiding these blemishes.

These natural assets have endured remarkably well in Honolulu over the seventy-five years since Mumford wrote, but as the city's larger natural beauty has been left unmanicured and uncultivated, the tropical beach vacation city has vied for ever-increasing attention in a global beauty pageant of beaches and weather. As regions such as Southeast Asia and South America came into their own as tourist destinations, middle-class vacation albums began to boast images of Singapore, Sydney, and Rio as "it" tropical cities unburdened by political repression, street crime, and inaccessibility. As Honolulu's weather and climate have become mass-produced consumer goods and its global market has been debated on the pages of *Travel & Leisure* and the Discovery Channel, it is Mumford's fourth asset of Honolulu that has become increasingly important—indeed central: the people of Honolulu themselves and the various cultures that meet and mingle in the city on a daily basis. As Mumford describes it, in the language of his time,

> The original Polynesian culture has left a beneficent trace on the entire life [of the city]: its kindly human sense, its love of healthful natural activities, its nutritive diet must all be reckoned with in any intelligent planning scheme. The high Oriental cultures that have also left their mark on the city, through the Japanese and Chinese, have a no less powerful contribution to make: already they have begun to influence the architecture; and their ceremonious cult of beauty, especially in their cultivation of flowers, has re-enforced the original Hawaiian inheritance. Finally, the systematic rationalism of the Western World, with its habits of close accountancy of time, money, and energy, has contributed an element of purposive activity that perhaps helps to counterbalance the more indolent, haphazard ways that are closer to the life-rhythm of the tropics. Hawaii is a significant experiment of that hybridization of cultures which will perhaps mark the future development of human society: it is a miniature experimental station.[6]

This cultural mix remains even seventy years later.

On the surface, the city of Honolulu still struggles with achieving both the specific material improvements Mumford recommended as well as the larger urban identity he advocated. *Whither Honolulu* would be an equally compelling document were it penned in 2008 rather than 1938, illustrating the difficulty of shifting the state's mind-set from a small-town one to a big-city one. The stakes for making such a shift, however, are higher than ever; in 1938, the state's beautiful beaches were unique, being within a single flight or cruise from the U.S.

mainland and under the protection of a safe, modern secular state. Today, the Caribbean, Thailand, the Philippines, and some places in coastal Africa all offer comparable beauty and safety at much cheaper prices and are more easily tacked on to business trips, family visits, or shopping splurges for cheap products. The middle-class tropical vacation experience, it turns out, has become more global; gone is Honolulu's "natural monopoly"—its monopoly over nature.

More than ever, it is the urban-ness and cosmopolitan character of Honolulu, and Hawai'i in general, that distinguishes the current visitor experience. Today, the reason visitors come to Hawai'i is not for the beautiful beaches—they can get that more affordably, in regard to both money and time, elsewhere. What brings them is the proximity of those beaches to taxi stands from which they can be whisked off to high-end shopping centers, theaters, cultural events, and educational institutions. There are many beautiful beaches in the world, but only a few have a symphony, major university, and convention center within walking distance. Listening to a live performance of Bach, or heading off to professional association meetings after a long day at the beach, is an experience hard to find in Thailand or the Caribbean. Ironically, in the twenty-first century, visitors come to Hawai'i because it is so urban, not because it is pristine and beautiful.

This shift from tropical paradise to city on the ocean has been largely driven by global changes in a global market, for visitors of all sorts, that have forced Honolulu to chart unfamiliar waters in recent years.

GLOBALIZATION OF THE TROPICAL VACATION AND THE GREY REVOLUTION: TOP-NOTCH SERVICES AT ROCK-BOTTOM PRICES IN BEAUTIFUL LOCATIONS

At the same time that Thai restaurants were becoming a fad in New York City, American holiday vacations to beaches outside Bangkok and Hilltribes surrounding Chiang Mai were getting to be all the rage. Several technological, demographic, and economic trends have enabled tropical regions, most notably Southeast Asia, to become playgrounds for both short- and long-term visitors,[7] and these trends have also reshaped cities across the Global South. Most notably, Thailand and Bangkok illustrate that powerful combination of "sun, sand, surf, and sex."[8] While the explicit sex-tourist economy no doubt has thrived since the 1970s, it is only one facet of a larger visitor economy that includes (largely male) retirees from Europe and North America settling in with younger Thai wives, for example. Additionally, older and predominantly rural Korean and Taiwanese men visit Thailand and other parts of the region on "marriage tours" to find eligible wives through broker services, and many of these new unions, as with those from North America and Europe, result in longer-term investments in small businesses and real estate. More recently, the same phenomenon has happened with young women from the Mekong Delta of Vietnam, and such personal connections in both Thailand and Vietnam have facilitated communities of foreign residents living there for personal reasons.

This personal engagement has been facilitated by the growth of higher-end "quality of life" industries and services such as top-notch health care, private schools, and excellent transportation infrastructure. Because the relative value of these services is so high compared to their costs, this package of goods has become extremely attractive not just to spouses but also to retirees and others on fixed incomes facing rapidly escalating costs of housing, health care, and education in their home countries.

To illustrate this point, a knee-replacement surgery, including six days of physical therapy, in Thailand costs about one fifth of the cost in the United States. A $200,000 heart-valve replacement in the United States costs about $10,000 in India. And, of course, nonessential surgeries have also become globally popular, as a $20,000 facelift in the United States costs about $1,250 in South Africa. In education, one can get an MBA from the University of Hawai'i at reduced cost in Vietnam. With these price differentials and quality similarities, the cost of transportation and accommodation slides far down the list of deciding factors.

While little research exists on the extent of these industries, indicators all suggest the likelihood of hearing more and more of these stories in the near future. The global market for medical tourism was estimated to have grown to $40 billion by 2010;[9] moreover, health care is the world's largest industry, estimated at over US$2.8 trillion per year for the United States alone.[10] Many health-care "purchasers" come from developed countries such as the United States and those of Western Europe, some of which face severe quality and cost dilemmas; so severe that about 43 million residents of the United States live without any health insurance at all and 120 million live without dental insurance. In developed countries, cost factors and quality concerns combine with a lack of coverage for both basic and specialized procedures, driving consumers to consider medical tourism.[11] With an increasing number of native-born, but U.S.-educated, medical professionals staffing these global health-care destinations, the industry seems poised to grow, especially with the coming demographic bulge of retirees reaching an age of high health-care needs. Like it or not, the global market for "outsourced" health care is very lucrative and increasingly feasible. So lucrative, in fact, that hospitals such as Bumrungrad and Bangkok International Hospital run advertisements in the local newspapers of Addis Ababa, and Ethiopian tour agencies facilitate their connection to paying customers. So lucrative that tourism company MedRetreat has operated consistently in the United States and Canada since 2003, and so lucrative that an online portal, onlinemedicaltourism.com, has made global facilities from Thailand to South Africa to Brazil searchable by type of procedure. This clearinghouse provides information on types of insurance covering international procedures, facilities (without endorsing any), and links to the accrediting organizations for the facilities listed. Major U.S. insurers such as Aetna and United Health have pilot programs experimenting with the cost savings of medical tourism as part of their standard plans, while European employers have—to date—seen less opportunity for cost savings.[12] Whatever the current status, the opportunities for medical tourism are growing and are increasingly important, particularly for those nations with poor health care and those with highly skilled medical professionals who are underpaid in the global market.

The economic opportunities presented by medical tourism, however, exist within a larger global demographic context that will accelerate their relevance. The laws of supply and demand in global health care argue for further integration along unexpected lines. Just as there is a growth in the quality and affordability of health services in developing countries such as Thailand and India, the need for health care and related services is booming in developed countries because of long-term demographic trends. Global health care, while important, represents a much larger set of "quality of life" industries growing in importance across Southeast Asia's cities and elsewhere across the Global South. How is it that health care, education, and other services have become so popular and competitive? A look at labor-force dynamics can help provide the answer.

For decades, demographers have worried about bell-shaped population distributions in developing countries, predicting Malthusian social and economic collapses in countries where supposed overpopulation was to put too much strain on natural and economic resources. While certainly relevant in principle, today the constraints of national boundaries play a much less important role, and global population dispersal has become somewhat the norm.

Today, demographers worry more about champagne-glass population distributions in which societies fail to reproduce themselves at sufficient levels to ensure regeneration of the labor force than they worry about bottom-heavy ones. Societies trapped today in these negative- and low-growth demographic trends find themselves with decreasing payments into retirement pensions and social security funds, fewer workers available for low-skilled service and health-care work, and increasing populations aging into the phase of life in which these services are critical for maintenance of quality of life. This mismatch between the coming bulge in demand for medical care and health services, and the rich countries' ability to provide it through payments into retirement funds and a young workforce, drives the coming demographic globalization over the next two decades. Developing countries able to provide high-quality and affordable services have begun to fill this gap and will own it within a generation. The roughly seven thousand Americans calling San Miguel de Allende, Mexico, home and over one million retirees living across various parts of Asia who are from other continents[13] are only the crest of a coming demographic wave that will transform the relationship between developed and developing countries, as well as the cities that connect their residents.

Some countries have seen the opportunity and taken steps accordingly. Malaysia, for example, began a "silver hair" program in 2002 that expanded to be the "Malaysia My Second Home" program in 2006. Under this program, any fifty-year-old with over $104,000 in assets and a monthly pension of about $3,000 can get a ten-year resident visa, can work up to twenty hours per week, and gains the right to purchase property.[14] Not bad when compared to what that same $3,000 might buy in Los Angeles or Honolulu, but when the low-cost, high-quality daily services are accounted for and the available high-quality medical care is thrown in, the option becomes almost a necessity. The Philippines was even sooner off the starting line, creating the Philippines Retirement Authority in 1985 with the mandate to facilitate foreign retirees' and former Filipino citizens' retirements in the island nation. Their clients find second homes in retirement communities across the country where monthly luxury apartment rents are $250/month, twice weekly maid service is $10/week (same for a cook), and a beer costs $0.60 ($1 in a bar).[15] The $1,000 airfare costs every couple of months, to visit old friends and family back home, seem to pale in comparison.

This demographic corollary of the Heckscher–Ohlin thesis on global factor endowment complementarity will only increase as people in rich countries get older and the Global South's baby boomers in developing countries age into the workforce. Figures 5.1–5.4 show that this phenomenon will be no passing trend. In 2010, Germany showed a one-sixth to one-fifth drop-off from its population aged twenty to twenty-five to that aged fifteen to twenty, a pattern similar to Japan's. On the other hand, the Philippines shows a classic bell-shaped population distribution, with about 25 percent more zero to five-year-olds than twenty to twenty-five-year-olds. Ethiopia is even more skewed toward the young, with a 50 percent gain between these two cohorts. While during the Cold War many of these young people might have remained on the farm toiling away on diminishing land, today they will either find jobs in the growing industries servicing the elderly in developed countries, or they will play hosts to the increasingly mobile elderly eager to maximize the value they can get on their fixed incomes.

For some countries with significant expatriate populations, it is not just the elderly who see the opportunities. U.S.-based diaspora investments in hometowns of the Global South topped US$98 billion in 2010,[16] and many more short-term visitors with local ties but nonlocal expectations of service quality are sure to bolster the availability and affordability of good services where these labor-market complementarities exist.

These retirees and other quality-of-life visitors, who have come from around the world, to date have focused on Southeast Asia, where economic development and governmental stability have reached a threshold that enables retirees to think about buying a second home there. As the populations of North America, Europe, Japan, Korea,

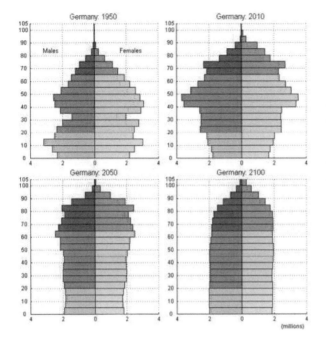

Figure 5.1. Population Trend Pyramids for Germany

Note: The flatter the pyramid, the greater the supply of affordable labor; the steeper the pyramid, the greater the demand for labor to service an aging population.

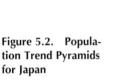

Figure 5.2. Population Trend Pyramids for Japan

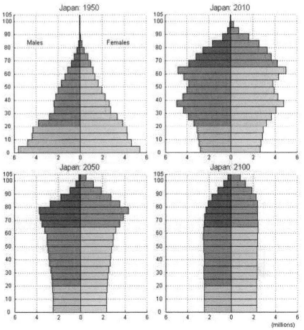

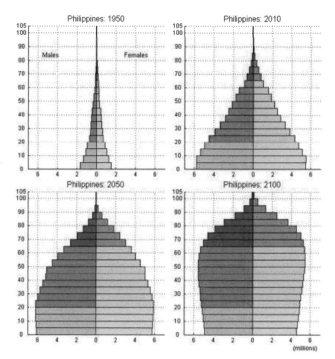

Figure 5.3. Population Trend Pyramids for the Philippines

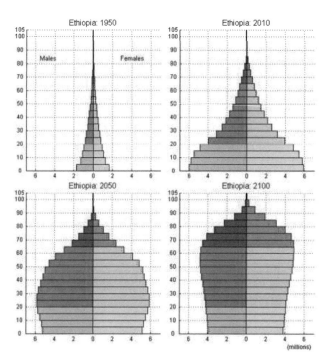

Figure 5.4. Population Trend Pyramids for Ethiopia

Source: UN Department of Economic and Social Affairs, Population Division, 2011.

and elsewhere age into retirement, this pool of long-term visitors and retirees to SEA is positioned to grow quickly in the coming decades.[17] The final piece of this puzzle—and by no means the least important— is the decline of western and northeast Asian youth. At the same time, adults of childbearing age in these countries show little interest in filling this gap internally with native-born children. Table 5.1 shows the fertility rates of the major industrialized countries. While the United States remains healthy in terms of its ability to reproduce itself, other wealthy countries face an astonishingly dire situation as their populations—literally—face disappearance. At 1.66, Western Europe faces a fertility rate at which each generation is only 79 percent of the previous one—equating to a loss of 20 percent of the cohort population with each successive generation. Japan (1.42) and Korea (1.35) are in even-more-dire demographic circumstances: each generation loses about 30 percent of its cohort population.[18] If this keeps up—statistically—Japan and Korea stand to disappear as meaningful descriptions of national populations in just over three generations. Even mighty China is not exempt from the trend—in part due to its one-child policy—with a birthrate of 1.56. On the other hand, the Philippines has a high fertility rate and a bell-shaped profile, as does Nigeria, Ethiopia, and, to some extent, Indonesia.

Table 5.1. Total Fertility (Children per Woman) for Selected Industrialized Countries, 1990–2015

	1990–1995	1995–2000	2000–2005	2005–2010	2010–2015
USA	1.99	1.96	2.04	2.07	2.08
FRANCE	1.71	1.76	1.88	1.97	1.99
GERMANY	1.3	1.34	1.35	1.36	1.46
ENGLAND (UK)	1.78	1.74	1.66	1.83	1.87
SPAIN	1.28	1.19	1.29	1.41	1.5
ITALY	1.28	1.22	1.25	1.38	1.48
Average of Five Previous Countries	1.47	1.45	1.48	1.59	1.66
JAPAN	1.48	1.37	1.3	1.32	1.42
KOREA	1.7	1.51	1.22	1.29	1.39
EUROPE	1.57	1.42	1.43	1.53	1.59
CHINA	2.01	1.8	1.7	1.64	1.56

Source: United Nations, Department of Economic and Social Affairs Population Division, Population Estimates and Projections Section, http://esa.un.org/unpd/wpp/unpp/Panel_profiles.htm.

Countries such as Vietnam, Thailand, and Myanmar, however, show a labor force (aged fifteen and above) with bell-like characteristics, but the demographics of the very young, aged fifteen and below, are more like those of Korea, Japan, and China. Which way they trend is yet to be seen.

Overall, the aging of the baby-boom generation and the lack of a young generation of workers in the United States, Europe, Japan, and Korea have led to a global generation of fixed-income retirees and vacationers searching for good deals, better care, and "bucket-list" experiences unavailable in their home countries or cities. In a strange way, SEA plays the global role of an "outsourced youth" as populations in the developed economies contract.

THE OLD-TIMERS: GREY REVOLUTION SUNBIRDS, NEW COMMUNALISTS, AND THE UNFULFILLED ASPIRATION OF AN ISLAND UTOPIA

At the beginning of 2012's popular film *The Descendents*, when talking about Honolulu, George Clooney remarks, "My friends on the mainland think just because I live in Hawai'i, I live in paradise. Like a permanent vacation. We're all just out here sipping Mai Tai's, shaking our hips, and catching waves. Are they insane? Paradise? Paradise can go fuck itself." Clooney's character, Matt King, with ethnic roots in a Native Hawai'ian culture that has been pushed off traditional lands and is rife with socioeconomic problems, is a wealthy landowner, and refers to himself when he quips, "Don't be fooled by appearances. In Hawai'i, some of the most powerful people look like bums and stuntmen." Honolulu's status as a tropical paradise allows it to ignore a lot of crime, homelessness, and houselessness. It is this tension between the soothing rhythms of tropical and indigenous life and the cold, hard steel of urban inequality that makes Honolulu part of this global urban ecosystem. It mirrors, in sharp definition, Lou Reed's quip contextualized in chapter 1: "I've been thinking of leaving . . . [New York] for, uh, 35 years now." It is a place to love and hate at the same time.

Honolulu's unique history cannot be replicated elsewhere. Its complex ethnic demography, particular land- and seascapes, as well as its position as a distinctive, but very real, one-fiftieth of the world's wealthiest country permeate the place. However, other states are now equally diverse, and Honolulu's tropical beaches are less exotic and the benefits of its U.S. political delegation less noteworthy, while other tropical locales become better serviced and more secure. Strange as it may seem, the direction of change prompts visions of washing out this uniqueness into a city that looks, more or less, like any other midsized American city, with the only major difference being its "equable climate." While other U.S. cities tout their aspirations with active nightlife and bustling downtowns, Honolulu plays these down in favor of the quiet life, community values, and its insularity from—as Thomas Friedman would have it—the flattening world.[19] As these threats of conformity to the United States loom, the deepest compliment in Honolulu is to be considered "local." Increasingly, the city is made up of the local born-and-bred who, indeed, have never left the islands for significant parts of their lives, and Kama'aina—naturalized locals—who are, in fact, global voyagers. In this way, the city reinvents itself in a historical image of the ancient Hawai'ian canoe voyagers rooted in island culture but jetting off across vast distances to do their daily, or monthly, business. Yesterday's canoes are soon to be today's Boeing Dreamliners and Airbus 380s, as the city is consistently reborn with new sets of young and fresh-faced, globe-trotting old-timers ready to champion the cause of local, nonglobal ways of living. What is more cosmopolitan than that?

These ideals, however, bump up against the ugly realities of the city that remind residents that they can never fully elude the trappings of modern urban life. Honolulu residents spend over fifty-eight hours stuck in traffic per year, on average, a traffic situation that is even worse than the vilified Los Angeles traffic situation;[20] in 2012, the city's Department of Environmental Services put a moratorium on new sewer connections on the fast-developing western side of the city, thereby severely limiting new construction, citing the fact that the city's aging sewer system could not accommodate any further stress; and the cost of new homeownership increased during the first decade of the twenty-first century to roughly 80 percent of household income, putting new homeownership out of the reach of most of the resident population and giving pause to those with big ambitions but smaller pocketbooks considering a move to the islands. While the ethic is a small-town, old-timer mentality, the problems are conventional and the result of big-city modernization and urbanization.

Three communities have come to call Honolulu home. Baby boomer retirees from the U.S. coasts looking for better weather, a culture of caring for elders, and numerous recreational activities to occupy their leisure time have come to characterize Honolulu, as have lifestyle-oriented young people from the continental United States, Japan, and elsewhere seeking a less-hectic approach to life, more environmental awareness, and a focus on community life that can be lacking in larger cities. I call these two communities "old-timers" because they each hearken back to neighborhood and small-scale community relationships that underlie the personality of the city. Sharing space with these New Communalists is a longer-standing Native Hawai'ian culture that embodies the true old-time culture of indigenous practices and identities formed prior to contact with Western and Asian settlers.

Honking your horn, speaking too loudly, and showing off your wealth are all frowned upon in Honolulu, perhaps because they threaten the community bonds that are so important in the local context, with excessively individualistic overtones. These community bonds are complicated, however, stemming not only from genuine interest in building human-scale relationships characteristic of a pre-"global" world but also from a desperate need to mobilize all collective resources in a global economy that loves the sand, surf, and symphony of Honolulu but cares little—and knows probably less—about an underworld of poverty-wage jobs, long hours, and some of the highest housing costs in the world. For some residents, the new communalism culture is a paradise of epic proportions and the preservation and reconstruction of a disappearing way of life. For others, however, that same identity comes of the need for poor people to pool their resources in a global economy. Every resident faces this universal question of the live-work balance, and the "Price of Paradise" often debated in the public eye is never far from a resident's mind.

THE GREY REVOLUTION:
THE PROMISE AND PERIL OF A RETIREMENT ECONOMY

Comprising 70 percent of the state's population, the city of Honolulu is, quite literally, a town of old-timers. In 2007, 14 percent of Hawai'i's residents were over the age of sixty-five, compared with a national average of 13 percent; by 2015, it is expected to be 17 percent. In fact, the anticipated growth rate of retirees between 2007 and 2035 is expected to be 112 percent—a doubling in twenty-eight years. This change is no general population increase or universal American pattern but a systematic greying of the state's and therefore the city's resident makeup: the number of working-age adults, aged eighteen–sixty-four, is expected to grow at only a 9.3 percent rate over the same period, and the number of young, aged zero–seventeen, at only a 14 percent rate.[21]

Add to these trends the fact that, according to the Pew Research Center, each and every day for the next nineteen years, ten thousand baby boomers will enter retirement age. With their savings, social security payments, and skills in tow, many of these sixty-nine million retirees will choose warm, small-scale, and community-oriented cities where symphonies, universities, open spaces, and good restaurants will keep them happy. There is a reason why the financial information website MoneyRates.com ranks Hawai'i in 2012 as the best state for retirement.[22]

Were the state of Hawai'i an independent country, this bulging group of retirees would spell disaster—in 2007 one working-age adult would have been needed to support about 0.25 senior-aged adult; projecting into the future, by 2035, this responsibility would have ballooned to almost twice that at 0.44. The growth of Honolulu's elderly population, however, represents an opportunity of sorts, born of the greying of both an in-place resident population and, importantly, newcomers to the city. In general, retirees' monthly incomes are comprised of state and federal benefits combined with personal savings and assets. Homegrown retirees spend federal income and personal savings, but the state increasingly sees the resident retirees as a potential drain on state fiscal resources, especially given relatively high proportions of public employees in Honolulu. On the other hand, it is migrants from other states that bring all three income sources—state and federal retirement packages, and personal assets—to spend in Honolulu that encourage the city to become more friendly to in-migration of the elderly. In general, greying populations are on the move, looking to escape cold winters, industrial environments, and impersonal communities: the adventurous and poorer ones are going to Southeast Asia and the tropics of the Global South; the more financially endowed and the homebodies are coming to places like Honolulu.

Because of its vibrant tourist industry and military bases, a relatively large percentage of people from the United States, Japan, and many other Organization for Economic Cooperation and Development (OECD) countries have been to Honolulu at least once. The numerous daily flights to the islands from cities as distant as New York, Tokyo, and Sydney, for example, give prospective retirees ample opportunities to visit Honolulu to explore options for retirement. The attractiveness of Honolulu, and Hawai'i in general, as a place to retire has definitely influenced the character of its urban culture. In his most recent book, *Who's Your City: How the Creative Economy Is Making Where to Live the Most Important Decision of Your Life,* urbanist Richard Florida characterizes the "personalities" of major American cities according to the typical profiles of people who move to be in them.[23] Not surprisingly, Honolulu ranks in the top four midsized regions for "empty-nesters" and retirees, but nowhere near that for young singles or professionals. Contrary to what many locals might claim, Honolulu also lags far behind for families with children, according to Florida, most likely because of the high cost of living and low-quality public education system.

While cost and affordability are major downsides of a migration to Honolulu for working-age people, mild weather, a slower pace, and Mumford's "universal verdure" significantly outweigh these aspects for those getting on in age. If ever there were a demographically mature big city, Honolulu is it. The demographics of globalization and the Grey Revolution make Honolulu's personality a hot commodity, but increasingly, for only the advanced in age and those who serve them. More subtly, though, it is not only the old in years who are attracted to Honolulu's personality but the "old-at-heart" as well, a group I term the "New Communalists."

THE NEW COMMUNALISTS

A new TV series titled *Portlandia* made an understated splash on cable TV in 2011 and instantly became a cult hit. This series, named after Oregon's urban jewel, might have been more aptly named after Honolulu because *Portlandia* is "the place where young people go to retire." The show's popularity gives narrative shape to an amorphous underlying current in American culture in which—as described by Richard Florida[24]—mobile urban residents are on the move to match their personalities with the places they call "home." In fact, a recent report by the Michigan Municipal League titled "The Economics of Place" found that about 65 percent of mobile young professionals decide where to live before they decide what job to look for. Cities such as Portland, Seattle, Austin, and Chattanooga have things that New York, Los Angeles, Chicago, and even San Francisco don't: a balanced quality of life.

Richard Florida is not the only one ranking American cities by who should be attracted to move there. Bloomberg News[25] ranked Honolulu as the third-best place to live in the United States in 2011, behind first-place Raleigh, North Carolina, and Arlington, Virginia, an affluent suburb of Washington, D.C. In that same year, the Quality of Living Worldwide Survey[26] ranked Honolulu as the city with the twenty-ninth-highest "quality of living" globally. While not immediately impressive, this position placed it as the highest-ranking American city, just ahead of San Francisco and Boston.

Designed as a metric for global corporations to assess the "degree to which expatriates enjoy the standard of living in each host location," criteria are broken down into ten areas ranging from economic environment to sociocultural environment, public transportation, schools, consumer goods, and housing, for example. Of all major American cities, the report argues, Honolulu is the most receptive to global migrants, counterintuitively illustrating how midsized cities can sometimes have an advantage over their "mega" counterparts in attracting a global resident base. In 2000, about 86,000 Japanese nationals lived in Honolulu, significantly more than in London or Los Angeles, and more than twice as many—in raw numbers—than in New York City, which is almost ten times its size! These Japanese nationals rubbed shoulders with over 170,000 Filipino nationals in Hawai'i;[27] a significant expatriate community of Koreans, who maintain a popular full-time Korean-language television station; and an expatriate community of Brazilians, who populate the local and global surfing scene.

Unlike other cities targeted by global migrants, Honolulu is not dominated by a powerful industry such as New York's Wall Street, San Francisco's Silicon Valley, or Shanghai's huge labor force of cheap workers. It has no major industrial plant or agricultural operations calling out to adventurous workers looking to test their fortunes. For sure, some come to take jobs in the tourist industry or in health care, but the true comparative advantage of Honolulu is the place itself. It is a place where weekends are spent at the beach, workdays end at five o'clock, and organized sports on the water, fields, and courts abound. As with seniors finished with the "rat race," these migrants from the continental United States and elsewhere are more interested in a balanced and personally satisfying and personally sustainable lifestyle as an alternative to the high-performance and high-maintenance lives of their peers in New York City, Tokyo, and Rio. No one comes to Honolulu to "make it"; from the New Communalist's point of view, to live in Honolulu is to *have* "made it."

It's not that those who choose Honolulu as home are slackers with no other options, though there certainly are some of these. Many are professionals, entrepreneurs, and holders of advanced degrees. In fact, 35 percent of the city's residents are college graduates, and it has ranked between fifteenth and fiftieth in terms of residents' educational achievements. Even beyond simple formal education, Honolulu ranks as the seventh "brainiest" metropolitan area, according to Lumos Labs, and the second—only to the San Francisco/Oakland/San Jose region— for cities with populations of over three hundred thousand.[28] Using a measure of individual cognitive performance in online game plays, Honolulu punches well above its weight, and not surprising for a remote island, its high performers are lighting up the Internet almost as well as is Silicon Valley.

While not among the elite, Honolulu is one of the brainier cities out there. If not for attractive jobs, what brings these educated residents, once they graduate from some of the best universities in the country, to Honolulu and keeps them there? In large part, it is the values and philosophy of the place's localism and sustainability that keeps them there. The state's motto is "*Ua mau ke ea o ka aina i ka pono*," or "The life of the land is perpetuated in righteousness," and this overall emphasis has taken material shape in the form of major public decisions such as those to prohibit billboards, popular inclinations to purchase local products, and an ingrained allergy—often justified—to further developing land. Hearkening back to a simpler time and place, the New Communalists' values, preferences, and habits mesh well with a community more deeply rooted in the land upon which Honolulu rests.

NATIVE HAWAI'IAN RENAISSANCE

Today, roughly 290,000 Native Hawai'ians live in Hawai'i. In 1990, about 162,000 did, and by 2000, 282,000 did. A 75 percent jump between 1990 and 2000 is one of those statistical disjunctures that make one do a double take, wondering if prodigious procreation or data entry errors led to the change. In fact, neither did. Rather, in 2000, the U.S. Census of Population and Housing challenged all respondents to consider their multiple ethnic origins by allowing more than one response to the questions related to ethnic background. With almost no fully Native Hawai'ians alive today, the 1990 figure, a number that boomed when the census' long form showing multiple ethnicity response categories was introduced in 2000, surely included many partially indigenous respondents. This change was a recognition, not just for Hawai'ians, that Americans can and should be proud of their mixed heritage. For Hawai'ians, this particularly meant that their indigenous heritage could be more fully valued as part of Hawai'i's and Honolulu's unique composition. The popularity of this choice of proudly claiming a Hawai'ian identity reflected a long-simmering and hard-fought political battle waged by Native Hawai'ians to bolster pride in their history, earn respect from the broader American society, and cultivate their indigenous traditions even within the context of globalized and dominating Western and Asian societies. The 3 percent change between 2000 and 2010 shows a building momentum of this pride and reflects the continued resurgence and renaissance of a Hawai'ian character to the state and, particularly notable, to the city of Honolulu.

Concurrent with this renaissance, however, is the awkward fact that about 237,000 Hawai'ians live on the continental United States, not counting those that live abroad. While certainly some follow in the entrepreneurially voyaging spirit endemic to the vast open spaces of Pacific cultures, undoubtedly many more feel the centripetal pressure of high living costs and few economic opportunities of Honolulu. Most Honolulans feel this centripetal force, but gentrification always affects those at the bottom of the socioeconomic ladder the most. Moderate-income families in Honolulu cannot "drive 'til they qualify" for mortgages, as well they might in comparable American cities. Therefore, the choice left to many Native Hawai'ians, who often have a powerful cultural attachment to their native lands (which is common to most indigenous communities) and who are struggling to reconcile aspirations for their and their kids' futures with the shockingly limited work and affordable housing options in Honolulu, is relocation. The options are a short move to the isolated big island of Hawai'i, where housing is cheap but unemployment runs consistently at about three percentage points above the rest of the state, or relocation to the continental United States. It is not surprising that one of the most popular destinations is Las Vegas, where housing has been historically cheap and working-class jobs plentiful. For a smaller number, the best choice is to join the growing homeless camps on the beaches just outside of the Honolulu city center.

Compounding these affordability challenges that Hawai'ians face in their own land, the Hawai'ian renaissance lies atop a community facing some major social challenges. Between 2000 and 2008, 147,000 Native Hawai'ians were arrested,[29] from which a significant number ended up incarcerated. Like their minority counterparts on the mainland, Native Hawai'ians have a complicated relationship with Honolulu's law enforcement. From both sides of the bars, Native Hawai'ians, sadly, end up with long-term engagements with the criminal justice system: at times as beat officers and judges but more often as arrestees, prisoners, and juvenile detainees. Even this engagement has an out-migration component; of about 6,000 incarcerated adults from Hawai'i in 2005, fully 29 percent were sent to the continent to serve their terms, mostly in Arizona facilities. Thus, not counted among the Native Hawai'ians on the continent, an additional 730 are housed in isolated correctional facilities far from friends and family. Ironically, there is not even any affordable housing for prisoners in the city of Honolulu.[30]

All these socioeconomic problems beset the Native Hawai'ian community, even though they—as a distinct community—are one of the financially richest in the country. To be sure, average incomes, educational levels, and crime statistics are well below local and national averages of other groups. As individuals and families, Native Hawai'ians face major challenges in daily life. However, this individual poverty masks a very powerful and resource-rich *community*. And I don't mean abstract or philosophical resources. Native Hawai'ians are served by two very large and important financial and political resources: Kamehameha Schools and the Office of Hawai'ian Affairs. Together, they represent assets of almost $8 billion—mostly attributable to Kamehameha Schools—and combined annual revenues of roughly $50 million. If these assets were divided up evenly among all Native Hawai'ians in Hawai'i, every man, woman, and child would receive about $25,000 as a one-time payment. Rightly, few believe that this kind of individual asset building would systematically improve opportunities; the community assets do, however, indicate that the issue is not one of individuals but one of community, and, more broadly, culture.

The financial and political power of Native Hawaiʻians, actually, is substantial, and the thorny question is how to deploy these resources in a way that identifies, preserves, and constructs an authentic Hawaiʻian identity within a modern American metropolis. Wealthy indigenous communities with severe individual poverty are nothing new to the United States. Tribal casinos and resorts have ensured that some Native Americans have new economic tools to counter the global and modernization forces flattening out cultural differences. The distinction for Native Hawaiʻians in Honolulu, however, is that these resources are deployed in a city of over one million indigenous and nonindigenous residents. As with its tropical assets, it is the proximity to the urbanness that makes the Hawaiʻian indigenous identity globally competitive. If Alexie's "urban Indian" is the contemporary reality of Native America, Honolulu represents America's best chance to build the "Indian urban," or an "Indigenous City," based on an identity of collective entrepreneurialism and the strength of community in a global society.

In the end, the Native Hawaiʻian question is not about money but about collective action. And it is this that the city of Honolulu is banking on. Honolulu is a cultural phenomenon, and it is on this that the city is forging its global identity as other tropical paradises come into their own and attract the tourists, visitors, and retirees, on which Honolulu depends so much, to other, more competitive locales. Developing this global identity, however, requires strategic growth and development at the citywide scale, two phenomena that have not come easy to Honolulu.

THE PROBLEM WITH GROWTH: ELEVATED RAIL, SOLID WASTE, AND THE BACKBONE OF A GLOBAL CITY

Honolulu's identity as a city of old-timers presents a development dilemma in an age of global migration and real estate investment. The global demand for an island paradise with a balanced quality of life, ample social and cultural amenities, and major educational institutions is—not surprisingly—healthy. Only the professionally ambitious and family oriented stay away, because of the city's relative isolation, high cost of living, and poor schools. The problem is that these are the kinds of residents most in demand by urban leaders. They pay more into the tax base, start new businesses, consume more goods and services, and pressure local school systems to perform better. They keep a city of old-timers and New Communalists from becoming a city of slackers.

Since Honolulu is coming off a century of backbreaking work in plantation agriculture, it is understandable that Honolulu might cherish its newfound appreciation for the city's natural assets that Mumford praised long ago. Nevertheless, some outward blemishes on the surface of Honolulu's urban paradise suggest some inner decay of the system.

The city and county of Honolulu has seen its fair share of development dilemmas over the past decade. At the start of the twenty-first century, the city confronted a number of big-city problems that brought its small-town residents out into the streets. These growth conflicts bubbled up into local debates about public transit, solid waste, and sewers—a familiar and gritty city narrative lying just below the glamorous veneer of Waikiki's swaying palm trees, rolling surf, and echoing Hawai'ian chants.

In a city without billboards, that famous Boston roadside advertisement for in-city development stating "If you lived here, you'd be home by now"[31] has no chance to quietly chastise driving commuters. In this one case, the city's restrictions on roadside billboards might be dysfunctional, since Honolulans spend so much time stuck in traffic. It is ironic that in a land more than five thousand miles from the nearest major landmass, Honolulu residents face some of the country's and world's severest traffic problems. According to the traffic analysis firm INRIX, Honolulu tops the charts on a composite index of traffic congestion measured at both the metropolitan and "corridor" level. Beating out Los Angeles, San Francisco, and New York City in that order, Honolulu is poised to become the largest parking lot not just in the middle of the Pacific but in the United States, the world's most auto-dependent nation. In real terms, residents lose over fifty hours of their time stuck in traffic each year, and this is not the kind of "big time" that the New Communalists had in mind.

To help alleviate this big-city problem, former mayor Frank Fasi began planning a high-speed rail project in 1977 with support from the federal Department of Transportation. With the election of Ronald Reagan, however, the project foundered with the withdrawal of federal funding, leaving potentially burdensome state tax obligations associated with the project—if it were to be approved—during a recessionary period.[32] The vigorous vocal opposition, resulting from this withdrawal, to an already controversial public transit project meant that this investment would need to wait until another day. By 2004, with the election of Mayor Mufi Hannemann, the project was back on the table because the traffic problem—especially between the growing western side of the city and downtown—was worse than ever. After years of heated debate, voters approved—by a narrow margin of 53 percent to 47 percent—a 2008 ballot-box decree to move forward with the transit project, even though the projected costs were over $5 billion, making it the most expensive public works project in the city's history.

The future holds numerous opportunities to derail Honolulu's rail project, as old-timers vying to preserve Honolulu's nonurban character clash with its more pragmatic New Communalists and others willing to make the trade-offs. In particular, it is the aesthetic concerns voiced by the local chapter of the American Institute of Architects, which opposes the project. For them, transit represents cold, concrete structures, interrupted viewsheds, and noise pollution. The end result of the rail project will be a good indicator of whether the city is prepared to make the transition from a local to a global city.

If Honolulans have rudely awoken to big-city transportation debates, the issue of what to do with the city's garbage has surely compounded this dilemma of how to retain a small-town character in an increasingly global world. When you buy a newspaper in a Honolulu Safeway, you will inevitably receive it back from the cashier in a plastic bag—this is the case whether you purchased eggs, milk, and bread, for example, along with that newspaper or just the paper alone. Convincing the cashier that a bag is unnecessary can sometimes make you appear to be some form of off-the-grid survivalist.

During the 2012 legislative session of the Hawai'i State Legislature, State Senator Mike Gabbard took inspiration from a Honolulu City Council and mayor–supported ordinance to reduce single-use plastic bags and introduced a long-awaited bill to limit their excessive use by Honolulu's retailers by requiring them to charge for single-use bags. With general support from lawmakers, supermarkets, and even the Girl Scouts, the local chapter of the Sierra Club mobilized public and private support for the measure. Their excitement stemmed from the fact that the state of Hawai'i produces 41 percent more solid waste per capita than do its national counterparts and that the waste disposal facilities in Honolulu are some of the dirtiest facilities on the islands.[33] To top it off, landfill space on the island of Oʻahu is at a premium, and debates about how to expand solid waste disposal sites have been contentious for years. Given the fact that plastic grocery bags are said to take over five hundred years to decompose,[34] it seemed like a slam dunk to get the bill passed with minimal opposition. Against all logic, House Bill 2483 effectively died when Speaker of the House Calvin Say failed to forward it to conference committee during the 2012 legislative session,[35] thereby letting the Safeway, Foodland, and Times Supermarket chains continue to import plastic bags into Honolulu and bury them in the city's landfills, burn them up in the city's incinerator, or let them float off into the sea and forests. Because it is a good idea, the proposal is sure to come around again, perhaps with a stronger political base, and who knows whether this obviously beneficial policy will survive Round 2? A city of old-timers trying to protect its natural environment this is not—at least in practice.

The broader problem of solid waste management came to a head in 2011, when the city council recognized that the city's waste had become too great to handle through its own landfills and made the decision that many American mayors and city councils have: to export its garbage. Some cities such as New York used to send their waste over to a neighboring part of the state but now ship it out to poorer rural communities in Pennsylvania, Ohio, and Virginia—communities faced with the Faustian choice of whether or not to be paid to clean up after others' messes. From time to time, a city's garbage will crisscross oceans looking for a port or country to accept it for a fee, as happened in the late 1980s with one of Long Island's garbage barges named the *Mobro 4000*. The Honolulu City Council's choice to become part of this trading system was both a philosophical blow to a sustainability-oriented philosophy valuing localism and a serious logistical challenge.

In late 2009, the Honolulu City Council voted to authorize a private firm to ship over one hundred thousand tons of solid waste to a landfill in Washington State. Ironically, this site would have been adjacent to the Yakima Indian Nation, which initiated a lawsuit against the proposed plan, thereby holding up all shipments. As the waste accumulated on the docks in Honolulu, city residents began to realize that its problems—and solutions—were not much different from other big cities'. In response to a ruling against the trash transfer, Honolulu city officials agreed to dispose of the steadily accumulating waste by burning it in the city's existing incineration plant, effectively postponing the problem to a later date.

The issue of solid waste sitting on the docks is emblematic of a big challenge that the city of Honolulu faces. The challenge is both technical and political, as the failure of the plastic bag bill illustrates. The city sits on an incredibly beautiful island about as far from any large, open land spaces as one can get. Because land in Hawai'i, and in particular in Honolulu, is at such a premium, it is difficult to identify sites that meet the economic and political threshold for a sufficiently cheap location to place a dump. Add to that fact the unpleasant neighborhood spillover effects—in the immediate form of unpleasant smells and inconvenient and noisy truck traffic, and in the longer term in the form of environmental contamination. In part, because of these characteristics—very high real estate values, virtually no "hinterland" to hide unpleasant externalities, and a political environment in which environmental concerns can affect the city's economic base of tourism—Honolulu has all the elements of a form of NIMBYism on steroids. Because it is an island, however, the only place that is not in Honolulu's "backyard" is somewhere as distant as Washington State.

This technical characteristic of Honolulu's geography, environment, and economy underlies an important political crisis of Honolulu's identity as an old-timer city. As with other forms of NIMBYism, the losers tend to be poor and generally "minority" neighborhoods. Despite its isolation from the continent, Honolulu has made choices similar to other big cities' and has placed both its primary landfill and its incineration plant on the Leeward Coast of O'ahu, a generally poorer and disproportionately Native Hawai'ian area. It is ironic that the intended destination for the exported garbage was next to Native American lands and the default destination is likely to be the Waimanalo Gulch, next to the largest concentration of Native Hawai'ians on O'ahu.

On the one hand, the problem is a technical issue of solid waste disposal and management on a piece of land that is more like Manhattan than Fresh Kills, the final destination for much of New York City's solid waste. On the other hand, the underlying problem is an issue of who bears the cost of waste disposal siting decisions. That is a political problem inherent to any city but especially to Honolulu, where, because of its island geography, hiding the city's trash out of sight and out of mind is not an option. Even if Honolulu had a large hinterland of cheap real estate, like other big cities, it would most likely do what has happened in so many other places, where housing for minority and disadvantaged communities lies in close proximity to toxic waste disposal sites: find the community with the smallest political voice to locate its dumps and simultaneously minimize economic and political costs. Ironically, the nascent Indigenous City was slapped on the hand for sending its trash to the continental indigenous countryside, but responds by sending it to its Hawaiʻian indigenous community. Without a fundamental restructuring of politics and urban infrastructure, the Indigenous City—even with a relatively vibrant community advocating for Native Hawaiʻian interests—looks a lot like other cities.

To be true to its ideals of localism, sustainability, and a less-complicated time when urban problems could be solved—at least in theory—by working together with neighbors, Honolulu needs to find ways to live with its trash and not foist it on distant others. The only way to deal with this problem of development, however, is through reducing waste production—a goal realizable only far in the future, if the fate of the plastic bag bill is any indicator. Until then, the city will continue to substitute sending its trash to distant communities with the other option—sending its trash to communities whose distance from the urban center is measured in political power rather than in miles: the Native Hawaiʻian communities. The real challenge of an island ecosystem, it turns out, is not a technical one at all. It is mostly political, in particular, a challenge of turning the political debate into an urban one where collective interests and decisions can be envisioned and made at the level of the citywide community rather than at the neighborhood or statewide level. In fact, Honolulu is a big-city community with small-town politics.

Urban infrastructure is the backbone of a strong and modern democracy and, therefore, a good window into the tensions between local politics and urban politics. Whether they live in the most rarefied enclave or the most hardscrabble housing project, urban residents depend on their city to provide them with the most basic services such as water and sanitation, electricity, and transportation. Urbanists have known this fact since the cholera epidemics forced London to build

extensive water and sanitation public works. It is these shared resources, investments, and interdependencies that keep every city
neighborhood, community, and resident engaged in productive discussions and negotiations; they all depend on a shared urban-service resource base. In the island context of Honolulu, the absence or decay of
these mutual interdependencies threatens the natural and social assets
that make the city unique.

In Honolulu, the importance of developing this backbone is often
lost in the debate. Fiscal naysayers and technical critics often dominate
public discourse about transit and waste disposal, but the underlying
questions are always larger and thornier. Technical reports and fiscal
analyses are more often rational documents used to overlay highly
emotional and partisan stances rather than materials to support effective decision making beyond a narrow band of highly trained technical
experts. Urban megaprojects are always about much more than dollars
and cents. The Sydney Opera House, New York's Empire State Building,
and Kuala Lumpur's Petronas Towers are all defining characteristics of
their respective cities, and all were major fiscal burdens. As visionary
projects, they were never meant primarily as sound financial investments to make a profit or to cover costs. In a narrow sense, the ways
in which they contributed to their respective urban economies could
never have been accurately specified a priori. They were investments to
create and develop each city's identity on a global stage by coalitions of
municipal and private interests. It is this identity that is the subtext of
the ongoing debate on Honolulu rail and the city's reluctance to invest
in big-city infrastructure, and the nature of the debate over whether
this city should spend what many estimate to be about $5 billion on
the project.

A project of this scale, with a time horizon of almost twenty years
into the future, will never come down to today's math—it is all about
ascertaining and creating the future. As even the first-time home buyer
knows, there are too many contingencies to determine if a purchase,
in the end, makes financial sense. Unemployment spells, fluctuations
in family size, and changing real estate values all affect the wisdom
of a thirty-year mortgage in retrospect—to think otherwise is hubris.
The difference is that a timely sale always waits in the wings as a viable exit option for home buyers. This option, however, is unavailable
to city mayors. On the other hand, political officials have significant

alternatives for revenue generation, savings, and refinance of the assets in which they invest. No one wants a city loan to go underwater, and besides, like the homeowner, city residents benefit from use in the meantime.

The true make-or-break variable is political leadership. During the city's most recent incarnation of leadership, Mayor Mufi Hannemann led the charge to reshape Honolulu's urban identity and turn it into a city worthy of being called "the Capital of the Pacific." As mayor, his strategy included embracing Kapolei as a "second city" of Honolulu and emphasized developing the city's walkable streets. However, after six initial years of progress, Hannemann left office to try his hand at an unsuccessful run for the governorship. With his departure came another blow to Honolulu's urban aspirations and the physical backbone of a world-class city.

The debate on elevated rail and Honolulu's investment in its urban infrastructure rests on good and committed leadership. And ironically, it is the collective horse-trading among the various political elites—the mayor, the governor, the city council, Native Hawai'ian organizations, and the civil society leaders—that will allow the city to break out of its paralysis and recognize itself as a big city with big-city challenges requiring big-city solutions. Without such kinds of political, economic, and civic leadership, Honolulu will never become its own destination rather than an appendage of Waikiki and the tourist industry. Achieving such unity of overarching purpose amidst such diversities of interest is challenging, but some recent events have shown promise at making this philosophical leap to a more-urban politics. Political leaders have upgraded the city's aspirations based on its identity as an old-timer city in a global and cosmopolitan region, opening the door for the city's old-timers to reconcile Honolulu's small-town character with a big-city reality.

CONSTRUCTING THE GOOD OLD DAYS: APEC, THE *AHUPUA'A*, AND *KAKA'AKO*

In 2008 the city and county of Honolulu embarked on an interesting but short-lived campaign to promote itself based on the idea of a "twenty-first-century ahupua'a," which showed some promise but suggested few actionable ideas. It proposed developing a new urban identity rooted in culturally and historically relevant practices. In doing so, it hoped to integrate the island's human and environmental resources into a broad development strategy by knitting mountains, plains, and oceans into a mutually dependent social, political, and ecological entity: the ancient Hawai'ian concept of land management called "the ahupua'a."

The powerful part of the ahupua'a concept is the structured diversity of land (and water) uses into a single region. Governance of those complex socio-ecological regions was through the brilliance of a traditional Hawai'ian society that saw the need to keep internal to the governance structure the diverse resources upon which all depended. This brilliance, however, was not born of some kind of indigenous affinity toward "sustainability" as some might now construe. Rather, it stemmed from a perceptive view of the limitations presented by life on an island with limited landmass and little connection to a larger society, as well as the limitations on mobility imposed by steep valley walls.

Today, Honolulu faces different limitations of isolation such as the physical discomfort of sitting through long flights, high transport costs for daily consumer goods, and an insufficient tax base due to its limited population. The city's choice to frame its efforts from the perspective of an ahupua'a reflects an affinity toward an old-timer identity likely to appeal to the disparate political interests of the city. The concept usefully oriented the city's sights outward toward its ocean-ward resources rather than inward—a useful political trope, but in the context of Honolulu, compelling and realistic.

This outward orientation bore major fruit in 2011, when Honolulu had the opportunity to showcase its unique culture and identity during the November 2011 Asia-Pacific Economic Cooperation (APEC) meeting—a meeting of almost twenty heads of state from the Asia Pacific region. Many local and international doubters questioned whether the city that foundered for over twenty years on a rail project could manage the logistics, security, and hospitality needed for U.S. president Barack Obama, Chinese premier Hu Jintao, the prime minister of Japan, and their counterparts and entourages. Seemingly much to the surprise of its residents, the event went off without a hitch and under budget. The only grumble heard locally was that visitor spending in Waikiki was down during the meetings even though the number of visitors was up. And in this fact lies one of the central dilemmas facing Honolulu. The short-term loss of tourist revenue rankles some old-timers more than do the long-term opportunities inherent in greater global integration.

For others, long-term investment is the necessary work of development. Aged old-timers often see little value in long-term investments sure to bear fruit only long after they are gone. A New Communalist old-timer, on the other hand, can view them cautiously as necessary trade-offs to enable a good quality of life for the future, and the indigenous old-timer can view them through the lens of intergenerational cultural identity. Following on after APEC 2011, the real question is whether the city can generate the will across these divergent old-timer interests to invest in its urban identity and, therefore, shape a contemporary reality consistent with its aspirations and potential.

As with any intriguing idea, Honolulu's twenty-first-century ahupua'a promoters risked overpromising and underdelivering. At the time, the city's website defined the twenty-first-century ahupua'a as: public transit, alternative fuels, green construction, sensitivity to host culture, reef and forest protection, recycling, and more agriculture. While none of these goals were objectionable, they didn't jump to mind as particularly "ahupua'a-ish," and therefore withered away with the election of a new mayor in 2010. Rather than be a rallying call for balancing urban development with local traditions, the effort came off more as a political co-optation of an ancient Hawai'ian concept in service of the general objectives of a broadly defined and universalizing concept of "sustainability."

The plans sounded like plain old sustainability and localism, which will never work as a strategy for the future now that others have claimed that mantle; Portland, Vancouver, and others have a leg up on Honolulu regarding sustainability. Where they fall shorter is in the more unique cultural characteristics of the place. With globalization and new technologies, today's scope of view stretches far beyond what could have been conceivable even one hundred years ago. Today, Honolulu's ahupua'as are the Pacific, the mainland United States, East Asia, Southeast Asia, and even South America. A city strategy for facilitating cheap and comfortable transportation up and down these ahupua'as for business, tourism, and family visits, for better integrating financial transactions between Honolulu and these ahupua'as, for developing labor market exchanges across them, for creatively thinking about cofinancing shared infrastructure to make the ocean between the Honolulu and offshore landmasses more productive, and for strengthening Honolulu's neighborhoods to reflect and encourage these identities through supporting the arts and businesses that strengthen these ties are ideas consistent with contemporary globalization and Honolulu's old-timer identity. If the city can manage its ahupua'as in any of these ways, it will have truly bridged the old with the new in a material way consistent with the philosophy of its residents.

Like the city's efforts to create a twenty-first-century ahupua'a, the case of development in Kaka'ako illustrates the dilemma of trying to respect the past while simultaneously growing the future. In November 2011, Hawai'i governor Neil Abercrombie announced a historic agreement with the Office of Hawai'ian Affairs to settle a thirty-year-old claim regarding the state's seizure of "ceded lands." This long-standing claim had been seemingly resolved through the allocation of prime real estate in Kaka'ako to the OHA on behalf of the Hawai'ian people. Nestled between Waikiki, the city's financial downtown, and the open shores of the South Pacific, the six-hundred-acre neighborhood of Kaka'ako represents a prime, yet undeveloped, neighborhood in a city where land is at a premium. By granting these lands to Native Hawai'ians, the state tied the issue of Native Hawai'ian sovereignty to urban development.

By facilitating a political coalition to create urban density in Kaka'ako, the governor hoped to limit sprawl on O'ahu, allow for more productive utilization of agricultural land, and create a third urban destination, after Waikiki and Kapolei, the neighborhood at the end of the proposed rail line. In 2012, however, Kaka'ako was far from being a destination itself, serving as home to a haphazard collection of car repair shops, struggling small businesses, empty lots, and streets without sidewalks all within a short stroll of those million-dollar views of the South Pacific. Although the area has been under the planning control of the Hawai'i Community Development Authority (HCDA) for decades, neighborhood change has been painfully slow. Supposedly environmental concerns with high-rises obstructing views, Native Hawai'ian concerns over disturbing traditional burial sites, and surfers' concerns over revealing and overcrowding a perfect surf break have all led to oppositional roadblocks to development in a neighborhood that could potentially connect the city's two major centers of activity.

As with many other urban revitalization projects, plans can often seem mismatched with demand for the types of high-end residential developments proposed. While disputes over burial grounds, beach access, and viewsheds dominate the public debate, it is the underlying demand for the neighborhood that keeps the project foundering in rough surf. The need to limit sprawl on a small island is acute, but doing so goes well beyond a neighborhood focus, which those "brainy" Honolulans sense but cannot quite articulate. Somewhere deep down, they realize that simple real estate deals to gentrify a neighborhood are not an urban strategy for growth and development.

The basic fear is a scenario in which developers are allowed to build luxury condos that locals cannot afford. With household incomes averaging only about $50,000 and supported in large part by a low-wage tourist industry, the city's residents increasingly compete for new housing with a large cohort of mobile and retirement-aged Californians, New Yorkers, and Japanese, supported by their Silicon Valley, Wall Street, and government savings. Honolulans are in a very weak position indeed; their salaries cannot compete with the wealth of these new migrants, it is very difficult to limit in-migration, and even if it were, the key to improving the city's position in a global economy lies in greater integration, not isolation. As has often been the case in paradise, snowbirds—and especially those retiring baby-boomer ones—will bid prices out of the reach of locals and swoop in to purchase investment properties, retirement homes, and pieds-à-terre in one of the most physically attractive neighborhoods in the world; and who can blame them? Without a sophisticated economic development strategy, Honolulans will always be priced out of their own neighborhoods. And in this way, all Honolulans share what is most acute for the true Native Hawai'ian old-timers: the feeling of being outsiders in their own land.

The global urban ecosystem is an urban world where individual interaction can directly engage across vast geographic and social divides, made possible not only by technology but also by the shared and increasingly universal practices of urbanity. The problem with this kind of urbanity, however, is the possibility it presents of washing out the local particularities that make residents comfortable. While local culture may be under threat in Saigon and Addis, their respective interests are backed by national populations of over eighty million each and independent national governments. Honolulu has no such demographic or political resources upon which to draw, and apparently reasonable development projects such as Kaka'ako often take on an underlying theme of carpetbagging by outsiders.

For example, an urban neighborhood with all the natural, cultural, and physical amenities possible in Kaka'ako requires a vibrant urban economy to match it. Wall Street incomes can support Soho and Tribeca with local residents and businesses; Silicon Valley can support Nob Hill and Noe Valley in San Francisco; a low-wage tourism industry will never be able to support the kind of dense Kaka'ako that would limit sprawl. To do that requires a big-city economy offering much more to workers than a tourism industry ever could. Honolulu will always attract those from the United States and elsewhere, and the affordability of the city rests not only on policies to keep costs down but also on policies to increase local purchasing power in a national and global economy. There is no going back to an isolated existence, and the question is how, not whether, Honolulu will grow in the context of an increasingly global and competitive market for tropical urban paradises.

Honolulans should know that such kinds of change do not come naturally. As in the past, Honolulans will have to create their own future much in the same way that they invested in and created a tourist economy, in years past, based on Mumford's "equable climate" and "universal verdure." There is little that is natural about Honolulu; even the pristine and beautiful natural environment of the city's major tourist destination, Waikiki, is a constructed past. Because the fact that most of Waikiki Beach's beautiful white sand is imported from as far away as the north shore of O'ahu and Los Angeles is well-known locally, Hawai'i Department of Land and Natural Resources administrator Sam Lemmo nonchalantly states, "[Waikiki] is almost completely manufactured."[36] There is little that is natural about Honolulu, and that is okay; the sooner Honolulu's old-timers recognize this and begin to create their future, the greater the city's chances of finding a unique spot in the global urban ecosystem.

CHAPTER 6

"FOR-ALL-TIMERS": NEW YORK CITY'S *EMPIRE STATE OF MIND*

One of the biggest hits of the twenty-first century so far is a quietly sentimental anthem originally composed by two native New Yorkers who were missing home in 2009. "Empire State of Mind" was picked up, rewritten, and recorded by rapper Jay-Z, who recruited fellow New Yorker Alicia Keys as his duet partner for the blockbuster song that went on to be played at Yankee games and in New York State promotional videos. The song's intense feeling of New York City as a place can only be conveyed through viewing the lyrics in their entirety. Much like an ecosystem itself, the constituent parts cannot be usefully extracted from the whole. However, because of restrictive copyright laws, I am unable to reproduce any part of this lyrical ecosystem. Thus, I would encourage readers to view the original CD sleeve or do an Internet search for the relevant lines of the song's ecosystem where I suggest. First, begin with the song's first four lines (Verse 1, lines 1–4), then move to Alicia Keys's chorus (Chorus, lines 1–7).

As Jay-Z fondly reminisces about the pathways that he carved out of the concrete jungle, noting landmarks as he goes, New Yorkers the world over will recognize the tense mix of survivalist bravado and creative inspiration that defines a place both celebrated and reviled. It is this state of mind that transforms everything around it and permeates the air of the city.

Like Honolulu, New York City pulls its geographically much-larger state along by the coattails. Unlike its distant cousin isolated in the middle of the Pacific, however, New York City is one of the first cities that come to mind in the context of globalization and urbanization. Even as the growing megacities of China and the developing world capture headlines, something unique remains about New York. Being more populous, Tokyo and Mexico City, for example, have exceeded New York in demographic weight for decades. Being globally diverse, Los Angeles and London better reflect the twenty-first-century demography of the rising BRICS (Brazil, Russia, India, China, South Africa), where Asia, Africa, and Latin America play increasingly important roles in the global economy. And being economically dynamic, Mumbai and Silicon Valley are much further ahead of New York in the kinds of innovations seen to be the most exciting of the twenty-first century.

What keeps this city at the forefront of globalization has more to do with culture—and in particular a culture of urbanity—than any of these simpler and more convenient metrics. This culture has two important components: a distinct physical form and a political quality born of this form that facilitates problem solving, transformation, and resilience. What today looks like a dynamic, exciting, and timeless city has not always been so. In fact, as recently as thirty years ago, it was all but dead, seen as a rotting shell of concrete and infrastructure crumbling through neglect; the object of suspicion from the federal government and residents alike.

At some points during the twentieth century, New York as a symbol of decay and hatred got so bad as to become the official federal stance. In 1975, the *New York Daily News* ran a front-page headline that has lived on even thirty years after the fact: "[President] Ford to City: Drop Dead!"[1] New York City's distinct urban identity has been contentious, and few other agglomerations have retained the kind of unique personality able to conjure up such scorn from the most powerful man in the world, yet also to weather its consequences. Digging deeper down into the mechanics of how this urban culture and identity function will reveal that a more universal set of characteristics underlies each of the unique cities in the global urban ecosystem, making them edgy and familiar; exciting, yet safe.

New York City is the quintessential city to which others are compared. It is old, but in a sense, it is globally quite new; contrary to the old saying, it is actually *new* wine in *old* bottles. Unlike contemporary major centers in Europe and parts of Asia, New York is the primary city that came of age as an economic entity rather than as a capital of a national empire. London, Paris, Tokyo, and now Beijing are political centers lying atop national geographies; an urban face flashing national powers. New York is a city formed by the chaos of "the market" rather than the order of nation-states and comparatively free of national ideologies embedded within colonial and Cold War histories that define even other economic city-states such as Hong Kong and Singapore. In part because of this openness and freedom from national ideologies, New York has developed a reputation for creativity, speed, and global trendsetting that has persisted for generations of residents who sometimes see their identities as New Yorkers first and Americans a close second.

One cannot begin to talk about globalization and New York City without first talking about its twenty-first-century creation story—9/11. In 2001, two Boeing 767s toppled the iconic World Trade Center buildings into a heap of flames, dust, and steel. By September 12, 2001, New York's context was completely different. Ironically, though, it was the software of the city rather than its hardware that had changed the most. Physical destruction of the buildings—terrible as it was—was only the tip of a much-larger social and psychological change that the city underwent, and which it still confronts.

As the magnitude of those terrorist events and the detailed planning necessary to pull them off came to light in the following days, New Yorkers were forced to confront some ugly truths about the city they called home. Educated in the *New Yorker* magazine's self-centered, west-facing map of the world depicting East Side, Central Park, West Side, Hudson River, New Jersey, western United States, and China all in decreasing importance, many New Yorkers woke up that day to realize how their locality has had an impact—both symbolic and material—on the world. They also realized that what it represented to those far corners of the globe was no longer just the shining light of the Statue of Liberty.

In the years following 9/11, the United States invaded Afghanistan and Iraq, and encountered serious challenges to its civil liberties as the Patriot Act emboldened law enforcement to chase down even a hint of fundamentalism or suspected disloyalty on both American soil and abroad. These global and domestic shocks literally changed the face of urban America and New York City as much as anywhere. Concrete barricades, security gates, and bulletproof glass popped up in front of federal buildings, mayor's offices, and other significant symbolic buildings—what Jon Coaffee has called "fortress architecture"[2]—new "smart city" technologies allowed for 24/7 remote observation of all public spaces, and police officers more regularly patrolled the most visible neighborhoods of cities. The feeling of security this engendered, while controversial, made up for the long waits in airport security and inconvenient traffic rerouting. With such a mysterious and threatening external enemy, New York became a physically and psychologically damaged city but also a softer, more understanding one. It was after this chastening and lull of a rebound that a second major crisis hit the city, shaking it free of some old but dysfunctional habits.

Lest the Wall Street banks, so hard-hit by the 9/11 attacks, forget their global exploits and impacts, the mortgage crisis of 2008 hit their pocketbooks as hard as the Boeing 767s hit their offices. As with 9/11, Wall Street survived, but New Yorkers came to realize the kind of havoc that a less-than-one-square-mile parcel of real estate tucked in between three sides of cold water and an unassuming crosstown street—packed full of millions of square feet of commercial office space—can have on the livelihoods and lives of people around the world. September 11 taught New Yorkers to pull together to survive, while the mortgage crisis taught them that they might have to clean up their act if they were to remain the "city of immigrants" that had defined it so well before. The collective response of the city to the turmoil of the twenty-first-century's early years has been a valiant and ongoing effort to reenvision and re-create the city to keep up in a more globally connected and indeed globally aware world. One cannot say whether today's New York

City is better or worse than the twentieth century's; we can only know that it is different.

URBAN RESILIENCE: REPURPOSING BOTH PEOPLE AND PLACES

The types of persons relocating to New York are as diverse as those of any city in the world. On the one hand, the city is a de rigueur stop on the professional trajectories of graduates of elite universities in the United States and elsewhere, looking to enjoy their twenties and thirties absorbing the excitement and thrill of being at one of the centers of global culture and economy, if not politics. On the other hand, working-class Dominicans, Africans, and other new immigrants fill the roles that southern Italians and Jews once played, coming to the city for work opportunities and political stability. Peppered in between the socioeconomic range defined by these two groups are the multigenerational locals, artists, authors, publishers, and professionals who fill out the ranks of the city's complex economic and cultural matrix.

The array of reasons that these immigrants come is similarly complex. Once a trading center of the colonial Dutch perched on the edge of a vast continent of natural resources, the city has somehow retained its attractive force even as changes in the global economy, development of the North American continent, and the rise of the American empire have changed its context. Most cities able to sustain their attractive force over the course of over one hundred years easily fall back on their role as political centers; New York has done it by continually re-creating itself and adapting to changing circumstances independent of national fortunes. Few other major cities have been so adept at driving painful transformations and managing the successive crises that result.

New York City has few physical and natural assets to draw in the numbers of immigrants and attention it gets. Its port, once the foundation for the city's connection to international trade, has long been eclipsed by others in the United States, and particularly those on the West Coast facing the production factories of Asia. Available cheap labor, once the foundation for important manufacturing industries, is long gone as well, first migrating to the South and West, and later across the Pacific. Nevertheless, the city has persisted as the quintessential urban center over time, continuing to attract people, jobs, and the cultural attributes made possible by demographic and economic growth; the secret to this ongoing vibrancy is a unique and attractive identity that permeates deeper than any physical attribute. It has become an "environment" in and of itself that draws others in, who in turn contribute to that attractive force. The particular factor, however, is a contradictory tension between contemporary material reality and that identity.

One of the public faces of New York is the *Late Show with David Letterman*. Each night, stand-up comic Letterman makes cracks about the rats, streetwalkers, and murders that tourists are sure to find lurking around every corner during their visit. This theme is so effective at garnering a reluctant chuckle night after night because it represents the urban "edge" that so many cities strive for—that fine line between urban excitement and true physical danger. His wry smile, however, belies the fact that by 2003, the U.S. Federal Bureau of Investigation ranked New York as the safest big city in the country and *Popular Mechanics* ranked it as the twentieth greenest of American cities of any size in 2008. Sometimes popular portrayals are slow to catch up with lived reality.

New York's current high quality of life, however, lies on a contentious history during which the city saw the flight of the largely white middle class in the 1970s and 1980s, the complete breakdown of social ties, and the abandonment of its physical stock. As in previous eras, the city was able to bounce back from the edge of collapse by repurposing its people and physical stock for the twenty-first century. The fact that the city has recovered on numerous occasions suggests that there is something more than just a "first-mover's" advantage driving its continued prominence.

What is the source of this resilience against all apparent odds? In the winter, New York ranges from rainy and overcast to bitterly cold. In the summer, urban heat suffocates even the most intrepid outdoor enthusiasts. The city does not even have the redeeming qualities of the beautiful autumn foliage of a Boston, nor the human physical scale and layout of a Washington, D.C. By most physical measures, New York falls far short as a choice location, especially as the reduction in costs of automobile and air transport have widened the possibilities for mobile people to choose cities with material attributes to their liking. Seemingly, to add to New York's disadvantage, the advent of telecommuting possibilities further increases locational choice so that the ills of New York City life can be easily left behind. Yet people still want to come to New York.

Contextual factors should have suffocated the city long ago, once its initial industrial economy foundered. When its world-famous factories fell silent in the 1970s along with those of other old industrial cities on the East Coast of the United States, neither centuries-old educational institutions nor significant governmental bureaucracies were there to keep the local economy afloat, as they had in many other successful cities in New England, the mid-Atlantic states, and the Midwest. Somehow, the city has survived and thrived in spite of its natural drawbacks.

Today, the city's cultural attributes are what sustain it against all of these strikes against it that grow ever larger as the global urban ecosystem spreads to the far corners of the globe. And while the city does have many world-class cultural institutions such as the Metropolitan Museum of Art, and neighborhoods such as the Broadway theater district, it is not those headlining names that enable the city to regenerate itself. Rather, it is a mature *culture of urbanity*, of familiarity with urbanization and urban life, that makes New York special among cities.

New York's functional urban culture can be illustrated in the way it resolves its own very material problems compared to other large megacities and, in particular, much younger ones with less of an urban culture. And as is often the case, it is the material backbone of the city at the center of those problems. In 2005, New York's Transport Workers Union Local 100 called for a strike against their employer, the Metropolitan Transit Authority (MTA) on December 20, which effectively halted all public transportation in the five boroughs of New York, sidelining roughly seventy thousand employees and leaving millions of commuters to fend for themselves on their way to work, while shopping, and while doing other essential errands. Similarly, on October 14, 2003, the Los Angeles Mechanics Union of the Los Angeles Metropolitan Transportation Authority announced a strike of all its bus and rail lines, sidelining about nine thousand essential city workers and abandoning about five hundred thousand commuters on the city's hot street corners. Similar grievances underlay each strike, but their resolution could not have been more different. Within two days, the New York City strike had been resolved and service resumed. The same result took thirty-five days in Los Angeles.

Since the two cities are major metropolitan municipalities with long histories of public-sector unions involved in local politics, the 2003 and 2005 strikes themselves were nothing new to them. In fact, major transit strikes had occurred in 1966 and 1980 in New York, and in 1974 and 1976 in Los Angeles. In New York City, the 1966 strike lasted 12 days and the 1980 strike lasted for 11 days. In Los Angeles, the 1974 strike lasted 68 days and the 1976 strike lasted 35 days. If the New York City average is 8.3 days and the Los Angeles average 46.3 days, does that mean Los Angeles' municipal authorities are five times better negotiators than are New York's? Mayors Bloomberg (2002–2013), Koch (1978–1989), and Lindsay (1966–1973) might disagree, though certainly Los Angeles mayors Hahn (2001–2005) and Bradley (1973–1993) would be flattered. Rather, New York's speedy recoveries from its strikes seem additionally surprising given that two of the mayors resolving the public-sector union strikes were Republican, and the lone Democrat (Koch) was generally thought of as a conservative liberal. Compare this to the record of the two Democratic mayors of Los Angeles, and it's clear that political party and urban union politics fail to explain New York City's relative ease of resolving major citywide conflicts. Party politics, historical periods of union activism, or municipal fiscal constraints are not the key elements of New York's problem-solving urban culture and identity. Rather, it is its urban form, its political culture, and, indeed, its differing urban cultures that explain the difference. And this difference can be summed up simply: Wall Street executives take the bus from time to time (or at least their families do), but Hollywood executives don't.

While Honolulu is a city filled with old-timer residents, New York is one filled with an old-timer urban politics. Founded in 1614 as "New Amsterdam," and developed and densified during a period before automobiles but after the elevator, New York has a physical form that is a kind of old-world European city on steroids—matching dense pre-automobile streets with high, post-elevator skyscrapers. Such densities force residents onto public forms of transportation and into scarce public spaces. It is in this kind of ecosystem that an urban culture has developed. The culture associated with this socio-spatial environment of density and diversity breeds children adept at negotiating: over a seat on a crowded subway car, for an open stretch of park space to play sports, or for a spot in the local charter school. The application of these skills to the metropolitan-wide problems of affordable housing, waste transfer, and—yes—union pay is what defines the culture of urbanity that has evolved in the city.

It is these shared infrastructures and spaces that have forced diverse residents to confront and negotiate with one another on an hourly basis. Just as meerkats are more social than tigers, New Yorkers—boisterous, rude, and cantankerous as they are—are more social than are Los Angelenos. And this is no critique of New York's West Coast sibling; few large cities have benefited from the fortuitous intersection of physical form, human immigration, and global connections. Surely, Los Angeles is as diverse in both ethnicity and nationality, and equally diverse socioeconomically, as is New York. Where the difference lies, however, is that the dispersed physical form of Los Angeles allows this diversity to remain latent in the fabric of the city, with residents never really being mobilized to confront one another and hash out a familiar way of interacting and negotiating, which is—ultimately—more important for solving metropolitan-scale problems than is becoming friends. Learning to live together socially and politically is the ultimate function of an urban culture, and this is what has made New York City so resilient even through the turmoil of recent years.

New Yorkers are famously nonchalant and unimpressed with crisis and excitement; they have seen it all before, and nothing is new—or so they say and convey. That is why the World Trade Center attack was such a game changer. Being completely new to the lived experience of everyday New Yorkers, the event had to be noticed and acted on. Terrorist attacks, however, are not the only crisis that the city has suffered, embraced, and then weathered. It is through these convulsions that New Yorkers have learned to live together and adapt to one another. Longtime residents have gone through periodic and painful initiation rites, during which the city's innards are torn out, examined, and reconstituted. If the city's buildings, streets, and bridges are its hardware, its human software has needed to be rebooted from time to time to ensure continued operation. Fiscal crisis, terrorism, and recession are the most important transformations that have flipped this switch in recent decades.

FISCAL CRISIS AND A SLOW CLIMB BACK INTO THE LIMELIGHT

New York City's contemporary story begins after World War II, when its European and Asian global competitors were left in ruins and the American industrial production machine was running at full tilt. With almost 4.5 million young disciplined soldiers, sailors, mechanics, pilots, and others returning home to their families between June 1945 and December 1946, the United States was poised to make major investments in itself and establish its economic and political footprint throughout the world.

A story of industrial prowess, suburbanization,[3] and westward expansion, this period for New York City meant a massive reenvisioning of its physical footprint. Chronicled in Robert Caro's magnum opus *The Power Broker*, City Parks commissioner Robert Moses built the physical backbone of contemporary New York through his construction of connective infrastructure such as the Triborough Bridge and the Brooklyn-Queens Expressway, as well as major city landmarks such as Shea Stadium and the United Nations complex. While oft reviled for his undemocratic modus operandi, Moses's projects did include public spaces such as Lincoln Center, Herald Square, Jones Beach, and all the way out to the eastern tip of Long Island's Montauk State Park,[4] softening the new contours of the city. When Moses's influence had waned by the mid-1960s, his physical footprint on the city had been substantial, and it was this physical footprint that conditioned the period to come.

In particular, it was both the physical footprint and the process of its construction that seeded collapse. As described by Caro, to build infrastructure on the scale that Moses did required a ruthless approach to neighborhood communities. In describing the construction of the Cross Bronx Expressway, Caro depicts a bulldozing city uprooting and destroying East Tremont, a working-class neighborhood of 1,530 largely Jewish families, without any attention to how this stable and long-term community might reconstitute itself elsewhere in the city. According to a 1981 interview with a former neighborhood resident:

> I remember Moses and the Cross Bronx well. They knocked my house down, 1005 East 176th Street. They told us we had to move. I was kind of happy about it. I know a lot of people were unhappy because they had to move, but don't listen to the complaints: they got paid nicely for those houses, those people. Nice money. They all moved out to Long Island.[5]

For both critics and supporters of Robert Moses, the major urban projects contributed to a hollowing-out of the city.

At the same time as these projects were under way, the construction of highways, like the Cross Bronx Expressway, connected other stable neighborhoods to the green fields of southern Connecticut, Long Island, and New Jersey, thereby giving every reason for urban residents to relocate outside the city limits that they had called "home," but it was also the city that had ruthlessly pushed some of them out. Their experience of the twinned forces of community destruction and the facilitation of suburban dispersal heralded a very steep decline; it marked the beginning of an era in which New Yorkers came to see their city as a wasteland, but one that also prompted a reenvisioning and reimagining of the city's character itself.

The reimagination of this city of over eight million can be readily seen through the lens of urban rioting and looting: an urban fiscal crisis of the 1970s culminated in major rioting and looting in the summer of 1977 during its first blackout in years. By the time the next major blackout struck the city in 2003, the social, political, and economic environment had calmed such that no significant social problems marred the infrastructural glitch. Even as New York's West Coast sibling, Los Angeles, repeated the cycle of violence culminating in riots in 1965 and then again in 1992, New York's history of mass urban uprising reflects not only its different material conditions and inequality, but also its ability to learn as a larger socio-spatial community and to reinvent itself. Such reinvention forestalled the repetition of urban violence but came at a cost. It all began with a fiscal crisis.

At around the time of the first transit strike in New York, the U.S. Navy closed the Brooklyn Navy Yards, laying off 9,000 employees and halting the operations of New York State's oldest continually active industrial plant. This closing hit the New York Harbor particularly hard because just four years before, Elizabeth, New Jersey, had opened the world's first containerized shipping port, which siphoned off much of the shipping business into neighboring New Jersey, where operations were much more efficient and access to national transportation routes was more convenient. The textile mills active until the 1960s in the neighborhood just south of Houston Street—later to be called "Soho"—had also closed up by the end of the decade, leaving empty factory buildings, cleared of their machinery and human capital. According to the New York State Department of Labor, the city's manufacturing began a steep decline around the late 1960s, dropping from about 870,000 jobs to about 540,000 by 1974, and then on to less than 200,000 by 2002.

These trends were certainly worse—on a percentage basis—elsewhere in the American Rustbelt, but the loss of manufacturing and port activities hit the city hard, as ominous macroeconomic trends rippled across the United States. The early 1970s brought about "stagflation"— a period during which high inflation combined with ongoing high unemployment and sluggish economic growth squeezed everyone, but especially residents of cities such as New York, where the loss of manufacturing and the high costs of living put a double squeeze on most residents that was not seen in other areas of the rustbelt.

In large part because of these pressures, New York City experienced a severe period of "white flight" during the 1970s and 1980s. Stagflation squeezed urban residents, and the highways and connectivity built by Robert Moses gave those middle-class residents of the city the opportunity to leave. Unlike the Okies and Arkies of the Midwest's Great Dust Bowl, middle-class residents of New York who were feeling the pressure could easily move out of the city to New Jersey, southern Connecticut, or Long Island, all the while keeping their city jobs and keeping their kids in their existing city schools if they chose. Many, however, preferred the more stable and better-funded suburban school districts where achievement was higher and facilities better kept. During this period, the New York middle class was largely white in ethnic composition, and of those minorities who could afford to leave, many were hampered by discriminatory housing covenants in suburban districts that made it extremely difficult or impossible for nonwhites to find homes outside of the city. As a result of this hollowing-out of the New York middle class, the city was left with a smaller tax base to support the same urban services. Of course, however, the city government's responsibilities actually increased because the loss of stable students from urban schools and stable residents from urban neighborhoods increased the challenges of those left behind without the steadying influences of the middle class—a situation among African American communities described so well by scholars in their discussions of spatially concentrated poverty.[6]

The loss of the manufacturing and middle-class tax bases, combined with the increased responsibilities of city services, placed city government in a precarious position that led to an acute fiscal crisis. This gradual hollowing out came to a head in 1975, when Mayor Abraham Beame (in office from 1974 to 1977), on the verge of announcing the city's default on its general obligations bond debts, was bailed out by the national United Federation of Teachers' union purchase of $150 million in Municipal Assistance Corporation bonds. On the verge of going into receivership by the state of New York (never a beneficent parent of its downstate child), New York City was bailed out by a union, a favor indirectly paid back to the transit union subsequently and partly the result of good negotiating with their union brethren earlier.

The twinned challenges of industrial decline and middle-class flight paired to hollow out the city. These challenges not only stressed the city government, but also had major impacts on the daily life of residents. The triad of crime, drugs, and prostitution, always issues for big cities, and other social problems faced a shrinking budget for public services of police, fire department, and health. The slow strangling of the city's material lifeblood—its urban services—was seen everywhere but nowhere more prominently than in the decline of Times Square.

As of the end of World War II, Times Square had become the active heart of the theater district and was a bustling neighborhood of culture and the arts. By the late 1970s, however, it had reached its nadir, becoming the center for peep shows, drug deals, and prostitution. A broader social and economic decline of New York was given a physical and visual form by this central neighborhood. In 1980, violent crime in the city had reached a high of 1,030 per 100,000 residents, including 13 murders—more than tripling the 1965 rate, a statistic mirrored in almost all crime categories.[7] Importantly, it was violent crime that had spiked the most sharply, suggesting that deterioration was less about material and economic challenges and more about frustration, anger, and social breakdown. It was also during the early 1980s that the crack cocaine and HIV epidemics hit poor neighborhoods and the gay community hard, further stressing already underfunded city agencies. For observers at the time, it seemed that President Ford's invitation for New Yorkers to "drop dead" was actually being accepted. It was in this physical and social context that the blackout of July 13–14, 1977, shut the city down. Amidst a sweltering heat wave, the 9:36 p.m. blackout triggered a wave of arson, looting, and violence that, when all was said and done, led to 3,776 arrests, 1,037 fires, and over 1,500 stores looted everywhere from Bedford-Stuyvesant to Madison Avenue. In this environment, it seemed that any small malfunction in the grid could lead to complete chaos.

Until the early twenty-first century, New Yorkers perceived the city was always a tense powder keg of social tension and physical decline on the verge of collapse, no matter what their personal experience told them. It is this New York, the one of filth, crime, violence, and chaos, that David Letterman memorializes night after night; and his audience adores him for it because hindsight shows how the subsequent transformation was truly something to be celebrated—at least for those who could afford it.

It wasn't until a blackout of similar scale happened on August 14, 2003, that New Yorkers got to see that their social core had changed, even though the physical stock had remained more or less the same. While the 2003 outage did shut down industry, businesses, and public services, ordinary citizens stepped up to direct traffic, restaurants opened their dining rooms to serve heavily discounted and free dinners to passersby, and spontaneous block parties erupted, which got people outside to beat the heat and pass the time. Although forty thousand police and the entire fire department were called in to preserve order, they were pleasantly surprised to see New Yorkers making do, enjoying themselves, and killing time instead of each other. Why the difference?

Some say it was Police Commissioner William Bratton's "broken windows" approach to policing in which beat cops used CompStat mobile computing technology to crack down particularly hard on "quality of life crimes" in the neighborhoods most plagued by drugs and violence. Others attribute the difference to an expansion of the U.S. economy, in the early 1990s, due at least in part to a dot-com boom that powered not just Wall Street stocks but also a host of start-up businesses looking to capitalize on the technology revolution. Still others, such as celebrity economists John Donohue and Steven Levitt, have even pointed to the 1973 *Roe v. Wade* Supreme Court decision allowing poor women the right to terminate unwanted pregnancies as the reason crime dropped so precipitously in the 1990s.[8]

The debate on the "whys" will never be fully resolved, but the fact that New York City turned itself around better than did most other contemporary declining cities in the United States is indisputable. By 2010, violent crime was down 62 percent from its 1980 levels to 392 per 100,000; murders were down by 65 percent to 4.5 per 100,000;[9] unemployment had hit an all-time low of 5 percent in 2007[10] prior to the Wall Street meltdown; and home values, generally considered to be the most robust indicator of neighborhood and community-level changes, had completed a remarkable turnaround. Some typical brownstones recorded a 500 percent increase in inflation-adjusted dollars between 1976 and 2012, and the overall average, even between 1995 and 2011, for one of the more expensive Manhattan neighborhoods was up 200 percent. A popular neighborhood in Brooklyn saw about a 120 percent increase over the same period, and even Queens—central New York's least-connected borough—saw greater than 88 percent gains.[11]

Seemingly against all odds, by the mid-1990s the city was on an uptick, cleaned out of its postwar white middle class, most of its industrial manufacturing, and the cynicism so prominently on display for the world to see during the 1977 blackout. Replacing them were a diverse class of professionals and new immigrants, a higher-tech economy, a resurgent Wall Street, and a general optimism about the excitement of urban life.

One of the ironic legacies of this period of fiscal crisis is that some urbanists made out like bandits, even with only pennies in their pockets. In 1980, when even the toniest areas of Manhattan's Upper East Side were on the skids, the "for all timers" stood their ground. Five-story brownstones on Seventieth Street were abandoned, and vacant co-ops and apartments were on—sometimes even literally—a "fire sale." With housing selling at prices as low as $140,000 for a four-story brownstone on the East Side, this was a time when some of the more perceptive and financially liquid of the "for all timers" were rewarded for their commitment to the city's urban life. Today, the same brownstone sells for over $4 million. The for-all-timers, weathering the garbage-clogged streets, poorly performing schools, and rampant crime, somehow knew the city would rebound; and if it didn't, they weren't going to either.[12]

And rebound it did. By the mid-1990s, local real estate agents had come to refer to Manhattan and Brooklyn's historically gritty and crime-plagued neighborhoods of Alphabet City, Hell's Kitchen, and Bedford-Stuyvesant by the newly invented upscale monikers of the "East Village," "Clinton," and "Clinton Hill," respectively. As real estate values here shot skyward, Wall Street and tech salaries flooded the city's crevasses, and energetic young newcomers flocked in; it seemed that the postwar "Go-Go years" of confidence were back.

This recovery marked New York City as a city "for all time." It demonstrated an uncanny ability to bounce back from adversity and defined a resilient metropolitan community. While Honolulu has strong neighborhood ties and community relationships, New York City's challenges during this period hardened the city's resolve, weeding out those residents there for material reasons alone. Like a forest cleared of underbrush by wildfires, New York showed itself as a metropolitan area that had evolved a sophisticated and pragmatic politics to get things done and to invest in its future. It wasn't until the twenty-first century that these skills would be needed to bring the city back from the brink of collapse again.

9/11, WALL STREET COLLAPSE, AND THE SOFTENING OF THE BIG CITY?

The 9/11 events, beyond their obvious human tragedy, topped off this gradual change from imploding to comeback city; the collapse of the Twin Towers, ironically, crystallized a social environment on the mend, forcing residents overnight to see themselves as a whole fabric interrelated by family, professional, and other ties rather than as disjointed fragments of the city each successful in their own right but largely disconnected from that larger urban identity. The city's literal rise from the ashes fired a kind of social activism that allowed the city and its residents to reinvent themselves as a "kinder and gentler" city and a city with a broader consciousness.

On the morning of September 11, 2001, two commercial airliners slammed into the World Trade Center buildings in New York City, killing thousands of innocent people and setting in motion a major long-term physical change in the neighboring communities of Chinatown, Wall Street, and Tribeca, but more important, a psychological change for the city as a whole. September 11 had multiple impacts on New York's neighborhoods and their residents—on the one hand consolidating them and creating a more cooperative and supportive community; on the other, scaring away jobs, businesses, and residents unable to keep up with the kind of city reenvisioned by the planners brought in to rebuild.

David Jones, president of the Community Service Association of New York, characterized the complicated response of New York well in an interview on the tenth anniversary of the attacks.

I think that when disaster strikes, New Yorkers pull together. We saw it when [Hurricane] Irene threatened the city last month. After 9/11, using our portion of a special Neediest Cases drive in 2001, CSA provided about $5 million in aid to about two thousand families who lost loved ones, jobs, or homes. That may not be true in everyday life. Public officials and the media don't often focus on the problems of the city's most vulnerable populations. They talk about "shared pain" in hard times, but budgets are still balanced on the backs of the poor.

To a certain extent [New York is still a gateway to opportunity for the poor, the persecuted, and the downtrodden]. But over the past several decades, economic mobility—the idea that with hard work you can rise from the working poor to the middle class, a historically American ideal—is no longer widely true. In fact, this latest recession has caused many black and Latino families who reached the middle class in terms of family income because of the boom times of the 1990s to fall back economically.

During times of crisis, New Yorkers tend to "pull together." This was seen in the 2003 blackout, during which everyday New Yorkers showcased their patience, equanimity, and goodwill. Ten years on, however, the cost of this community goodwill remains to be seen. In some ways, the city pulled together by "opening its doors," but in other ways, by "circling the wagons." The former reached out to a changing world; the latter closed ranks to protect itself.

Immediately following 9/11, the city welcomed an outpouring of national and global sympathy. And in particular, New York City's "finest"[13] were indeed seen as the finest, as consumers from Paris to Pittsburgh, Pretoria, and Peking all proudly sported shirts and caps honoring the fallen public-sector workers who had so bravely entered the fiery, dusty, and chaotic towers, many knowing full well that their chances of returning to their families were slim. Beyond simply a faddish trend, the letters NYPD and NYFD on these personal style symbols announced to everyone who saw them around the world that their wearer felt some solidarity with and sympathy for New Yorkers. This goodwill and desire for a stronger community was more than cynically symbolic. It pulled spatially and socially disparate people together not just to grieve but also to plan.

Not since the days of the epic debates between Robert Moses and Jane Jacobs had New Yorkers looked past their fears of the decline of, and excitement at the booming of, the economy to think about what their city should physically look like. And it is the difference between the ways in which New York was built by Moses versus the ways in which it is being built at the Lower Manhattan site of the 9/11 tragedy that suggests New York—or at least Manhattan—can convert the post-9/11 warm feelings illustrated during the 2003 blackout into the steel and concrete structure of the city.

The debate over what to do on the site of the Twin Towers began almost immediately after the dust cleared. Many called for a permanent memorial to the 9/11 victims by leaving the site undeveloped, while others called for the reconstruction of the Twin Towers in their original form as a symbol that New Yorkers will come back as before. Tellingly, neither of these options was deemed viable by either the owner of the site, the Port Authority and its leaseholder—Larry A. Silverstein—or the communities surrounding it. For native New Yorkers, developing the site was necessary not only from a pragmatic standpoint (to create material value on the spot) but also from a symbolic one, as leaving it empty would signify that non–New Yorkers could erase an important landmark of the city. Rebuilding the Twin Towers as they once stood, while a pragmatic option that might have shown the city's persistence and pride, would also have been uncharacteristic. New York is a city of "for all timers" not because it preserves and re-creates the past but because it churns itself through crises to adapt to contemporary conditions. For these reasons, something big, and something new, had to be built on the site, even though to do so required a very complicated, and very public, planning process, with citywide, national, and global interests all trying to influence the process.

Through fits and starts, the planning process became an opening of doors to urban decision making, very much unlike the historical roots of New York's Moses-built landscape. As Lisa Chamberlain describes it in *Planning*, the magazine of the American Planning Association, a first attempt at redesigning the site by the Port Authority of New York and New Jersey was ill-advised.[14] After contracting with a private firm to propose alternatives, the resulting design charrette, which included five thousand participants, torpedoed the plans, because they had been developed without significant public input. Gone were the days of centralized, rational planning in which technical experts drove the process, with communities trailing behind on the coattails or dragged in kicking and screaming. Rather, the Port Authority's second effort reflected a city with a stronger and more collaborative base to make decisions. While mostly contentious, the debate included "competing interests" ranging from Silverstein to the Port Authority (controlled by the states of New York and New Jersey), the New York City mayor, the families of the September 11 victims, designers, and the general public. As Chamberlain wrote in 2006, "Those are a lot of competing interests, and without a Herculean consensus-building effort, it seems clear that the process was doomed to stagnate."[15]

Stagnation, it turned out, would have been better termed "growing pains," as the complex of constituencies for the site's development eventually reached an agreement that led to breaking ground in 2006. The Herculean task of planning included numerous missteps, miscommunications, and misunderstandings among these constituents, as described ten years after the attacks by William Menking, founder and editor in chief of the *Architect's Newspaper*. Nevertheless, as of September 11, 2011, construction had begun on all eight of the major elements of the site plan, and all were on schedule to be completed by 2015. In the end, post-9/11 New Yorkers were able to "pull together" and translate abstract good feelings after the attacks into a physical structure representing a wide range of the city's constituents. This was something new, and a process mirrored years later in a subsequent 2010 debate over efforts to build Cordoba House, a thirteen-story multi-faith community center that included a memorial to 9/11 victims on the grounds of what had been a mosque. Opponents of the project argued that the development constituted a mosque built by Muslims just two blocks from the Twin Towers and was a slap in the face to all the victims of 9/11 rather than a memorial.

Owned by Soho Properties, which was led by CEO Sharif El-Gamal, and backed by Imam Feisal Abdul Rauf, the Cordoba project ran into public debate immediately after the local community board reviewed its plans and the proposed development became public. The project was planned as a community center with prayer space, and the board's approval of the center sparked public protests across the country, lawsuits against the development, and a larger debate about whether New York had a space for moderate Islam after 9/11. A renamed Cordoba House, under the new moniker "Park51"—named after the site's address—opened its doors on September 21, 2011, with no controversy, and plans for completion seem on track for the coming years.

Even with national figures such as Sarah Palin, John McCain, Mitt Romney, and former New York mayor Rudy Giuliani publicly opposing the development, New Yorkers' negotiation of this conflict reinforced a new kind of open, pragmatic, and deliberative process for development in Manhattan. Even in the face of polarizing national politics, New York had become a more collaborative and open environment—its resilient culture of urbanism had triumphed in pragmatically moving forward and getting things done.

The debates over Lower Manhattan embody the material and symbolic functions of the city. Lewis Mumford's claim that "the city is a magnet before it becomes a container" is nowhere more apparent than at One World Trade Center. Ancient nomadic societies planted memorials to the deceased to which they returned periodically to pay their respects. Even in today's most urbanized neighborhood, this role of the city as memorial to people, communities, and societies looms large in the values underlying material decisions; with almost forty-seven million visitors each year, New York City does play an important symbolic and magnetic node for a global community with which its eight million residents must negotiate. And it is because New York has been reminded of these connections between the physical and the spiritual that it has been able to regenerate itself.

But at what cost? The story of post-9/11 Chinatown is illustrative of some of the larger trends challenging the city. In the immediate aftermath of 9/11, Chinatown experienced job loss, business decline, and out-migration in large part due to policies to limit people's movements in a neighborhood dominated by low-income immigrants and racio-ethnic minorities. In the years following 9/11, the traditional Chinatown industries of manufacturing and restaurants suffered declines that never completely recovered, reducing job opportunities for the resident population, which had a pre-9/11 poverty rate of over 30 percent. These socioeconomic pressures were compounded by city security policies such as restricting an already limited supply of parking in the neighborhood and increasing congestion through tighter monitoring of traffic. These policies exposed the weak infrastructure of Chinatown that had long been masked by high levels of economic activity but low accumulations of assets characteristic of the working and immigrant poor. The overview chronicled by the Asian American Federation in 2008 exposed Chinatown's relatively weak capacity to rebound in the longer term from this crisis when compared to other neighborhoods adjacent to the World Trade Center.

In September 2011, the *New York Times* reported that even ten years after the attacks, Chinatown's economy lagged behind its neighbors due to the loss of downtown office workers and tourists. While certainly improved over the years of the immediate aftermath, Chinatown has changed the type, as well as the amount, of its economic activity. Instead, according to the Asian American Federation's Howard Shih, now the growing Chinatowns of Flushing, Queens, and Sunset Park, Brooklyn, show greater concentrations of Chinese as younger and whiter residents move into the Manhattan Chinatown. A classic story of gentrification laid atop the newer sympathetic attraction and draw of the 9/11 neighborhoods, the recovery and resilience of New Yorkers post-9/11 can sometimes seem a bit more like a circling of the wagons around those who can afford to live in the city than the opening of a deliberative process that post-9/11 planning showed.

THE CITY AND THE GREAT RECESSION

The goodwill and unity brought about by the attacks, however, were severely tested during the Wall Street collapse of 2007 and the loss of jobs, bonuses, and goodwill that accompanied it.

In March 2008, New York investment bank Bear Stearns was sold to JPMorgan Chase for $10 per share, far below its value of $133.20 per share of the previous year. The precipitous collapse of the seventh-largest investment firm—in business for over eighty years—with assets greater than $350 billion in 2006 was not an isolated event; the following September, Lehman Brothers Holdings Inc., the fourth-largest investment bank in the United States, filed for bankruptcy. The precipitous collapse of these long-standing Wall Street firms was the result of their overreliance on a new financial instrument called the "mortgage-backed security," which revealed massive amounts of formerly solid assets that became "toxic" as the subprime mortgage crisis became increasingly apparent. Following a meeting between U.S. Secretary of the Treasury Hank Paulson and the CEOs of the remaining major Wall Street investment banks, the federal government authorized a $700 billion bailout of Wall Street banks called the "Temporary Asset Relief Fund (TARP)," which eventually transferred over $400 billion worth of these "toxic" assets onto the federal government's books. Combined with subsequent efforts at "quantitative easing," Wall Street survived the crisis intact but, according to the *Washington Post*, lost almost $7 trillion in assets[16] and by the end of the year, the American economy had lost almost 2.5 million jobs. The originators of this crisis also took their hit: in mid-October 2008, the New York City comptroller estimated that thirty-five thousand Wall Street workers would lose their jobs.[17]

As important, Wall Street lost an aura of flash, invincibility, and stability as young graduating math whizzes and engineers began to look elsewhere for employment. For an industry built on freewheeling firms flaunting government regulation and touting the efficiency of the market, going on corporate welfare was a psychological shock and a blow to their confidence—at least for a time—if not for the most committed bankers themselves, then for the New Yorkers and others who admired them and aspired to be one of them.

The Great Recession made public a brewing trend that had also transformed the city's software. While most New Yorkers have reveled in their history of being America's welcoming gateway to immigrants, the city has become the gateway of a different sort in recent years. Indeed, it is believed that up to 40 percent of all Americans today have a relative that came through New York City's Ellis Island, a port of entry that received 12 million immigrants between 1892 and 1954. In 2010, however, the Immigration Policy Center reports that the state of California alone was home to 10.2 million immigrants, a fact reflecting that Los Angeles and other cities have become attractive points of entry; and even small states are now the fastest-growing ports of entry according to the Center for Immigration Studies. Instead, it is New York City's attraction of investment and capital that has been the underappreciated, yet more significant, part of the city's early twenty-first-century dynamics. While immigrant points of entry have diversified since the time Ellis Island was processing new families day and night, global capital in the United States remains remarkably consistently focused on New York: whether measured by the Global Financial Centres Index,[18] the International Financial Centres Development Index,[19] the Worldwide Centres of Commerce Index,[20] or the listing of "Most Economically Powerful Cities,"[21] New York City is ranked either first or second, and the next closest American city is Chicago, which holds a fifth position regarding commerce. And this fact became huge, as global investment capital doubled between 2000 and 2006 to $72 trillion. The cause? Economic growth in Asia and the Middle East.[22]

The Great Recession began with the ballooning availability of these massive pools of capital searching out investments with stable and predictable financial returns, highlighted by the stable and reliable returns of American real estate. When the Federal Reserve cut its interest rates to 1 percent in the lead-up to the mortgage crisis, this capital flooded U.S. banks looking to finance mortgages for an ever-wider range of borrowers looking to purchase homes. The laws of supply and demand being what they are, this investment capital became cheap for borrowers to secure, and the U.S. property market became a sector with virtually no barriers to entry. With millions of overly risky investments made in real estate, the capital flowing through Wall Street pumped up a real estate bubble that exploded magnificently with the failure of Bear Stearns in 2008. Triggering layoffs, high unemployment, and a sustained recession, this latest crisis, in its aftermath, was also centered on New York City, as the city lost about two hundred thousand jobs[23] and countless small businesses closed up shop for lack of credit.

New York has not yet figured out how to negotiate and adapt to this most recent crisis, but, surely, it will. It has already begun to do so by welcoming immigrants and the financial and entrepreneurial resources they bring with them. The revitalization of 125th Street in Harlem, for example, is driven by small African traders making their way—much as they do in Ho Chi Minh City—by purchasing cheap goods for sale back home and opening businesses on profit margins that work for them, even though they may be too low for more-established immigrants.

Flushing and Sunset Park surely represent much more than the displacement of Manhattan's Chinatown. Nestled within countless restaurants, markets, and workshops is an informal and undocumented, yet very real, financial investment in the city. In fact, through its neighborhoods, New York City has brought the Global South into the inner workings of a global center. At the same time, these neighborhoods have projected out the values of New Yorkers to their inhabitants' homelands. It is through these urban spaces that the city churns individuals up and down a vertical global urban demography.

Newcomers to Chinatown represent both illegal migrants from Fujian and Vietnamese refugee families eking out lives of both economic opportunity and political freedom. Gentrifying Brooklyn holds some of the highest concentrations of Caribbean expatriates and children of expatriates outside of the region itself, and presents opportunities for middle-class Black and Latino minorities to settle in comfortable neighborhoods without the stress of overly segregated communities or being a "minority." One Hundred Twenty-Fifth Street in Harlem has become a node for African immigrant businesses, similar to Chinatown, where small entrepreneurs can do business with a growing middle class of African Americans and others and escape corruption, health, and other problems in their homelands. Finally, Wall Street is the quintessential economic driver of New York, but its attraction to legions of highly educated young professionals lies not only in making money but also in its role as a larger marker of global success. Such kinds of transnational neighborhoods hearken back to the city's history of vibrant, chaotic immigrant neighborhoods of the Lower East Side and Little Italy, where a previous generation of outsiders had breathed new life into the city. These neighborhoods are the engines that allow New York to plow forward and reinvent itself and, in the process, reestablish its global relevance. This cycle of growth, decline, and reinvention permeating the city's neighborhoods, as far as can be perceived today, has gone on, does go on, and will go on "for all time."

IMMORTALITY THROUGH REINVENTION

New York today is every bit as cosmopolitan, gritty, and refined as it was in the times of Robert Moses, of industrial decline and social dysfunction, and of 9/11. It is just that these environments have varied over the years; throughout, however, the city has retained its "edge"— that magical space between excitement and danger that makes a city universally attractive. Even as early as the late 1980s, Manhattan's Chinatown was on the rise. The Festival of San Genarro, which takes place each September on Mulberry Street just north of Canal Street, is the hallmark event of a Little Italy that is mostly an immigrant space of the past. While the restaurants remain mostly Italian, the mobile vendors are almost all Chinese; Chinatown is succeeding Little Italy.

A few miles north of Canal Street, 125th Street has seen a similar neighborhood change. What was once the cultural center of the Harlem Renaissance, with its Apollo Theater, soul food, Cotton Club, and

Duke Ellington, is now a similarly active strip of trading for African—
not African American in the traditional sense—businesspeople and
entrepreneurs. One of the homes of contemporary African American
culture has been succeeded by a continental African energy. As Asia
and Sub-Saharan Africa grow in global prominence, the newly arrived
residents have replaced the immigrants of decades past, using the city's
hardware—the built environment—as a platform to improve their lives
and catapult the city into a new era, just as their predecessors did during years past.

Perhaps most surprisingly, Brooklyn's most persistently poverty-
and crime-plagued Red Hook neighborhood—often seen as a quaint,
isolated relic of old New York—now simultaneously has an Ikea and
a Fresh Fields grocery mega-store targeting the professional class and
serves as the public space for the city's exploding working-class Latino
population. After generations down in the dumps, neighborhoods such
as these are reaping the rewards of the post-9/11 era. Through the fiscal crisis, 9/11, and the Great Recession, neighborhoods such as these,
filled with resilient New Yorkers, both young and old, have developed
an ability to adapt; to attract, survive, and "own" those big events that
enable a place like New York City to claim its identity as a city "for all
time."

In 2009, after the success of the original "Empire State of Mind"
hit, Alicia Keys recorded her own version of the song—"Empire State
of Mind (Part II)"—because she wanted to express her own New York.
Less explicitly celebratory of the place, Keys's version carves out her
own pathways through the concrete jungle, replacing Jay-Z's sports,
neighborhood, and people references with more explicit judgments of
New York's street scenes. Again, please see the original CD sleeve for
the relevant lines (Verse 1, lines 1–4; Verse 1, lines 5–6; Verse 2, lines
1–4) to get a sense of this lyrical ecosystem.

Even with all its problems, noise, and hunger deeper than an empty
stomach, New York is for all time. It is that hunger that keeps one
pushing through the meanness, disappointments, and drugs toward
reinvention—and some would say "redemption."

CHAPTER 7

THE GLOBAL URBAN ECOSYSTEM: A GLOBALLY INTEGRATED ECOLOGY OF EVERYDAY LIFE

This book began with an overview of how ecosystem science can help us make sense of contemporary globalization by enabling us to see the physical environments in which the complexities of globalization are unfolding. Such an approach points directly toward cities and, in particular, those kinds of cities that are the gathering places of twenty-first-century globalization. Rather than treat each of these cities on its own terms, I have by necessity simplified their characteristics to illustrate how very different types of urban forms can show surprising street-level and historical contradictions to convention. In this way, my cases illustrate the insufficiency of the global-cities literature's notion of a global city as just the most economically vibrant, culturally triumphant, or beset by poverty. In some ways, *every* city is now a global city. While some certainly sit on the global economic margins, many small, physically remote, and culturally isolated cities *do* exist within a global system of cities. This system, like a metropolitan transit system, forms a kind of global urban ecosystem of "patches" and "corridors" in constant flux, none relinquishing or rejecting their particular spot in this ecosystem.

THE GLOBAL CITY REVISITED: ARE WE ALL GLOBAL CITIES NOW?

In chapter 1, I briefly reviewed some of the literature claiming that there is such a thing as a global city. While not inherently problematic, I do suggest that this kind of designation obscures much more than it illuminates. In today's world, a new global political economy has brought significant portions of the "globe"—its peoples, foods, political institutions, and norms—into the everyday lives of residents of a surprising range of cities. The holding of the APEC meeting of the leaders of many of the world's most influential economies in an aging plantation settlement in the Pacific and the establishment of the African Union in the continent's most infrastructurally challenged city suggest that urbanity reaches much farther than the world cities literature would suggest.

Also in chapter 1, I discussed the mix of science and aesthetics that underlies the character of cities, arguing that they become mini-planets with gravitational forces drawing people, goods, services, and even fauna and flora into their orbits. Chapter 2's review of the natural history of the city identified some of the reasons this gravitational force has persisted and grown over time; a prehistory of ceremonial symbolism followed by the establishment of a market system able to accelerate collective human intelligence and innovation that enabled traditional societies to broaden their horizons beyond localism and the inefficient limits imposed by reliance on political diplomacy. Global colonialism brought this scope of capitalism to the far corners of the earth, and once that expansion had been exhausted, urban industrialization gave rise to the manufacturing city that we can see even today. Today, however, these cities of production coexist with postindustrial cities driven more by consumption.

Throughout each of these periods of growth, the city has been driven by major shifts in the political economy of human civilization, and there is no reason to believe that the twenty-first century will be any different. The cities described in this book are intended to illustrate how new and inevitable forces of global economic complementarity are reshaping many of the relationships among nations and their constituent cities, pushing the world toward a global system in which some of the most remote and seemingly backwater cities can rightfully find their unique place in a new world, should they choose to claim it.

These points in the global system, however, are more than simply unique locations dispersed across space but linked logistically. There are important functions that they play as sophisticated and macro-level technologies facilitating individual human interactions. Just as a metropolitan transportation system, with its standardized signage and like-minded passengers, allows individuals to traverse relatively wide distances without knowing exactly—through prior lived experience—what lies at the other end of the line, the city itself lies on a global system facilitating comfortable interaction across vast physical and cultural distances. It is the city that allows African footballers in Saigon to comfortably bring their homelands into the global consumption economy, Chinese engineers to keep up their massage regimens even in the rough-and-tumble of Addis, Honolulu's New Communalists to enjoy *both* the beach and the symphony, and New Yorkers born and bred on urban collapse to recognize the post-9/11 version of the city.

Also described in chapter 1 was the need to "identify the pitch" of contemporary globalization. My description of the four cities is not intended to simply deconstruct the notion of global cities. Rather, it is to outline the broad contours of an urban skyline of the future so that policy makers, planners, activists, and all kinds of urbanists can think more clearly about the challenges they are likely to face in the coming decades. Thus, my characterization of the global urban ecosystem depicts a world of vertically integrated urbanization that spans a decreasingly relevant Global North/South divide.

THE ALTERNATIVE PITCH: VERTICALLY INTEGRATED URBANIZATION

Describing the long-term and irreversible trends of contemporary global political economy sets the stage for an understanding of the unlikely communities of people found in cities throughout the globe. The long-term trends that contextualize Saigon, Addis, and Honolulu are understudied precisely because they contradict established notions of North America–Europe-centered cognitive maps of the world, the assumption that food, families, and leisure activities are—and can remain—"local," and that the political and development challenges of Africa are insurmountable. The case of New York, on the other hand, describes a city that has in the past developed its own unique character of resilience that has charted it through the kinds of global changes on the horizon.

In a surprisingly whimsical and broad vision, *The Economist* tackled the question: what is natural and what is man-made in its May 26, 2011 issue. Devoted to fleshing out what some scientists are coming to call the "Anthropocene," the *Economist* makes the argument that the earth itself is entering a geologic age characterized by human manipulation and management. To some, no longer are we all living in the Holocene— meaning "entirely new"—but now we have entered the Anthropocene— meaning "new human." Nowhere is the new human more easily seen than in contemporary cities. For this reason, an examination of the global urban ecosystem and its micro-ecosystem of daily life—the interactions among species, physical structures, and human institutions in places— provides a window not only into some of the major physical transformations underway but also into the changing ways that humans are relating to one another—and in the process changing themselves.

In many ways, the global urban Anthropocene is an emerging human culture of urbanism facilitating global exchanges. This culture does not directly compete with the more traditional local cultures of language, families, religion, and foods to be found in Saigon, Addis, Honolulu, or New York, but lies under them as a newer set of practices and assumptions that allow urban residents and visitors to use the physical and social infrastructures of the city. This urban quid pro quo is a set of social infrastructure that enables legibility across vast physical and cultural distances. African footballers and Chinese engineers have used these norms of urban lifestyles—a kind of global urbanism—to establish businesses and families in new contexts, even as have retirees to Honolulu from the United States and Japan to bravely venture out into the middle of the Pacific to live out their silver years. And in many ways, the gruff, direct New York culture of pragmatic reinvention is the convergence of the more traditional local culture with that of the global urban ecosystem; New York City is a place where the local culture *is* global urbanity. At its root, the urbanity that allows for these kinds of pragmatic connections is enabled by the existence of patches and corridors of exchange around the globe that enable periodic disturbances, reinventions, and transformations of individuals.

The larger twenty-first-century political economy visualized through growing South-South relationships, the globalization of what has long been thought of as local markets for basic goods such as food, and demographic—or grassroots—globalization provides an analytic backdrop that helps to explain why the twenty-first century is characterized by the urban shift, and why cities and their urbanism are so important as the physical and institutional manifestation of globalization. The fact that most people now live in cities is much less interesting than the reasons why the *particular composition* of a global urban ecosystem exists. Identifying this new global political economy as the driver of what makes any particular city "global" breaks down stereotypes of urban agglomerations and their host nations; moreover, the scholar's task is not just to deconstruct these stereotypes but also to reorganize them into categories more appropriate to the contemporary context.

The trends of contemporary globalization are fundamentally about diversity—the branching out of individuals, nations, and economies into new and unfamiliar territories. Following the economic tradition of Jane Jacobs, a focus on cities is the best window into these larger political processes. Beyond simply being the physical access points of this diversification, cities themselves are about diversity, a fact often glossed over by a narrow focus on global urban percentages. The political economy identified with each of the four cities underlies today's global urban ecosystem precisely because the cities not only build on today's (and tomorrow's) inevitable factor endowment complementarity but also extend beyond the veneer of economic growth to drive new social, cultural, and political engagements that create new opportunities for individuals.

These trends enable the kinds of close encounters and unlikely relationships that have always characterized cities, especially those that break down regional or social barriers. Breaking these barriers down creates new kinds of geographic and social juxtapositions that might best be seen as vertically integrated globalization—the flattening out of national differences as the world becomes more "spiky" with urban clusters everywhere. While Mumbai is a huge concentration of people and economic activities, for example, to what extent is it truly "global" for the average resident? Most inhabitants are sequestered far away from people and things not native to the locality or to India. Certainly, there is a global economy in the city, but the likelihood of the average resident directly encountering it is relatively low. Likewise, Shanghai, where the economy is global but language, culture, and strict political divisions erect barriers to grassroots interactions, is a different sort of *economically* global but not a truly global city. With these intentional and unintentional barriers in place, cities such as Shanghai retain social and cultural diversity yet are unable to mobilize it into the creativity, innovation, and organic change that characterize truly "global" cities.

Thus, rather than size, economic prowess, or physical infrastructure defining the importance of the city, it is actualization of deep economic and intimate social complementarities that makes a city part of the global urban ecosystem. Natural environments of monocrops are unsustainable, just as cities built on simple industries, closed to external influences, and divorced from changing social mores and composition have all withered in their time. In sum, the global cities described in the previous chapters are surprising, but they share an element of cosmopolitanism that far exceeds other, more-conventionally defined, global cities *precisely because they are surprising.* While size, history, and economy play important roles, perhaps the best measure of the globalization and urbanization of a city is the probability an average resident has of bumping into the globe through his or her interaction with residents, visitors, products, and services, and through his or her experience of the built environment——that is the best way to characterize the contemporary global city.

Rather than plunge into exploratory searches for empirical relationships, this book's approach has been to describe ways in which globalization and urbanization have been related through history and, in particular, the ways in which contemporary global trends have strengthened particular types of these connections. It presents a hypothesis to be assessed and critiqued. The intent of the book has not been to develop a science of urbanization but rather to illustrate the commonalities that would allow the formulation and testing of why urbanization is an important phenomenon. Certainly, vast agrarian and rural parts of the world remain important as food production systems, tourist destinations, and ecosystem services, even if they *are* quickly being depopulated. Because cities are the places where most humans now live, they must be the centers of globalization—at least demographically. Even the globalization of environmental problems such as climate change has an urban focus. While drought, flooding, and sea level rise do affect agrarian regions, the vast majority of the vulnerable regions lie in the areas where people actually live, which is, now, in an urban and periurban context. To compound this simple fact of vulnerability, where people congregate, they transform the landscape and alter the natural environment, often compounding risk. Even of those that cannot yet be called "cities," many are on their way to becoming cities or their periurban rings.

If we are interested in understanding the environments in which humans live during this era, we have to understand the diversity of places where they are. The four case studies serve as a hypothesis that global cities should be seen as the locales where human interactions span the greatest physical and social distances. Of course, the choice of only four illustrative case studies limits the universality of their common factors. However, the diversity of their geographic, cultural, and economic locales illustrates the power and utility of a global-urban-ecosystem lens for understanding contemporary globalization.

BUILDING BLOCKS OF
THE GLOBAL URBAN ECOSYSTEM

In the previous chapters, I outlined four disparate cases as "do-your-timer," "old-timer," and "for-all-timer" cities, focusing on the human personalities, physical imprints, and institutional habits driving each one's collective culture. One model suggested by this frame is that of ecosystem succession, a process through which an ecosystem evolves predictably over time, and in which a recently burned-down or cleared forest, for example, is first colonized by "pioneer species" of trees, which are soon outcompeted by more resource-demanding but stable species, and finally colonized by "mature" forest trees able to live for hundreds of years. Understanding cities in this way, Saigon and Addis—as they appear today—will eventually develop into Honolulu or New York, depending on both human trends and natural conditions. Honolulu itself is going through a period of trying to figure out its next phase—if any—while New York has undergone successive transformations and survived successfully. Convenient as it might be, however, technological change and Murphy's Law warn against making predictions based on an increasingly tenuous knowledge of how the past connects with the future.

Certainly, one cannot prepackage a model of development independent of cycles and unforeseen events, but one can usefully contour some possible alternatives. Such an approach to understanding the urban form is attractive for its simplicity and clarity and because we are generally familiar with a model for growth and development that, if not entirely linear, shows consistent development and modernization. In 1960, W. W. Rostow[1] proposed the five stages of economic growth to explain how poor countries develop. To summarize the transitions between these stages, traditional agricultural societies industrialized, expanded their trade networks, and reinvested surplus, thereby creating the preconditions for "take-off."

In his third stage, poor countries sustained manufacturing growth and created the private and public institutional framework for managing it, followed by a fourth stage in which the majority of people shifted from agriculture into industry, and cumulating with an age of high mass consumption. While Rostow's definition appears quaint and outdated today, his efforts to understand development, and the commonalities inherent in it globally, had significant impacts not only on how we think about development but also—for better or worse—on how decision makers invest in some policies and not others.

One alternative approach toward understanding the analytic connections between Saigon, Addis, Honolulu, and New York might propose a similar explanation. And beyond my characterizations of the four cities, a healthy literature on cities reinforces a shared model for urban growth and development: modernization theory,[2] neighborhood placemaking,[3] and deindustrialization.[4] During stage 1, for example, rural economies and communities transform and transition into urban ones in which a nascent industrial sector grows, as does agriculture. However, the bulk of human productive activity becomes urban as technology obviates the need for labor on farms and shifts it to urban settlements where the returns on human endeavors generate greater material returns. Both Saigon and Addis to a lesser extent exhibit these characteristics, and both have taken the physical shape of a city dominated by these trends: slums, rapidly erected and unserviced neighborhoods, and communities filled with residents unfamiliar with urban lifestyles. A possible stage 2, for example, might see Honolulu as a city in which the economy and residents have put agriculture behind and have committed to an urban life. However, in Honolulu, a newly recognized city of urbanism, the imprint of human-scale communities necessary to soften urban life dominates relationships and debate. Here, the physical layout is modern, yet the city lacks major backbone infrastructures such as public transit and waste management systems, and struggles to even recognize the need to invest in these systems.

Following a conventional understanding of the comparison, a third stage would show hierarchical differentiation across urban spaces, conventionally known as "suburbanization" and "white flight" of the kind seen in New York during the 1980s. Here, the physical city is a relic of a manufacturing heyday populated only by those unable to escape. Finally, a fourth stage would be the consumerist city of New York, where residents return, neighborhoods become cleaner and sometimes more diverse, and real estate values reflect not only the improved amenities but also the human need to be close together for both economic and social reasons.

While this four-stage model of urbanization may neatly package the cases into a coherent narrative, it surely obscures much about *why* global urbanization happens. It conveniently captures the connections between the diverse cases discussed in the preceding chapters, but ultimately it dissatisfies. It is fraught with both conceptual inadequacies—despite its elegant simplicity—and practical dangers. There are too many intervening conditions in the development of human settlements that render such efforts of a conceptual unity for such an infinitely complex entity as a city severely limited. Perhaps more dangerously, such unified theories of urban development—as with modernization theory—can put decision makers in a formulaic mind-set in which they deliberately try to reproduce the successes of other cities. The proliferation of urban planning "*best* practices" instead of "*informative* practices" or "*suggestive* practices" is emblematic of a standardized model for understanding urban development. This problem has wasted huge amounts of public resources and dislocated countless city residents, as high-tech tax credits in low-tech regions and slum clearance for illusory luxury developments destroy the human and built elements of what makes cities great. Such utopian dreams are well intentioned but often fall far short of their stated goals.

The evidence presented here might, to a rushed observer, suggest a neat model for urbanization across the globe. However, the complexity and sheer number of cities, combined with the elusive definition of what "city" is, as described in the first chapter, equally suggest that there are as many that don't fit the model as there are those that do. More important, it fails to capture the notion that cities are great because each has a unique character, and, in particular, the truly great ones are great because they capture human elements unavailable anywhere else. The four cases described in this book are really interesting and truly unique. Should we just leave it at that? This alternative interpretation of the cases—that they should each be taken on their own terms, undiluted by comparison—also dissatisfies. If every city is unique, then why do we care about urbanization in general rather than any particular case? The level of public interest and ubiquitous use of the term "urban" surely suggest that this placeholder term is important as a conceptual unifier rather than as a distinguisher. The analytic challenge, however, is to parse out the commonalities of cities without shackling them into unrealistic categories.

The staged explanation of my four cases dissatisfies in its mechanistic implication of a common development trajectory blissfully but dangerously ignorant of novel events and leapfrogging technologies. The classification of unique cities around the world dissatisfies because it willfully ignores the fact that, in a fundamental way, these cities are much more alike than they are different. Despite differing languages and cultures, they all value public buses, a municipal police force, and the convenience of finding a variety of food and entertainment options in close proximity.

Rather than throw up our hands and shy away from the task of analytically classifying cities in the new urban century, it is important that we make an attempt to understand how they reconcile the universalizing conformity of integration into a single urban system with the isolating and unrealistic prospect of urban autarky in an increasingly integrated world. A return to the ecosystem lens can help us corral the diversity of cities without suffocating the dynamism and educational weight of their complexity.

Certainly, the complexity of human economies, politics, society, and culture mirrors the complexities of natural ecosystems, but ecosystems also retain significant differences that matter. Just as a desert ecosystem differs fundamentally from a forest one, city spaces can take very different forms and successional dynamics. We can separate out developing cities, industrial cities, Asian cities, and African cities, but the added analytic value seems illusory, groping for some concepts that only partially ring true because the agency of human beings cannot be simplified by human beings as observers. Atlanta and Los Angeles look remarkably similar even though one is in a desert and the other in a forest environment. Delta-located Saigon exhibits many characteristics common to Addis, which is up in the Ethiopian highlands. Cities are human systems and we need to understand human dynamics to understand them. It is not the natural environment that shapes them, but the social, political, cultural, and economic ones that do.

Just as flora, fauna, and water are present in any ecosystem, there are some foundational building blocks of the contemporary global city, a kind of "urban DNA" that runs through "do-your-timer," "old-timer," and "for-all-timer" cities.

THE BUILDING BLOCKS OF THE CITY

To understand any system requires an understanding of its core, building-block elements; and just as the complex human body has numerous genotypic variations resulting in a vast diversity of phenotypes, the complex city has its own building blocks, its own DNA. The four case studies described in this book rarely appear in the same category, yet most would consider them part of what we would call a "city." This classification based on difference, I argued earlier, is what makes an understanding of their commonalities an advance in our understanding of global urbanization. Our understanding of cities is a bit like Associate Supreme Court Justice Potter Stewart's understanding of the definition of "hard-core" pornography, of which he famously stated, "I know it when I see it." As scholars, observers, and decision makers we need to do better than this.

To sum up the urban commonalities described in the previous chapters, each city punches above its weight class, whether it is Saigon (and the Africans eking out a living there), Addis as the standard-bearer for the African continent, Honolulu's Indigenous City, or New York's reincarnations. Each is also an "edgy" landscape with residents comfortable but not satisfied: Saigon's dynamic growth on top of the exploitation of its workforce of livability, Addis' uneasy billionaires looking out over their neighbors living in shacks, Honolulu's completely man-made "natural" environment, and New York's popular image of dysfunction even as the city has become softer. The surprises and contradictions of these two characteristics—comfortable yet unsatisfied—however, would mean little on their own. It is the sense of intentionality, especially those intentions that extend across the globe, that mobilize these characteristics into a kind of urban "potential energy." Each actively thinks about its future, with both Saigon's and Addis' forcing their transition to a fully industrialized city with adequate services for all, with Honolulu's efforts to carve out a local identity in a globally connected world, and with New York's surprising itself over and over in its ability to push onward through severe crises. Without this kind of intentionality, punching above one's weight class and an edgy characteristic are more accurately considered dysfunction and a waste of resources. Without this potential energy, we are left with Potemkin villages such as Celebration, Florida, a city that has many of the technical features of urban life with none of the human ones. These cities will seldom be confused with a global city.

And like all truly great cities, even ones "for all time," the four cities presented here are more interesting for what they are becoming than for what they are. They each have unresolved questions about the future that require their residents to engage, negotiate, fight, and sometimes resolve among themselves. It is these questions that pump new lifeblood into their hearts, the new residents eager to build anew and construct the future, whether that future shape is economic, political, cultural, or physical. In this way, the contemporary global city is a city filled with millions of city builders, each actively making his or her own contributions to the physical and social shape of the city.

While each city has its own history, region, culture, and pathway, the attractive ones, such as Saigon, Addis, Honolulu, and New York, are great because they each benefit from a triad of mutually reinforcing characteristics that attract these human-scale city builders: economic and productivity efficiencies born of agglomeration, a central role for difference and diversity, and a global connectivity that is able to renew these characteristics over time.

What makes global trends so compelling in driving urbanization in these great cities is that each brings with it those three important characteristics that enable a city to reinvent itself: economic efficiency, difference and diversity, and connectivity. Global economic complementarities provide sufficient material resources to meet everyday needs; national, ethnic, racial, and philosophical differences provide residents ongoing opportunities to do the hard work of learning, encouraging residents out of the cells they naturally create for themselves as part of their daily routines; and connectivity allows residents to continuously change their daily routines through new foods, services, and physical environments.

It is this vertical integration of the social, connective, and physical structures of a city that allows for full and exciting experiences in micro spaces. The combination of these foundational elements, these DNA building blocks, enables a city to ask new questions, collaboratively engage and negotiate progress, and reinvent itself. As with biological DNA, every city has elements of each, but it is the particular combination and concentrations that give individuality to any case.

Saigon and Addis are dominated by do your timers, but every city has them; Honolulu by old-timers, but every city has them; and New York by for all timers, even though every city certainly has them as well.

DO YOUR TIMERS, OLD-TIMERS, AND FOR ALL TIMERS REVISITED

Just as Malcolm Gladwell's understanding of social epidemics has "connectors," "mavens," and "salesmen" driving society past important thresholds,[5] I believe that the general personality types of city dwellers and the cities that they disproportionately influence will drive many of the latent trends of globalization past thresholds of surprising and significant change. The existence of medical tourism connecting patients in Addis with a Bangkok hospital, foreign retirement communities of the Grey Revolution in Mexico and Malaysia, Chinese traders in small African markets, African footballers in Saigon, and the competing interests of catfish producers in the Mekong Delta and their American counterparts illustrates a snowballing phenomenon facilitated by the interactions of three types of cities: do-your-timer, old-timer, and for-all-timer cities and their residents.

Saigon and Addis Ababa share some basic economic questions about the future as well as some distinct ones regarding the types of environments enabled by economic growth and the provision of basic needs.

They are both on a pathway toward modernization and growth, trying to transform an agrarian economy and society into a modern urban and industrial one. The former, however, is an economic center driven by globalization of trade, while the other is a political center driven by the globalization of formerly marginal Africa. Both are, to use Mumford's[6] words, cities that serve as meeting places for migrants from the rural hinterlands, global professionals, and local communities. Saigon is driven by an attractive force of economic opportunity that is underlaid by less significant political forces pushing residents to move there. Addis, on the other hand, is a political capital underlaid by a very gradually improving economic environment.

Vietnam's excitement and fast-paced life driven by very rapid rates of economic growth, and the hopeful presence of an emerging continent's African Union, give both Saigon and Addis, respectively, a feeling of "becoming," in which it is relatively easy to mix across national, ethnic, racial, and philosophical differences. They are places where it is easy to make friends, but just as easy to lose—or lose track of—them. And how can it be otherwise when the future shape and culture of these cities are so much in flux?

For Saigon, the big questions are how to mitigate the high cost of living among the poor, with inflation reaching 25 percent and a looming crisis in social inequality; and what will happen once other cheap-labor-producing countries outcompete the Vietnamese workforce, as China, Bangladesh, and others are beginning to do. For Addis, the questions are more basic: pride and culture cannot put food on the table. Despite its rich history, Ethiopia (and Addis Ababa) faces serious challenges, of not just basic services but even food security and disease prevention, in regard to much of its population. At the same time as Addis is proud of its history and independence, residents' attitudes toward colonialism are surprisingly complex. Rather than simple pride of independence, many residents express a fleeting twinge of regret at the lack of a colonial patron. For all the crimes and tragedies of colonial rule, European powers tended to make some investments in infrastructure and education in other African cities that were never made in Ethiopia, hence Addis is—in some ways—at the bottom of a heap atop which it used to sit during Selassie's time. And in the absence of these relationships, the uneasy relationship with Chinese contractors who are making those investments is ever more important.

The diplomats and international staff have a good time in Addis because for them it is cheap and they can live like royalty. Whether they like it or not, however, they end up living a colonial life in Addis even as they may be working toward undoing the remnants of a neocolonial history. The Chinese here are no less contradictory. They are outsiders and hated because of cultural misunderstandings and a self-exploitative pragmatism that contradicts Ethiopian habits; on the other hand, their efforts have resulted in important improvements, a fact overlaid by local complaints about poor-quality Chinese goods.

As seen through the lenses of Saigon and Addis, the do-your-timer city is exciting but unsustainable; a place where opportunities abound, but only if one has a clear and accurate vision of the future. What this future holds is the basic question on the minds of the various residents in these cities because if they are wrong, the investments made today will be a colossal waste of resources rather than an astute investment in their, and their children's, futures.

Like Saigonese and Addis Ababans, Honolulans also think about the future; it's just that their concerns hinge on different types of questions. Two questions are central to this community: what to do with culture and how to resolve the problem of an old-timer economy.

The values embedded in Honolulu's DNA require a bit of cognitive dissonance that many hope will pay off in the end. The basic question is whether a New Communalist way of life can succeed in a global economy and culture. Can it reinvent itself as either an Indigenous City or as an environmentally sustainable one, either of which might allow it to retain a sense of identity in a world where "tropical paradise" is increasingly a boilerplate label? While old-timers certainly aspire toward both, realizing these goals contradicts almost all past experience. Garbage transfer, investment in public transit, and numerous other challenges to collective visioning and decision making have yet to be realized on an implementation level, even though many residents share an affinity for local, traditional, and sustainable ways. How can preservationists reconcile the city's needs for alternative energy with airplane-sized wind turbines on formerly pristine hills? Does Honolulu become a warehouse for people "getting away from it all," or does it develop its place at the geographic center of the twenty-first century's most dynamic economic region into a social, economic, and cultural center of it. Can it use its tradition as a platform for innovation and guidance of the global economy and society rather than as a cover for a kind of NIMBYism? Many of these challenges come down to one of governance, and at root, the most important underlying question remains: Honolulu is good at small-community governance, but will it ever become an "urban-level community" as a forum for collective decision making?

On the surface, it would seem that a city such as New York might be self-satisfied, comfortable in the knowledge that the city has the power and capacity to reinvent itself and attract a global resident base even as its position within a global network of cities sees ever more challenges to its primacy. For all of New York's demonstrated ability to independently weather transformational changes, New Yorkers remain a neurotic bunch; but it is not a neuroticism born of insecurity. This is one attuned to the ever-changing nature of social life, and one that requires being comfortable in uncomfortable situations.

Certainly, there are New Yorkers wedded to its past, those wedded to particular neighborhoods, and those wedded to specific types of diversities. But true "for all timers" must be committed to the place itself, not to any particular incarnation of it. They were New Yorkers when the city was collapsing under the triad of fiscal meltdown, industrial decline, and skyrocketing crime; they were New Yorkers amidst the rubble of the Twin Towers; and they were New Yorkers as Wall Street drove the country's credit to ruin. Each of these periods saw mass exodus from New York's neighborhoods, its economy, and its social life, but each also served as a purification reaction that sorted out those there for only the ephemeral qualities of a job, a social life, or a neighborhood.

Surely, Saigon and Addis also have their residents ready to stick it out through thick and thin. The difference is that—for the time being at least—they are cities defined by particular identifiable characteristics and reasons to be there. Surely, their growth will slow, just as surely as Honolulu's comparative advantage as an island paradise will lose its luster. The question for these cities is what happens after that. For New Yorkers, more familiar with the ups and downs of a city, the questions center on how to prepare to weather them. New Yorkers like the city but cannot easily identify why they like it; the economic and political characteristics dominating Saigon and Addis are relatively inconsequential in the minds of New York's for all timers, and a decreasing percentage of Honolulans would point toward any natural resource or other physical attribute as the reason they love their city.

Thus, the questions of for all timers are not about the city at all; they are about each person's ability to "go with the flow," to weather the changes, and to find the opportunities where none seem to exist. To return to that quintessential New Yorker Lou Reed again, the for all timer constantly asks whether he wants to stay in the city. He is constantly struggling to justify his commitment to it, and for so many, constantly trying out Reed's own words: "I don't know very many people who live in New York . . . who don't also say, 'But I'm leaving. And I've been thinking of leaving . . . for, uh, 35 years now.'" To outsiders, this may appear as neurotic insecurity, but to for all timers, it is the most comfortable thing in the world.

In this way, the for all timer is a partner in marriage. Fight as you may over the small stuff, it is the long-term commitment itself that ends up being the reason to love it, rather than any particular set of characteristics. This characterization of an emergent DNA that most certainly will come to characterize a diverse but connected global urban ecosystem mirrors E. B. White's original description of New York:

> There are roughly three New Yorks. There is, first, the New York of the man or woman who was born there, who takes the city for granted and accepts its size, its turbulence as natural and inevitable. Second, there is the New York of the commuter—the city that is devoured by locusts each day and spat out each night. Third, there is New York of the person who was born somewhere else and came to New York in quest of something. . . . Commuters give the city its tidal restlessness, natives give it solidity and continuity, but the settlers give it passion.[7]

Rather than listing categories of people who should choose to live in any given city because it is the "retirement" city, or the one for "artists" or "tech-savvy professionals," I believe that cities as diverse as Saigon and New York are filled with diversities of people; most important, these people are diverse in their attitudes toward their city. It is the tension among these diverse personality types that makes a city unique.

The do your timers connect cities across the world in their efforts to prepare for the future, old-timers cultivate local traditions and habits that stem the universalizing pressures of globalization, and for all timers synthesize the two into an "edgy" feeling of adventure without danger. Taken together, they connect complex, place-based arrangements of people, structures, flora, and fauna that are unique, but not so different as to be foreign. This system of patches and corridors defines a global urban ecosystem from which very rapid changes are likely to burst.

GLOBAL URBAN GOVERNANCE: SCIENCE AND POETRY

Cities are the places where cultural and socioeconomic gaps yawn the widest. They are where both the global elites and, increasingly, the poor are concentrated; where minority cultures are both strong and undergoing the greatest change. Cities are at the crossroads of cultures where social experiments blossom or wither on the vine. However, the myth of an integrated mosaic of cultures and differences peacefully coexisting in close quarters and participating confidently in this global system should never cloud out skepticism of how difficult it is to achieve urban social and political cohesion. Cities are the spaces where residents move in and out of urban subcultures in which language, religious, cultural, and other influences constantly try to penetrate deep into the hardened exteriors of residents, thereby shaping their personal cultures.

These interjections are not merely the personal challenges to individual residents that make daily life a series of headaches and confrontations to negotiate. Rather, they are seeds planted among individuals that civic leaders hope will find broader manifestation in collaborative negotiations over shared tax burdens and the distribution of scarce physical resources and infrastructures; over affordable housing, clean air, or a seat on a rush-hour bus. If one spends one week in Saigon or Addis, one can easily see that a focus on the economic and political future permeates the air. In Honolulu, reference to the past, in the form of a Hawai'ian chant, begins every professional meeting; in New York City, it is assumed that the city drives the rest of the world. Newbies soon realize that their ability to function effectively depends on their ability to center themselves in these characteristics. At the same time, they challenge residents, through their daily negotiations, to rethink and adapt their personalities in an endless dance of mutual adjustment. Each must become comfortable with being uncomfortable.

Only at crossroads such as these vertically integrated cities, where the whole of global life is experienced, does one practice this kind of global personal transformation. Unable to simply gloss over these differences, civic leaders in these places hope that their diverse residents can come

to negotiate a mutually acceptable public sphere and begin to shape an-
swers to each of their city's important questions about the future.

In sum, effective governance requires envisioning an inclusive future in which these diverse individuals can agree upon some foundational principles of change. Without a vision, questions about how to
change quickly degenerate into chaos and conflict. It is for this reason
that utopian visions are born of crisis. Ebenezer Howard's response to
the squalor of the turn-of-the-century cities in the industrial world, So-
viet- and Chinese-modeled Socialism after colonialism, and American
efforts to create "Empowerment Zones" have all served as convenient
policy solutions that defined a crisis of development. Their visions,
narrow and unrealistic as they were and continue to be, have provided
the spark that ignites the fire driving change: a clear human vision of a
preferred future. Without such visions, residents are only disinterested
parties, unable to see the whole as something more than disparate
parts; for the contemporary global city, the whole extends beyond city
boundaries, incorporating global disparities of both people and places.

Despite the failure of these visions, they continue to be promoted
by planners, developers, historic preservationists, and utopians worldwide. The proliferation of eco-cities across Asia, the construction of
Masdar City and the existence of Dubai/Abu Dhabi themselves in the
Middle East, and the New Urbanist movement in the United States are
the top-down manifestations of a human beaverlike intensity in the
desire to transform their physical environments to serve contemporary
material and symbolic desires. These utopian visions have usually been
defined by well-meaning architects and engineers rather than embedded within the minds, attitudes, and character of city residents, and
perhaps this provides some indication of their prospects for success. As
Mike Davis, Robert Neuwirth, and Jeb Brugmann all point out, it is the
residents of cities themselves that are transforming the face and internal
organs of cities around the world.[8]

It is those being personally transformed every day through mutual
adjustment with their neighbors that may come to define the Anthropocene: the age of humans. Just as Mumford suggests that the city
originated due to the simple fact that humans had emotional needs to
reconnect with their ancestors in specific gathering places, the shape of
today's cities reflects deeper human desires than merely material efficiency. In addition to being a connection with the past, today's cities are

the sites where deep motivations for improvement—material, physical, spiritual, emotional, and even psychological—are manifest. They are the gathering places not only of globalization but also of development: people move to cities to *escape* their communities of origin, but then to *rebuild* their communities of origin in new places. In making this argument, I hope this book challenges the assumptions that—as the late, great urbanist Jane Jacobs argued so effectively—urban communities are long-standing and stable entities. Without refuting Jacobs' important focus on community stability, I argue that without these utopia builders of "New Communities" associated with urbanization and globalization, the city holds little attraction and falls into disrepair, starved of the revitalizing elements of hope and reinvention. It is these builders that have led to some of the most impressive human achievements in history; it is also these builders who have created the most spectacular failures. In either case, it is in cities across the globe where these utopians and visionaries will work their stuff in the twenty-first century.

Utopians are creative, inspired by the human condition, but anchored to earth by a realism about material life and the ways to get things done; they are about *both* poetry *and* engineering. They provide material opportunities as well as human meaning. This book began with a question: what is a city? Perhaps the most universal ways to express this complexity is to say that a city is, as both Jay-Z and Alicia Keys proudly sing, in the first version of the song (see Chorus, lines 1–7). And, of course, it's not just New York that is this kind of place: Saigon, Addis, and Honolulu each have their own budding young superstars expressing their love of the cities from which they take their inspiration.

In all cities that can lay claim to the global urban ecosystem, artists like Jay Z and Alicia Keys are on an urban edge: the inhabitants of places on the verge of breaking through to a better life for their residents in Saigon or Addis; on the verge of stemming a gradual decline with a creative reinterpretation of what it means to be local in Honolulu; or, in New York, always on the verge of something new. The corridors that connect cities such as these to other urban patches exist on the edge of comfort and complacency. It is this ecology of daily life that distinguishes the organic urbanism of the coming Anthropocene from cookie-cutter developments, "Disney-fied" neighborhoods, and remote but stable—or static—settlements.

Notes

INTRODUCTION

1. World Bank: Finance, Economics & Urban Development Department; Sustainable Development Network, "Systems of Cities: Harnessing Urbanization for Growth & Poverty Alleviation," The World Bank Urban and Local Government Strategy, 2010.

2. As reviewed in John Rennie Short, *Global Metropolitan: Globalizing Cities in a Capitalist World* (London and New York: Routledge, 2004).

3. The China-Africa Project estimates that between 750,000 and 1 million ethnic Chinese immigrants currently reside on the African continent. This figure places Chinese immigrants at a higher number than the number of French immigrants in Africa during the height of the French colonial period.

1 URBANIZATION AND THE CONSTRUCTION OF THE GLOBAL URBAN ECOSYSTEM

1. Author calculations based on the United Nations, Department of Economic and Social Affairs Population Division, *World Population Prospects: The 2005 Revision* (New York: United Nations, 2006).

2. United Nations, Department of Economic and Social Affairs Population Division, *World Population Prospects: The 2005 Revision* (New York: United Nations, 2006).

3. B. Mbiba and M. Huchzermeyer, "Contentious Development: Peri-Urban Studies in Sub-Saharan Africa," *Progress in Development Studies* 2 (2002).

4. John Friedmann, "Becoming Urban: Periurban Dynamics in Vietnam and China—Introduction," *Pacific Affairs* 84 (2011).

5. For example, Erik Harms, *Saigon's Edge: On the Margins of Ho Chi Minh City* (Minneapolis, MN: University of Minnesota Press, 2011); or James H. Spencer, "An Emergent Landscape of Inequality in Vietnamese Cities," *Globalizations* 7, no.3 (2010): 431–43.

6. For example, Mike Davis, *Planet of Slums* (London: Verso, 2006).

7. For example, Robert Neuwirth, *Shadow Cities: A Billion Squatters, a New Urban World* (New York: Routledge, 2005).

8. It is likely no coincidence that the city as a subject of study has imprinted itself on both Glaeser's and my own professional careers, since we both grew up in the same neighborhood and attended the same high school in New York City.

9. A close observer, like a former student from Malaysia, might notice that even now cows have come to be "urban," carefully watching traffic patterns before venturing to cross the street.

10. Some of my own work with colleagues at the University of Hawai'i and the East West Center has begun to flesh these concepts out (e.g., see Spencer 2013 for an empirical analysis; Kapan et al., "Avian Influenza [H5N1] and the Evolutionary and Social Ecology of Infectious Disease Emergence," *EcoHealth* 3, no. 3 [2006]: 187–94 for a conceptual overview). But for a popular review of human urbanization, development, and the ecology of disease, see Jim Robbins' excellent article in the *New York Times*, July 14, 2012.

11. See *The Economist*, special issue, *The Anthropocene: A Man-Made World*, May 26, 2011.

12. Gabriel García Márquez, *Love in the Time of Cholera* (New York: Vintage Books, 1988), chap. 3.

13. Ayi Kwei Armah, *The Beautyful Ones Are Not Yet Born* (Boston, MA: Houghton Mifflin, 1968).

14. John Friedmann, "Reflections on Place and Place-Making in the Cities of China," *International Journal of Urban and Regional Research* 31, no.2 (2007): 257–79.

15. David Harvey, *Justice, Nature and the Geography of Difference* (Oxford, UK: Blackwell, 1996); David Harvey, *Spaces of Global Capitalism: Towards a Theory of Uneven Geographical Development* (London and New York: Verso, 2006).

16. Edward W. Soja. *Thirdspace* (Malden, MA: Blackwell, 1996).

17. AnnaLee Saxenian, *Regional Advantage: Culture and Competition in Silicon Valley and Route 128* (Cambridge, MA: Harvard University Press, 1996).

18. Michael Storper, Lena Lavinas, Alejandro Mercado-Célis, "Society, Community, and Development: A Tale of Two Regions," in *The Economic Geography of Innovation*, edited by Karen R. Polenske (Cambridge, UK: Cambridge University Press, 2007).

19. For example, Aprodicio Laquian, *Beyond Metropolis: The Planning and Governance of Asia's Mega-Urban Regions* (Ann Arbor, MI: The University of Michigan Press, 2005).

20. For example, Edward L. Glaeser, "A Tale of Many Cities," in *Economix: Explaining the Science of Everyday Life* (blog), *New York Times*, April 20, 2010.

21. Ebenezer Howard, *Garden Cities of Tomorrow* (London: Swan Sonnenschein & Co., 1902).

22. "China Urbanization in Shenzhen," Public Radio International, July 7, 2008.

23. Peter Calthorpe, *The Next American Metropolis: Ecology, Community, and the American Dream* (New York: Princeton Architectural Press, 1993).

24. John D. Kasarda and Greg Lindsay, *Aerotropolis: The Way We'll Live Next* (New York: Farrar, Straus and Giroux, 2011).

25. Brian J. Cudahy, *Box Boats: How Container Ships Changed the World* (New York: Fordham University Press, 2006).

26. See, for example, J. P. Grime, "Competitive Exclusion in Herbaceous Vegetation." *Nature* 242 (1973), 344–47; or J. H. Connell, "Diversity in Tropical Rain Forests and Coral Reefs." *Science* 199 (1978): 1302–10.

27. Lewis Mumford, "What Is a City?," *Architectural Record* 82 (November 1937).

28. Thomas L. Friedman, *The World Is Flat: A Brief History of the Twenty-First Century* (New York: Farrar, Straus and Giroux, 2005); Saskia Sassen, *The Global City: New York, London, Tokyo* (Princeton: Princeton University Press, 1991); Manfred Steger, *Globalization: A Very Short Introduction*, 2nd ed. (Oxford, UK: Oxford University Press, 2009); Jan Nederveen Pieterse, *Globalization and Culture: Global Mélange* (Lanham, MD: Rowman and Littlefield, 2003).

29. Steger, *Globalization*.

30. Philip McCann, "Globalization and Economic Geography: The World Is Curved, Not Flat," *The Cambridge Journal of Regions, Economy and Society* 1 (2008); Richard Florida, "The World Is Spiky: Globalization Has Changed the Economic Playing Field, but Hasn't Leveled It," *The Atlantic Monthly*, October 2005.

31. "Charter cities," a concept promoted by scholar Paul Romer, are cities established as administratively autonomous political entities in poor countries for the purpose of promoting economic development in those countries. The idea has been implemented with mixed results in places such as Honduras. Sebastian Mallaby, "The Politically Incorrect Guide to Ending Poverty," *The Atlantic*, July/August 2010; Elisabeth Malkin, "Plan for Charter City to Fight Honduras Poverty Loses Its Initiator," *New York Times*, September 30, 2012.

32. Richard Florida, *Who's Your City: How the Creative Economy Is Making Where to Live the Most Important Decision of Your Life* (New York: Basic Books, 2008).

33. Allen J. Scott, *Metropolis: From the Division of Labor to Urban Form* (Berkeley and Los Angeles: University of California Press, 1988); Michael Storper, *The Regional World: Territorial Development in a Global Economy* (London and New York: Guilford Press, 1997); and AnnaLee Saxenian, *Regional Advantage: Culture and Competition in Silicon Valley and Route 128* (Cambridge, MA: Harvard University Press, 1996).

34. Edward Glaeser, *Triumph of the City: How Our Greatest Invention Makes Us Richer, Smarter, Greener, Healthier, and Happier* (New York: The Penguin Press, 2011).

35. Richard Florida, *Who's Your City*.

36. Saskia Sassen, *Global Networks, Linked Cities* (New York: Routledge, 2002).

37. Mike Davis, *Planet of Slums* (New York: Verso, 2006).

38. Vinit Mukhija, *Squatters as Developers?: Slum Demolition and Redevelopment in Mumbai, India* (Aldershot: Ashgate Publishing Limited, 2003); Neuwirth, *Shadow Cities*.

39. Jeb Brugmann, *Welcome to the Urban Revolution: How Cities Are Changing the World* (New York: Bloomsbury Press, 2009).

40. John Friedmann, *China's Urban Transition* (Minneapolis: University of Minnesota Press, 2005).

41. Aprodicio Laquian, *Beyond Metropolis: The Planning and Governance of Asia's Mega-Urban Regions* (Washington, DC: Woodrow Wilson Press, 2005).

42. Toyin Falola, "An Overview," in *Globalization and Urbanization in Africa*, edited by Toyin Falola and Steven J. Salm (Trenton, NJ: Africa World Press, 2004), 1–6.

43. Edward Soja, *Postmetropolis—Critical Studies of Cities and Regions* (Oxford: Wiley-Blackwell, 2000).

44. Maliqalim Simone, *City Life from Jakarta to Dakar: Movements at the Crossroads* (New York: Routledge, 2010).

45. Richard Grant, *Globalizing City: The Urban and Economic Transformation of Accra, Ghana* (Syracuse: Syracuse University Press, 2008).

46. John Friedmann and Goetz Wolff, "World City Formation: An Agenda for Research and Action," *International Journal of Urban and Regional Research* 6 (1982): 309–44; John Friedmann, "The World City Hypothesis," *Development and Change* 17 (1986): 69–83.

47. Sassen, *The Global City*.

48. John Rennie Short, *Global Metropolitan: Globalizing Cities in a Capitalist World* (London and New York: Routledge, 2004).

49. World Health Organization and UNICEF, *Meeting the MDG Drinking Water and Sanitation Target: The Urban and Rural Challenge of the Decade* (Geneva: WHO, 2006).

50. Fergal O'Brien, "European Unemployment Rate Rises to Highest in Almost 15 Years," *Bloomberg News*, May 1, 2012.

51. And for the time being, American baseball is almost exclusively a male activity.

52. Lewis Mumford, *The City in History: Its Origins, Its Transformations, and Its Prospects* (New York: Harcourt, Brace & World, 1961), 573.

53. Jennifer Robinson, *Ordinary Cities: Between Modernity and Development* (London, UK: Routledge, 2006).

54. Janet L. Abu-Lughod, *Before European Hegemony: The World System A.D. 1250–1350* (Oxford, UK: Oxford University Press, 1989).

55. Malcolm Gladwell, *The Tipping Point: How Little Things Can Make a Big Difference* (New York: Little, Brown, 2000).

56. As legend has it, Peter Minuit, director of the Dutch West India Company purchased Manhattan for sixty guilders, approximately $24.

2 URBAN HISTORIES: ARRIVING AT THE GLOBAL URBAN ECOSYSTEM

1. Lewis Mumford, *The City in History: Its Origins, Its Transformations, and Its Prospects* (New York: Harcourt, Brace & World, 1961), 9.

2. Mumford, *The City in History*, 9.

3. The World Bank, Urbanization website, accessed November 26, 2012, http://web.worldbank.org/WBSITE/EXTERNAL/EXTABOUTUS/0,,contentMDK:23272497~pagePK:51123644~piPK:329829~theSitePK:29708,00.html.

4. Mumford, *The City in History*, 64–70.

5. In recent years, competition among rapidly growing Asian and Gulf State cities has led to "starchitect" development projects such as Petronas Towers in Malaysia, Taipei 101 in Taiwan, and Dubai's Burj Khalifa.

6. The "Birdnest" stadium of Beijing and the United Arab Emirates' proposed "Rock" stadium built into the side of a mountain are two of the most notable.

7. This tendency to enshrine has become more complex, as the structure is increasingly seen at the neighborhood—or the city—level. American New Urbanists have shaped hundreds of neighborhoods in the United States and abroad into an image of pre–World War II housing and commercial settlements, while forward-looking architects and engineers in Abu Dhabi and China have begun to build whole cities completely from scratch to meet environmental and sustainability objectives.

8. Mumford, *The City in History*, 14.

9. Jane Jacobs, *The Nature of Economies* (New York: Vintage Books, 2001).

10. Charles Lindblom, *The Market System: What It Is, How It Works, and What to Make of It* (New Haven: Yale University Press 2001).

11. Albert O. Hirschman, *The Passions and the Interests: Political Arguments for Capitalism before Its Triumph*, 20th anniversary ed. (Princeton: Princeton University Press, 1997), x.

12. See Steven Johnson, *Emergence: The Connected Lives of Ants, Brains, Cities, and Software* (New York: Scribner, 2001).

13. Jacobs, *The Nature of Economies*, chap. 1.

14. See Jane Jacobs, *The Death and Life of Great American Cities* (New York: Random House, 1961); *The Economy of Cities* (New York: Random House, 1969); and *Cities and the Wealth of Nations* (New York: Random House, 1984).

15. Alfred Crosby, Ecological Imperialism: *The Biological Expansion of Europe, 900–1900* (Cambridge, UK: Cambridge University Press, 2004).

16. Charles C. Mann, *1493: Uncovering the New World Columbus Created* (New York: Alfred A. Knopf, 2011), 23.

17. Carol Rose, *Property and Persuasion: New Perspectives on Law, Culture, and Society* (Boulder, CO: Westview Press, 1994).

18. Mann, *1493*, 31.

19. Most important to this school of central place theory was Walter Christaller. Walter Christaller, *Die zentralen Orte in Süddeutschland* (Jena: Gustav Fischer, 1933).

20. William Cronon, *Nature's Metropolis: Chicago and the Great West* (New York: W. W. Norton, 1991).

21. Douglass North, "Location Theory and Regional Economic Growth," in *Regional Development and Planning*, edited by John Friedmann and William Alonso (Cambridge, MA: The MIT Press, 1964), 256.

22. Steven Johnson, *The Ghost Map: The Story of London's Most Terrifying Epidemic—and How It Changed Science, Cities, and the Modern World* (New York: Riverhead Books, 2006).

23. Robert Fishman, *Urban Utopias in the Twentieth Century: Ebenezer Howard, Frank Lloyd Wright, and Le Corbusier* (Cambridge, MA: MIT Press, 1982, 1977).

24. Barry Bluestone and Bennett Harrison, *The Deindustrialization of America* (New York: Basic Books, 1982).

25. In particular, see William Julius Wilson, *The Truly Disadvantaged: The Inner City, the Underclass, and Public Policy* (Chicago: University of Chicago Press, 1987); and *When Work Disappears: The World of the New Urban Poor* (New York: Vintage Books, 1996).

26. See, in particular, R. T. T. Forman and M. Gordon, "Landscape Ecology Principles and Landscape Function," in *Methodology in Landscape Ecological Research and Planning*, vol. 5, edited by J. Brandt, and P. Agger (Proceedings of the First International Seminar of the International Association of Landscape Ecology, 1984); and R. Kerry Turner, Jeroen C. J. M. van den Bergh, Tore Soderqvist, Aat Barendregt, Jan van der Straaten, Edward Maltby, and Ekko C. van Ierland, "Ecological Economic Analysis of Wetlands: Scientific Integration for Management and Policy," *Ecological Economics* 35 (1995): 7–23.

3 SAIGON'S "DO-YOUR-TIMERS": RURAL TRANSFORMATION AND THE URBAN TRANSITION IN SAIGON

1. As of early 2014, this growth rate has dropped significantly, as has that of much of Asia and the rest of the world.

2. Ho Chi Minh City website, last accessed November 18, 2012, http://www.eng. hochiminhcity.gov.vn/Pages/default.aspx.

3. Hy Van Luong, "Wealth, Power and Inequality: Global Market, the State, and Local Sociocultural Dynamics," in *Postwar Vietnam: Dynamics of a Transforming Society*, edited by Hy Van Luong (Oxford: Rowman and Littlefield, 2003), 81–106; Benedict J. Kerkvliet, *The Power of Everyday Politics: How Vietnamese Peasants Transformed National Policy* (Ithaca: Cornell University Press, 2005).

4. Clare Arthurs, "One Million Jobs Created by New Enterprise Law in Viet Nam," United Nations Development Program Newsroom, UNDP, accessed December 14, 2012, http://content.undp.org/go/newsroom/choices-one-million-jobs-created-by-new-enterprise-law-in-viet-nam2003-06.en.

5. Peter Van Der Eng, "Productivity and Comparative Advantage in Rice Agriculture in Southeast Asia since 1870," *Asian Economic Journal* 18 (2004).

6. July 22, 2003.

7. December 18, 2001.

8. Nguyen Xuan Thanh, "Catfish Fight: Vietnam's Tra and Basa Fish Exports to the U.S.," paper prepared for the Vietnam Program of the John F. Kennedy School of Government, Harvard University, 2003, http://www.fetp.edu.vn/Research_casestudy/CaselistE.htm.

9. Le Cong Dinh, partner YKVN Law Firm and White & Case LLP affiliate, interview by author (James H. Spencer, Globalization Research Center, University of Hawai'i at Manoa), Ho Chi Minh City, Vietnam, July 2005; Duong Nhut Long, deputy director of Can Tho University Department of Aquaculture, interview by author (James H. Spencer, Globalization Research Center, University of Hawai'i at Manoa), Can Tho, Vietnam, July 2005.

10. Can Tho City Statistical Office, *So lieu kinh te xa hoi dong bang song cuu long* [Economic and social data of the Mekong Delta] (Can Tho City: Can Tho City Statistical Office, 2005).

11. Van Bui, Fulbright Economics Teaching Program, University of Economics, interview by author (James H. Spencer, Globalization Research Center, University of Hawai'i at Manoa), Ho Chi Minh City, Vietnam, July 7, 2005; Hong Van, "Leather Shoe Exporters Grapple with Anti-dumping Lawsuit," *Sai Gon Times Daily*, July 15, 2005.

12. From the "development assistance" side, Jeffrey Sachs, in *The End of Poverty: How Can We Make It Happen in Our Lifetime* (London: Penguin Books, 2005) argues for a focus on agriculture; and from an "open markets" perspective, Philippe LeGrain makes the same case in *Open World: The Truth about Globalization* (London: Abacus, 2002).

13. Chantal Pohl Nielsen, "Vietnam's Rice Policy: Recent Reforms and Future Opportunities," *Asian Economic Journal* 17 (2003).

14. Figures based on data from the Food and Agricultural Organization (FAO) Statistics Division, http://faostat.fao.org/site/339/default.aspx.

15. Denise Hare, "The Origins and Influence of Land Property Rights in Vietnam," *Development Policy Review* 26 (2008).

16. P. L. Pingali and V.-T. Xuan, "Vietnam: Decollectivization and Rice Productivity Growth," *Economic Development and Cultural Change* 40 (1992): 697–718.

17. Adam Fforde and Stefan de Vylder, *From Plan to Market—The Economic Transition in Vietnam* (Boulder, CO: Westview Press, 1996).

18. State Planning Committee (SPC), Socialist Republic of Vietnam, UNDP, FAO, and the World Bank, *Vietnam: Agricultural and Food Production Sector Review* (Hanoi, Vietnam: 1989).

19. Benedict J. Kerkvliet, *The Power of Everyday Politics: How Vietnamese Peasants Transformed National Policy* (Ithaca, NY: Cornell University Press, 2005); Hy Van Luong, "The Marxist State and Dialogic Re-structuration of Culture in Rural Vietnam," in *Indochina: Social and Cultural Change*, edited by David W. P. Elliott et al. (Claremont, CA: Keck Center for International and Strategic Studies, Claremont McKenna College, 2005).

20. SPC, *Vietnam: Agricultural and Food Production Sector Review*.

21. According to the State Planning Committee (1989), the decision was made in 1986, but Pingali and Xuan, in "Vietnam: Decollectivization and Rice Productivity Growth," associate Resolution No. 10 with its year of implementation, 1988.

22. Brian van Arkadie and Raymond Mallon, *Viet Nam: A Transition Tiger?* (Canberra, Australia: ANU Press, 2003); Adam Fforde and Stefan de Vylder, *From Plan to Market*.

23. SPC, *Vietnam: Agricultural and Food*; Pingali and Xuan, "Vietnam: Decollectivization and Rice Productivity Growth."

24. Figures calculated from International Monetary Fund, Balance of Payments Statistics Yearbook, vol. 61, part 1, country tables, 1.

25. Truong Si Anh, Patrick Gubry, Vu Thi Hong, and Jerrold W. Huguet, "Migration and Employment in Ho Chi Minh City," *Asia-Pacific Population Journal* 11 (1996).

26. James H. Spencer, "Water and Environmental Security in Globalizing Viet Nam: Emerging Risks in the Mekong Delta," issue brief for the Foundation for Environmental Security and Sustainability, 2007, www.fess-global.org/.

27. General Statistics Office of Vietnam, "Area, Population, and Population Density in 2011 by Province," accessed December 19, 2012, http://www.gso.gov.vn/ default_en.aspx?tabid=467&idmid=3&ItemID=12941.

28. Patrick Gubry, Vu Thi Hong, and Le Van Thanh, eds., *Les Chemins Vers la Ville: La Migration Vers Ho Chi Minh Ville a Partir d'une Zone du Delta du Mekong* (Paris: CEPED).

29. Department of Planning and Investment, Ho Chi Minh City, data calculated by author based on original data, last accessed November 17, 2012, http://www.dpi. hochiminhcity.gov.vn/invest/html/eco1.html.

30. Michael Waibel, Ronald Eckert, Michael Bose, and Volker Martin, "Housing for Low-Income Groups in Ho Chi Minh City between Re-Integration and Fragmentation: Approaches to Adequate Urban Typologies and Spatial Strategies," *ASIEN* 103 (2007).

31. Thi Cam Van Cao and Takahiro Akita, "Urban and Rural Dimensions of Income Inequality in Vietnam," GSIR Working Papers, Economic Development and Policy Series (EDP08-2), Graduate School of International Relations, International University of Japan, 2008.

32. Unlike the cases of Huong and Thao, their real names have been changed.

33. Ho Chi Minh City Department of Planning and Investment, "Foreign Direct Investment in HCMC," accessed December 15, 2012, http://www.dpi.hochiminhcity. gov.vn/invest/html/eco3.html.

34. For a taste of some of this literature, a good starting point would be the following: Le Ly Hayslip, *When Heaven and Earth Changed Places: A Vietnamese Woman's Journey from War to Peace* (New York: Doubleday, 1989); a memoir turned into a film by Oliver Stone, *Heaven and Earth*, 1993; James Freeman, *Hearts of Sorrow: Vietnamese-American Lives* (Palo Alto: Stanford University Press, 1991); Min Zhou and Carl L. Bankston, *Growing Up American: How Vietnamese Children Adapt to Life in the United States* (New York: Russell Sage Foundation, 1998); Uyen Nicole Duong, *Daughters of the River* (Las Vegas, NV: AmazonEncore, 2010); and *Mr. Cao Goes to Washington* (film).

35. My mother, Dao Nguyen Spencer, was one of the first to cautiously test the waters in newly Socialist Vietnam in 1985. Having emigrated from Vietnam in the 1960s for her education and, therefore, not considered a refugee, my mom was in a unique position regarding the new regime. Not having left the country under political stress, she presented a potential bridge between a politicized Viet Kieu diaspora and the government of Vietnam that had treated them poorly in the past. With the political sanctions of officials in Hanoi, she was given leeway to develop humanitarian programs ranging from youth exchanges to environmental protection, which brought her to Saigon several times a year. By the late 1980s, she had developed strong personal ties with leaders in the city such that her son was allowed to spend a year living in the home of a Vietnamese family—a politically unheard-of practice at the time. While my mom was the first to walk through the newly opened door policy in Saigon, she would not be the last.

36. Erik Harms, *Saigon's Edge: On the Margins of Ho Chi Minh City* (Minneapolis: University of Minnesota Press, 2011).

37. Kathy Chu, "Vietnam's Economy Lures Some Who Left in the 1970s," *USA Today*, August 18, 2010, accessed December 17, 2012, http://usatoday30.usatoday.com/money/world/2010-08-18-1Avietnam18_CV_N.htm.

38. Kathy Chu, "More Vietnamese Abroad Send Money Back to Their Homeland," *USA Today*, August 17, 2010, accessed December 17, 2012, http://usatoday30.usatoday.com/money/world/2010-08-18-vietnamremittances18_ST_N.htm.

39. Trung Phan, "The Nigerian Union by Trung Phan. From the Word Ho Chi Minh," Nigerian Union of Vietnam, November 26, 2010, accessed December 17, 2012, http://nuvietnam.blogspot.com/2010/04/nigerian-union-by-trung-phan-from-word.html.

40. Solomon Bamidele Jr., "Solomon Bamidele Junior (President NUV) Reply to the Recent Article by *Thanh Nien* Newspaper on Nigerians in Vietnam," Nigerian Union of Vietnam, September 16, 2010, http://nuvietnam.blogspot.com/2010/09/solomon-bamidele-junior-president-nuv.html#comment-form.

41. "Tough Times: Nigerians Flee to Ghana, Vietnam," *Modern Ghana*, February 16, 2009, accessed December 17, 2012, http://www.modernghana.com/news/202691/1/tough-times-nigerians-flee-to-ghana-vietnam.html.

42. Tuoi Tre, "Foreigners in HCMC Settle into Fashion Business: A Group of Nigerians Have Found a Stylish New Niche in Ho Chi Minh City," *Thanh Nien News*, July 22, 2008, accessed November 18, 2012, http://web.archive.org/web/20080822082845/http://www.thanhniennews.com/features/?catid=10&newsid=40473.

43. Trung Phan, "The Nigerian Union by Trung Phan."

44. Sean Geary, "Vietnamese Economy Showing Signs of Growth," *Emerging Money*, accessed December 17, 2012, http://emergingmoney.com/frontier-markets-2/vietnamese-economy-strength-vnm/; Nguyen Thi Lan Huong and Luu Quang Tuan, "Policy Coherence Initiative on Growth, Investment and Employment—the Case of Viet Nam Investment, Growth and Employment," report prepared for the International Labor Organization Regional Office for Asia and the Pacific, Bangkok, 2009.

45. Le Van Thanh, "Population and Urbanization in Ho Chi Minh City (Vietnam): Towards New Policies on Migration and Urban Development," paper prepared for the IUSSP Regional Population Conference, Siam City Hotel, Bangkok, Thailand, June 10–13, 2002.

46. Numbers calculated based on the Ho Chi Minh City General Statistics Office figures for 2010.

47. Colliers International, *Global Office Real Estate Review: Second Half, 2010*, last accessed March 4, 2014, http://www.colliers.com/~/media/Files/EMEA/UK/research/industrial/201012-global-office-real-estate-review.pdf.

48. Annette Kim, *Learning to be Capitalists* (Oxford, UK: Oxford University Press, 2008).

49. Translated as "native village," the concept is a strong thread through Vietnamese culture, providing a historical anchor to families and spatially and regionally oriented communities.

50. Erik Harms, *Saigon's Edge.*

4 "DO-YOUR-TIMERS" AFRICAN STYLE: ADDIS ABABA, THE UNLIKELY CAPITAL OF AFRICA

1. Tewodros Tigabu and Girma Semu, "Addis Ababa Urban Profile," UN Habitat Regional and Technical Cooperation Division, 2008.

2. United Nations, Department of Economic and Social Affairs Population Division, *World Population Prospects: The 2005 Revision* (New York: United Nations, 2006), figures calculated on a three-period moving average to smooth out sharp changes.

3. Ethiopia = 10 percent, Uzbekistan = 8.5 percent, China = 8.4 percent, India = 8.2 percent, Tanzania = 7.1 percent, Vietnam = 7.0 percent, Angola = 7.0 percent ("A More Hopeful Continent: The Lion Kings?" *The Economist*, January 6, 2011).

4. It is also important to note here that GDP growth measures only the growth of the economy, not its distribution.

5. Deborah Brautigam, *The Dragon's Gift: The Real Story of China in Africa* (Oxford, UK: Oxford University Press, 2009); Li Anshan, "China's New Policy toward Africa," in *China into Africa: Trade, Aid, and Influence*, edited by Robert I. Rotberg (Washington, DC: Brookings Institution Press, 2008), 29–30; Zhou Jianqing, "Sino-African Economic and Trade Cooperation Develops Steadily—Survey of 2005 and Prospects for 2006," *West Asia and Africa* 1 (2006), 15–18 (as cited in Li Anshan, "China's New Policy toward Africa").

6. Wenran Jiang, "China's Emerging Partnerships in Africa," in *China into Africa: Trade, Aid, and Influence*, edited by Robert I. Rotberg (Washington, DC: Brookings Institution Press, 2008).

7. Division of Coordination, Department of West Asia and Africa, Ministry of Commerce, "The Economic and Trade Relations between China and African Countries in 2004," in *China Commerce Yearbook, 2005* (Beijing, 2005), 182–83 (as cited in Li Anshan, 2008).

8. See Princeton Lyman, "China's Rising Role in Africa," accessed November 26, 2012, www.cfr.org/publication/8436; Lindsey Hilsum, "China's Offer to Africa: Pure Capitalism," *New Statesman*, July 3, 2006, 23–24.

9. Robert I. Rotberg, ed., *China into Africa: Trade, Aid, and Influence* (Washington, DC, and Cambridge, MA: Brookings Institution Press and World Peace Foundation, 2008), 3.

10. Ministry of Foreign Trade and Economic Cooperation, *Almanac of China's Foreign Economic Relations and Trade: 2001* (Beijing, 2001), 503 (as cited in Anshan, 2008).

11. Peng Mo, Ryan J. Orr, and Jianzhong Lu, "Addis Ababa Ring Road Project: A Case Study of a Chinese Construction Project in Ethiopia," paper prepared for the International Conference on Multi-national Construction Projects, "Securing High Performance through Cultural Awareness and Dispute Avoidance," Shanghai, China, November 21–23, 2008.

12. Terence McNamee, "Africa in Their Words: A Study of Chinese Traders in South Africa, Lesotho, Botswana, Zambia and Angola," discussion paper of the Brenthurst Foundation (2012).

13. Ndubisi Obiorah, Darren Kew, and Yusuf Tanko, "Peaceful Rise and Human Rights: China's Expanding Relations with Nigeria," in *China into Africa: Trade, Aid, and Influence*, edited by Robert I. Rotberg (Washington, DC: Brookings Institution Press, 2008).

14. Obiorah, Kew, and Tanko, "Peaceful Rise and Human Rights."

15. Li Anshan, "China's New Policy toward Africa," 29–30.

16. See Deborah Brautigam, *The Dragon's Gift*, 314.

17. Li Anshan, "China's New Policy toward Africa," 35–36.

18. Zhou Jianqing, "Sino-African Economic and Trade Cooperation Develops Steadily—Survey of 2005 and Prospects for 2006," *West Asia and Africa* 1 (2006), 15–18 (as cited in Li Anshan, "China's New Policy toward Africa").

19. Niall Ferguson, *Civilization: The West and the Rest* (New York: Penguin Books, 2012).

20. Obiorah, Kew, and Tanko, "Peaceful Rise and Human Rights," 287–89.

21. In particular, see George Friedman's chapter on "Africa: A Place to Leave Alone" to see the current arguments on the continent's supposed global irrelevance in *The Next Decade: Where We've Been . . . and Where We're Going* (New York: Doubleday, 2011).

22. Obiorah, Kew, and Tanko, "Peaceful Rise and Human Rights."

23. Yang Yang, "African Traders in Guangzhou: Routes, Reasons, Profits, Dreams," in *Globalization from Below: The World's Other Economy*, edited by Gordon Matthews, Gustavo Lins Ribeiro, and Carlos Alba Vega (New York: Routledge, 2012).

24. Nita Bhalla, "The Town That Rastafarians Built," BBC, November 5, 2001, accessed December 17, 2012, http://news.bbc.co.uk/2/hi/africa/1639646.stm.

25. For a comprehensive review of this period, see Edmond J. Keller's excellent book, *Revolutionary Ethiopia: From Empire to People's Republic* (Bloomington, IN: Indiana University Press, 1989).

26. Prime Minister Meles Zenawi died on August 20, 2012, as this book was in its final stages, and his passing will surely mark many changes in the political and economic future of Ethiopia. However, there remains no question as to the future of Addis Ababa as the centerpiece of the country's bright long-term future.

27. Central Intelligence Agency, *CIA World Factbook, 2012*; "Addis Ababa City Council," (London, UK: Ethiopia Embassy 2012), accessed November 17, 2012, http://www.ethioembassy.org.uk/about_us/regional_states/addis_ababa_city_council.htm.

28. The modern country's founding ruler, Menelik I (905 BCE), is said to be the son of King Solomon of Israel and Queen Sabah—often known as the "Queen of Sheba" in English—who ruled over an area ranging from Yemen to modern-day Eritrea, but the cultural connections to the ancient Middle East predate that. Most Ethiopians believe, for example, that the ancient Judaic Ark of the Covenant was transported to and laid to rest in a church in Axum, the ancient capital of Ethiopia, about one thousand kilometers north of Addis.

29. Krista Larson and Martin Vogl, "Africans Remember Gadhafi as Martyr, Benefactor," Associated Press, October 24, 2011.

30. "Bole International Airport (ADD/HAAB), Ethiopia," Airport-Technology.com, accessed December 17, 2012, www.airport-technology.com/projects/bole/.

31. John D. Kasarda and Greg Lindsay, *Aerotropolis: The Way We'll Live Next* (New York: Farrar, Straus and Giroux, 2011).

32. Kasarda and Lindsay, *Aerotropolis*.

33. Feyera Abdissa and Terefe Degefa, "Urbanization and Changing Livelihoods: The Case of Farmers' Displacement in the Expansion of Addis Ababa," in *The Demographic Transition and Development in Africa: The Unique Case of Ethiopia*, by Charles Teller and Assefa Hailemariam (London and New York: Springer, 2011), 215–35.

34. UN Habitat, "Urban Inequities Report: Addis Ababa," 2003.

35. UN Habitat, "Urban Inequities Report: Addis Ababa," 2003.

36. Sonja Fransen and Katie Kuschminder, "Migration in Ethiopia: History, Current Trends and Future Prospects," Migration and Development Country Profiles Paper Series, Maastricht Graduate School of Governance, 2009.

37. Marc Angelil and Dirk Hebel, eds., *Cities of Change: Addis Ababa: Transformation Strategies for Urban Territories in the 21st Century* (New York: Birkhauser Architecture, 2009).

38. Peng Mo, Ryan J. Orr, and Jianzhong Lu, "Addis Ababa Ring Road Project."

39. Mary Harper's "Ethiopia's 'Cupcake Divide' in Addis Ababa," November 10, 2012, condenses these contradictions of a fast-globalizing society in Addis into a brief popular piece on the unlikely cutting edge of Africa's recent development.

40. "Ethiopia—Addis Ababa Ranks as One of the Cheapest Cities for Expats to Live in the World," nazret.com, accessed December 18, 2012, http://nazret.com/blog/index.php/2010/06/29/ethiopia_addis_ababa_ranks_as_one_of_the.

41. Central Intelligence Agency, *CIA World Factbook, 2012*.

42. "Real Estate as an Investment," Access Capital's Real Estate Sector Report, May 2010, accessed December 18, 2012, http://www.accessrealestatesc.com/index.php?option=com_content&view=article&id=79:real-estate-as-an-investment&catid=36:general-&Itemid=55.

5 THE INDIGENOUS CITY? RECONCILING AN OLD-TIMERS' HONOLULU WITH A GLOBAL SOCIETY

1. The tenures of senatorial duo of Daniel Inouye and Daniel Akaka have come to a remarkable close. On December 12, 2012, Senator Akaka attended his final session in the U.S. Senate, having announced his retirement well over a year beforehand. Within one week, Senator Daniel Inouye passed away unexpectedly while in office and intending to run for his ninth term in office again in 2016. With his passing, the U.S. Senate lost its second-longest-serving representative. These two events threw the state of Hawai'i, and its population center, Honolulu, into a period of deep reflection on the future. The combined seniority of the senatorial delegation, especially that of Senator Inouye, has long been a lifeblood of the state's aspirations and development. With the loss of these deep ties to Washington, D.C., the role of the city and county of Honolulu in a global economy has become even more important in determining the lives of its residents. Until these deep relationships and seniority in the state's congressional delegation can be rebuilt, Honolulu will need to be creative in its efforts to find support for the essential major investments in its future that are described in this chapter.

2. United States Census Bureau, *2010 Census*, (U.S. Census Bureau, 2010), accessed March 4, 2014, http://www.census.gov/2010census/data/.

3. Frank Hirtz, "It Takes Modern Means to be Traditional: On Recognizing Indigenous Cultural Communities in the Philippines," *Development and Change* 34, no. 5 (2003).

4. Dennis Lim, "Displaced and Adrift in Los Angeles," *New York Times*, July 6, 2008, accessed December 18, 2012, http://www.nytimes.com/2008/07/06/movies/06lim.html?_r=0.

5. Sumner La Croix, "Economic History of Hawai'i," *EH.Net Encyclopedia*, edited by Robert Whaples, September 27, 2001, accessed November 26, 2012, http://eh.net/encyclopedia/article/lacroix.hawaii.history.

6. Lewis Mumford, *Whither Honolulu: A Memorandum on Park and City Planning*, prepared for the Honolulu City and County of Honolulu Park Board (Honolulu: Honolulu City and County Park Board, 1938).

7. P. Teo, T. C Chang, and K. C. Ho, eds., *Interconnected Worlds: Tourism in Southeast Asia* (Oxford: Pergamon, 2001).

8. C. Ryan and C. M. Hall, *Sex Tourism: Marginal People and Liminalities* (London: Routledge, 2001).

9. Adrienne Sevilla, "Medical Tourism: An Informed Choice May Present a Safe and Realistic Alternative to Expensive Treatment at Home," *Annals of Health Law: Advance Directive* 18 (2009).

10. Plunkett Research Ltd., "Introduction to the Health Care Industry," accessed November 20, 2012, http://www.plunkettresearch.com/health-care-medical-market-research/industry-trends.

11. Devon M. Herrick, *Medical Tourism: Global Competition in Health Care*, National Center for Policy Analysis Report No. 304 (Dallas, TX: National Center for Policy Analysis, 2007).

12. Ian Youngman, "Will the Boss Pick Up the Bill for Medical Travel?," *International Medical Travel Journal*, 2009, accessed December 18, 2012, http://www.imtj.com/articles/2009/company-funded-medical-travel/.

13. "Retirement Homes in SE Asia," *Deccan Herald*, accessed November 9, 2011, http://www.deccanherald.com/content/52065/retirement-homes-se-asia.html.

14. "Retirement Homes in SE Asia"; Mayumi Ono, "Long-Stay Tourism and International Migration: Japanese Retirees in Malaysia," edited by Yamashita et al., in "Transnational Migration in East Asia," *Senri Ethnological Reports* 77 (2008).

15. Will Irvin, "Retirement Villages," weblog, accessed November 9, 2011, http://retirementvillages.blog.com/2010/02/17/retirement-villages/.

16. "2012 Global Diaspora Forum: Moving Forward by Giving Back," accessed November 17, 2012, http://diasporaalliance.org/featured/global-diaspora-forum/.

17. Ian L. Gardner, Colette Browning, and Hal Kendig, "Accommodation Options in Later Life: Retirement Village or Community Living?," *The Australasian Journal on Ageing* 24, no.4 (2005): 188–95.

18. Estimates calculated based on data available from United Nations, Department of Economic and Social Affairs: Population Division, Population Estimates and Projections Section, http://esa.un.org/unpd/wpp/unpp/Panel_profiles.htm.

19. Thomas L. Friedman, *The World Is Flat: A Brief History of the Twenty-First Century* (New York: Farrar, Straus and Giroux, 2005).

20. Suzanne Kane, "The Worst Traffic in America? It's Not Los Angeles," *The Traffic Connection*, May 24, 2012, accessed November 17, 2012, http://autos.yahoo.com/news/the-worst-traffic-in-america--it-s-not-los-angeles.html.

21. State of Hawai'i Office of Planning, Department of Business, Economic Development and Planning, *Hawai'i Comprehensive Economic Development Strategy*, 2010, 9.

22. Richard Barrington, "10 Best States to Retire 2012," MoneyRates.com, October 22, 2012, accessed December 19, 2012, http://www.money-rates.com/research-center/best-states-for-retirement/2012.htm.

23. Richard Florida, *Who's Your City: How the Creative Economy Is Making Where to Live the Most Important Decision of Your Life* (New York: Basic Books, 2008).

24. Richard Florida, *Who's Your City*.

25. Vanessa Wong, "Which Is America's Best City?," *Bloomberg Businessweek: Lifestyle*, September 20, 2011.

26. Mercer Survey, "2011 Quality of Living Worldwide City Rankings," November 29, 2011, last accessed March 2, 2014, http://www.mercer.com/press-releases/1436950.

27. United States Census Bureau, *2010 Census*, (U.S. Census Bureau, 2010), accessed March 4, 2014, http://www.census.gov/2010census/data/.

28. Richard Florida, "America's Brainiest Cities," *The Atlantic Cities*, June 6, 2012, http://www.theatlanticcities.com/neighborhoods/2012/06/americas-brainiest-cities/2132/.

29. The next most populous group of arrestees was Filipinos at sixty thousand. All statistical data on Native Hawai'ians in the criminal justice system were generated through a research project I conducted on behalf of the Office of Hawai'ian Affairs of the Hawai'i Criminal Justice Data Center, summarized in the report titled "The Disparate Treatment of Native Hawaiians in the Criminal Justice System 2010," accessed November 26, 2012, http://www.oha.org/sites/default/files/ir_final_web_rev.pdf.

30. Hawai'i Criminal Justice Data Center, Office of Hawaiian Affairs, "The Disparate Treatment of Native Hawaiians in the Criminal Justice System 2010."

31. Alex Dodds, "NPR: Study Says Americans Prefer Walkable Neighborhoods," Smart Growth America website, May 29, 2012, accessed December 19, 2012, http://www.smartgrowthamerica.org/2012/05/29/npr-study-says-americans-prefer-walkable-neighborhoods/.

32. The state of Hawai'i never experienced the 1990s economic boom.

33. "Capitol Watch: Opala (Waste)," Sierra Club of Hawaii website, accessed December 19, 2012, http://www.sierraclubhawaii.com/opalacw.php.

34. The debate on how long plastic bags actually take to biodegrade is interesting because they have only been in existence for fifty years. See Juliet Lapidos, "Will My Plastic Bag Still Be Here in 2057?" *Slate*, June 27, 2007.

35. Sophie Cocke, "Single-Use Bag Bill in Political Death Throes," *Civil Beat*, April 18, 2012, accessed December 19, 2012, http://www.civilbeat.com/articles/2012/04/18/15608-single-use-bag-bill-in-political-death-throes/.

36. Dawn Southard, "Shifting Sands," *Hana Hou, the Magazine of Hawaiian Airlines*, June/July 2012, 98.

6 "FOR-ALL-TIMERS":
NEW YORK CITY'S *EMPIRE STATE OF MIND*

1. This comment, though not a word-for-word description of what then president Gerald Ford actually told New York City officials, was the federal response to City Hall's request for financial assistance right before the city was about to go bankrupt. While the city never actually did go bankrupt, the fiscal situation at the time was dire. The city has never really come close to bankruptcy since.

2. Jon Coaffee, *Terrorism, Risk and the Global City: Towards Urban Resilience* (Burlington, VT: Ashgate Publishers, 2009).

3. Kenneth T. Jackson, *Crabgrass Frontier: The Suburbanization of the United States* (New York: Oxford University Press, 1987).

4. Moses' influence stretched way beyond the boundaries of the city proper, but it is important to note that his public recreation areas were intended to be part of the city's makeup. While controversial in their origins, Jones Beach and Montauk Park, in contrast to their Hamptons counterparts, today are dominated by working-class New Yorkers looking for affordably priced fresh air and respite from the city.

5. "Cross Bronx Expressway: Historical Overview," nycroads.com, accessed December 19, 2012, http://www.nycroads.com/roads/cross-bronx/.

6. For example, William Julius Wilson, *The Truly Disadvantaged: The Inner City, the Underclass, and Public Policy* (Chicago: University of Chicago Press, 1987); Paul Jargowsky, *Poverty and Place: Ghettos, Barrios, and the American City* (New York: Russell Sage Foundation, 1997).

7. "New York Crime Rates, 1960–2010," The Disaster Center, accessed December 19, 2012, http://www.disastercenter.com/crime/nycrime.htm.

8. John J. Donohue and Steven Levitt, "The Impact of Legalized Abortion on Crime," *The Quarterly Journal of Economics* 116, no.2 (2000).

9. "New York Crime Rates, 1960–2010."

10. Matthew C. Hayes, "City's Unemployment Rate Hits an All Time Low," *New York Sun*, January 19, 2007.

11. Calculations based on Neglia Appraisals, Inc. figures and the Bureau of Labor Statistics inflation calculator.

12. I remember as a child, my mom badgering my dad on numerous occasions to purchase one of the abandoned brownstones on Seventieth Street and Third Avenue on Manhattan's Upper East Side at what I recall was about $100,000. Ever the budget-conscious father, my dad successfully parried these suggestions, given the high and unpredictable costs of raising three children in New York City. In retrospect, however, making the purchase would have been one of the best decisions of his life, given that the value of these properties runs in the multiple millions. Not all for-all-timers could translate their feelings into material benefit.

13. For generations, the New York City Police Department has been colloquially referred to as "New York's Finest." After 9/11, this general sentiment could easily be applied to the New York Fire Department and other front-line service agencies.

14. Lisa Chamberlain, "Idling at Zero: Politics and Planning Collide at the World Trade Center Rebuilding Site," *Planning* 72, no. 7 (2006): 12–15.

15. Lisa Chamberlain, "Idling at Zero."

16. Renae Merle, "Wall Street's Final '08 Toll: $6.9 Trillion Wiped Out," *The Washington Post*, January 1, 2009.

17. Scott Reeves, "Quick Hits: Wall Street Job Losses Cause Citywide Panic," *Minyanville Business News*, October 15, 2008, accessed November 6, 2012, http://www.minyanville.com/businessmarkets/articles/GS-lehman-aig-ms-Brothers/10/15/2008/id/19530.

18. "The Global Financial Centres Index 11 (United Nations, 2006)," Long Finance.net, March 2012, accessed November 7, 2012, www.longfinance.net/Publications/GFCI%2011.pdf.

19. Xinhua and Dow Jones, "Xinhua-Dow Jones International Financial Centers Development Index 2012," accessed November 7, 2012. www.djindexes.com/mdsidx/downloads/meth_info/Xinhua_Overview.pdf.

20. Xinhua and Dow Jones, "Xinhua-Dow Jones International Financial Centers Development Index 2012."

21. Xinhua and Dow Jones, "Xinhua-Dow Jones International Financial Centers Development Index 2012."

22. "The Giant Pool of Money," This American Life website, May 8, 2008, accessed December 19, 2012, http://www.thisamericanlife.org/radio-archives/episode/355/the-giant-pool-of-money.

23. Calculations based on data from the New York State Department of Labor (2008–2010).

7 THE GLOBAL URBAN ECOSYSTEM: A GLOBALLY INTEGRATED ECOLOGY OF EVERYDAY LIFE

1. W. W. Rostow, *The Stages of Economic Growth: A Non-Communist Manifesto* (Cambridge: Cambridge University Press, 1960).

2. For example, Rostow, *The Stages of Economic Growth*.

3. For example, Friedmann, "Reflections on Place and Place-Making in the Cities of China," *International Journal of Urban and Regional Research* 31, no. 2 (2007): 257–79.

4. For example, Barry Bluestone and Bennett Harrison, *The Deindustrialization of America* (New York: Basic Books, 1982).

5. Malcolm Gladwell, *The Tipping Point: How Little Things Can Make a Big Difference* (New York: Little, Brown, 2000).

6. Lewis Mumford, *The City in History: Its Origins, Its Transformations, and Its Prospects* (New York: Harcourt, Brace & World, 1961).

7. E. B. White, *Here Is New York* (New York: Little Bookroom, 1999).

8. Mike Davis, *Planet of Slums* (London: Verso, 2006); Robert Neuwirth, *Shadow Cities: A Billion Squatters, a New Urban World* (New York: Routledge, 2005); and Jeb Brugmann, *Welcome to the Urban Revolution: How Cities Are Changing the World* (New York: Bloomsbury Press, 2009).

BIBLIOGRAPHY

Abdissa, Feyera, and Terefe Degefa. "Urbanization and Changing Livelihoods: The Case of Farmers' Displacement in the Expansion of Addis Ababa." In *The Demographic Transition and Development in Africa: The Unique Case of Ethiopia*, by Charles Teller and Assefa Hailemariam. London and New York: Springer, 2011.

Abu-Lughod, Janet. *Before European Hegemony: The World System A.D. 1250–1350.* Oxford, UK: Oxford University Press, 1989.

"Addis Ababa City Council." (London, UK: Ethiopia Embassy 2012). Accessed November 17, 2012. http://www.ethioembassy.org.uk/about_us/regional_states/addis_ababa_city_council.htm.

Angelil, Marc, and Dirk Hebel, eds. *Cities of Change: Addis Ababa: Transformation Strategies for Urban Territories in the 21st Century.* New York: Birkhauser Architecture, 2009.

Arthurs, Clare. "One Million Jobs Created by New Enterprise Law in Viet Nam." United Nations Development Program Newsroom, UNDP. Accessed December 14, 2012. http://content.undp.org/go/newsroom/choices-one-million-jobs-created-by-new-enterprise-law-in-viet-nam2003-06.en.

Ayi Kwei Armah. *The Beautyful Ones Are Not Yet Born.* Boston: Houghton Mifflin, 1968.

Bamidele, Solomon, Jr. "Solomon Bamidele Junior (President NUV) Reply to the Recent Article by Thanh Nien Newspaper on Nigerians in Vietnam." Nigerian Union of Vietnam. September 16, 2010. http://nuvietnam.blogspot.com/2010/09/solomon-bamidele-junior-president-nuv.html#comment-form.

Barrington, Richard. "10 Best States to Retire 2012." MoneyRates.com, October 22, 2012. Accessed December 19, 2012. http://www.money-rates.com/research-center/best-states-for-retirement/2012.htm.

Bhalla, Nita. "The Town That Rastafarians Built." BBC, November 5, 2001. Accessed December 17, 2012. http://news.bbc.co.uk/2/hi/africa/1639646.stm.

Bluestone, Barry, and Bennett Harrison. *The Deindustrialization of America.* New York: Basic Books, 1982.

"Bole International Airport (ADD/HAAB), Ethiopia." Airport-Technology.com. Accessed December 17, 2012. www.airport-technology.com/projects/bole/.

Brautigam, Deborah. *The Dragon's Gift: The Real Story of China in Africa.* Oxford, UK: Oxford University Press, 2009.

Brugmann, Jeb. *Welcome to the Urban Revolution: How Cities Are Changing the World.* New York: Bloomsbury Press, 2009.

Calthorpe, Peter. *The Next American Metropolis: Ecology, Community, and the American Dream.* New York: Princeton Architectural Press, 1993.

Can Tho City Statistical Office. So lieu kinh te xa hoi dong bang song cuu long [Economic and social data of the Mekong Delta]. Can Tho City: Can Tho City Statistical Office, 2005.

"Capitol Watch: Opala (Waste)." Sierra Club of Hawaii website. Accessed December 19, 2012. http://www.sierraclubhawaii.com/opalacw.php.

Central Intelligence Agency. *CIA World Factbook, 2012.*

Chamberlain, Lisa. "Idling at Zero: Politics and Planning Collide at the World Trade Center Rebuilding Site." *Planning* 72, no. 7 (2006): 12–15.

"China Urbanization in Shenzhen." Public Radio International, July 7, 2008.

Christaller, Walter. *Die zentralen Orte in Süddeutschland.* Jena: Gustav Fischer, 1933.

Chu, Kathy. "More Vietnamese Abroad Send Money Back to Their Homeland." *USA Today*, August 17, 2010. Accessed on December 17, 2012. http://usatoday30.usatoday.com/money/world/2010-08-18-vietnamremittances18_ST_N.htm.

———. "Vietnam's Economy Lures Some Who Left in the 1970s." *USA Today*, August 18, 2010. Accessed on December 17, 2012. http://usatoday30.usatoday.com/money/world/2010-08-18-1Avietnam18_CV_N.htm.

Coaffee, Jon. *Terrorism, Risk and the Global City: Towards Urban Resilience.* Burlington, VT: Ashgate Publishers, 2009.

Cocke, Sophie. "Single-Use Bag Bill in Political Death Throes." *Civil Beat*, April 18, 2012. Accessed December 19, 2012. http://www.civilbeat.com/articles/2012/04/18/15608-single-use-bag-bill-in-political-death-throes/.

Colliers International. *Global Office Real Estate Review: Second Half, 2010.* Last accessed March 4, 2014. http://www.colliers.com/~/media/Files/EMEA/UK/research/industrial/201012-global-office-real-estate-review.pdf.

Connell, J. H. "Diversity in Tropical Rain Forests and Coral Reefs." *Science* 199 (1978): 1302–10.

Cronon, William. *Nature's Metropolis: Chicago and the Great West.* New York: W. W. Norton, 1991.

Crosby, Alfred. *Ecological Imperialism: The Biological Expansion of Europe, 900–1900.* Cambridge, UK: Cambridge University Press, 2004.

"Cross Bronx Expressway: Historical Overview." nycroads.com. Accessed December 19, 2012. http://www.nycroads.com/roads/cross-bronx/.

Cudahy, Brian J. *Box Boats: How Container Ships Changed the World.* New York: Fordham University Press, 2006.

Davis, Mike. *Planet of Slums.* London: Verso, 2006.

Department of Planning and Investment, Ho Chi Minh City. Data calculated by author based on original data. Last accessed November 17, 2012. http://www.dpi.hochiminhcity.gov.vn/invest/html/eco1.html.

Division of Coordination. Department of West Asia and Africa, Ministry of Commerce. "The Economic and Trade Relations between China and African Countries in 2004." *China Commerce Yearbook, 2005*. Beijing, 2005. As cited in Li Anshan, "China's New Policy toward Africa."

Dodds, Alex. "NPR: Study Says Americans Prefer Walkable Neighborhoods." Smart Growth America website, May 29, 2012. Accessed December 19, 2012. http://www. smartgrowthamerica.org/2012/05/29/npr-study-says-americans-prefer-walkable-neighborhoods/.

Donohue, John J., and Steven Levitt. "The Impact of Legalized Abortion on Crime." *The Quarterly Journal of Economics* 116, no. 2 (2000).

Duong Nhut Long. Deputy director of Can Tho University Department of Aquaculture. Interview by author (James H. Spencer, Globalization Research Center, University of Hawai'i at Manoa), Can Tho, Vietnam, July 2005.

The Economist, special issue. *The Anthropocene: A Man-Made World*, May 26, 2011.

"Ethiopia—Addis Ababa Ranks as One of the Cheapest Cities for Expats to Live in the World." nazret.com. Accessed December 18, 2012. http://nazret.com/blog/index. php/2010/06/29/ethiopia_addis_ababa_ranks_as_one_of_the.

Falola, Toyin. "An Overview." In *Globalization and Urbanization in Africa*, edited by Toyin Falola and Steven J. Salm. Trenton, NJ: Africa World Press, 2004.

Ferguson, Niall. *Civilization: The West and the Rest*. New York: Penguin Books, 2012.

Fforde, Adam, and Stefan de Vylder. *From Plan to Market—The Economic Transition in Vietnam*. Boulder, CO: Westview Press, 1996.

Florida, Richard. *Who's Your City: How the Creative Economy Is Making Where to Live the Most Important Decision of Your Life*. New York: Basic Books, 2008.

———. "The World Is Spiky: Globalization Has Changed the Economic Playing Field, but Hasn't Leveled It." *The Atlantic Monthly*, October 2005.

Forman, R. T. T., and M. Gordon. "Landscape Ecology Principles and Landscape Function." In *Methodology in Landscape Ecological Research and Planning*, vol. 5, edited by J. Brandt and P. Agger. Proceedings of the First International Seminar of the International Association of Landscape Ecology, 1984.

Fransen, Sonja, and Katie Kuschminder. "Migration in Ethiopia: History, Current Trends and Future Prospects." Migration and Development Country Profiles Paper Series. Maastricht Graduate School of Governance, 2009.

Freeman, James. *Hearts of Sorrow: Vietnamese-American Lives*. Palo Alto: Stanford University Press, 1991.

Friedman, George. *The Next Decade: Where We've Been . . . and Where We're Going*. New York: Doubleday, 2011.

Friedmann, John. "Becoming Urban: Periurban Dynamics in Vietnam and China—Introduction." *Pacific Affairs* 84 (2011).

———. *China's Urban Transition*. Minneapolis: University of Minnesota Press, 2005.

———. "Reflections on Place and Place-Making in the Cities of China." *International Journal of Urban and Regional Research* 31, no. 2 (2007): 257–79.

———. "The World City Hypothesis." *Development and Change* 17 (1986): 69–83.

Friedmann, John, and Goetz Wolff. "World City Formation: An Agenda for Research and Action." *International Journal of Urban and Regional Research* 6 (1982): 309–44.

Friedman, Thomas L. *The World Is Flat: A Brief History of the Twenty-First Century.* New York: Farrar, Straus and Giroux, 2005.

García Márquez, Gabriel. *Love in the Time of Cholera.* New York: Vintage Books, 1988.

Gardner, Ian L., Colette Browning, and Hal Kendig. "Accommodation Options in Later Life: Retirement Village or Community Living?" *The Australasian Journal on Ageing* 24, no.4 (2005): 188–95.

Geary, Sean. "Vietnamese Economy Showing Signs of Growth." *Emerging Money.* Accessed December 17, 2012. http://emergingmoney.com/frontier-markets-2/vietnamese-economy-strength-vnm/.

General Statistics Office of Vietnam. "Area, Population, and Population Density in 2011 by Province." Accessed December 19, 2012. http://www.gso.gov.vn/default_en.aspx?tabid=467&idmid=3&ItemID=12941.

"The Giant Pool of Money." This American Life website, May 8, 2008. Accessed December 19, 2012. http://www.thisamericanlife.org/radio-archives/episode/355/the-giant-pool-of-money.

Gladwell, Malcolm. *The Tipping Point: How Little Things Can Make a Big Difference.* New York: Little, Brown, 2000.

Glaeser, Edward. *Triumph of the City: How Our Greatest Invention Makes Us Richer, Smarter, Greener, Healthier, and Happier.* New York: The Penguin Press, 2011.

Glaeser, Edward L. "A Tale of Many Cities." In *Economix: Explaining the Science of Everyday Life* (blog). *New York Times*, April 20, 2010.

"The Global Financial Centres Index 11 (United Nations, 2006)." Long Finance. net, March 2012. Accessed November 7, 2012. www.longfinance.net/Publications/GFCI%2011.pdf.

Grant, Richard. *Globalizing City: The Urban and Economic Transformation of Accra, Ghana.* Syracuse: Syracuse University Press, 2008.

Grime, J. P. "Competitive Exclusion in Herbaceous Vegetation." *Nature* 242 (1973): 344–47.

Gubry, Patrick, Vu Thi Hong, and Le Van Thanh, eds. *Les Chemins Vers la Ville: La Migration Vers Ho Chi Minh Ville a Partir d'une Zone du Delta du Mekong* (Paris: CEPED).

Hare, Denise. "The Origins and Influence of Land Property Rights in Vietnam." *Development Policy Review* 26 (2008).

Harms, Erik. *Saigon's Edge: On the Margins of Ho Chi Minh City.* Minneapolis: University of Minnesota Press, 2011.

Harper, Mary. "Ethiopia's 'Cupcake Divide.'" *Addis Ababa'*, November 10, 2012.

Harvey, David. *Justice, Nature and the Geography of Difference.* Oxford, UK: Blackwell, 1996.

———. *Spaces of Global Capitalism: Towards a Theory of Uneven Geographical Development.* London and New York: Verso, 2006.

Hawai'i Criminal Justice Data Center. Office of Hawaiian Affairs. "The Disparate Treatment of Native Hawaiians in the Criminal Justice System 2010." Accessed November 26, 2012. http://www.oha.org/sites/default/files/ir_final_web_rev.pdf.

Hayes, Matthew C. "City's Unemployment Rate Hits an All Time Low." *New York Sun*, January 19, 2007.

Hayslip, Le Ly. *When Heaven and Earth Changed Places: A Vietnamese Woman's Journey from War to Peace.* New York: Doubleday, 1989.

Herrick, Devon M. *Medical Tourism: Global Competition in Health Care.* National Center for Policy Analysis Report No. 304, Dallas, TX: National Center for Policy Analysis, 2007.

Hilsum, Lindsey. "China's Offer to Africa: Pure Capitalism." *New Statesman,* July 3, 2006, 23–24.

Hirschman, Albert O. *The Passions and the Interests: Political Arguments for Capitalism before Its Triumph.* 20th anniversary ed. Princeton: Princeton University Press, 1997.

Hirtz, Frank. "It Takes Modern Means to be Traditional: On Recognizing Indigenous Cultural Communities in the Philippines." *Development and Change* 34, no. 5 (2003).

Ho Chi Minh City Department of Planning and Investment. "Foreign Direct Investment in HCMC." Accessed December 15, 2012. http://www.dpi.hochiminhcity.gov.vn/invest/html/eco3.html.

Hong Van. "Leather Shoe Exporters Grapple with Anti-dumping Lawsuit." *Sai Gon Times Daily,* July 15, 2005.

Howard, Ebenezer. *Garden Cities of Tomorrow.* London: Swan Sonnenschein & Co., 1902.

Hy Van Luong. "The Marxist State and Dialogic Re-structuration of Culture in Rural Vietnam." In *Indochina: Social and Cultural Change,* edited by David W. P. Elliott et al. Claremont, CA: Keck Center for International and Strategic Studies, Claremont McKenna College, 2005.

———. "Wealth, Power and Inequality: Global Market, the State, and Local Sociocultural Dynamics." In *Postwar Vietnam: Dynamics of a Transforming Society,* edited by Hy Van Luong. Oxford: Rowman and Littlefield, 2003.

Irvin, Will. "Retirement Villages." Weblog. Accessed November 9, 2011. http://retirementvillages.blog.com/2010/02/17/retirement-villages/.

Jackson, Kenneth T. *Crabgrass Frontier: The Suburbanization of the United States.* New York: Oxford University Press, 1987.

Jacobs, Jane. *Cities and the Wealth of Nations.* New York: Random House, 1984.

———. *The Death and Life of Great American Cities.* New York: Random House, 1961.

———. *The Economy of Cities.* New York: Random House, 1969.

———. *The Nature of Economies.* New York: Vintage Books, 2001.

Jargowsky, Paul. *Poverty and Place: Ghettos, Barrios, and the American City.* New York: Russell Sage Foundation, 1997.

Jiang, Wenran. "China's Emerging Partnerships in Africa." In *China into Africa: Trade, Aid, and Influence,* edited by Robert I. Rotberg. Washington, DC: Brookings Institution Press, 2008.

Johnson, Steven. *Emergence: The Connected Lives of Ants, Brains, Cities, and Software.* New York: Scribner, 2001.

———. *The Ghost Map: The Story of London's Most Terrifying Epidemic—and How It Changed Science, Cities, and the Modern World.* New York: Riverhead Books, 2006.

Kane, Suzanne. "The Worst Traffic in America? It's Not Los Angeles." *The Traffic Connection,* May 24, 2012. Accessed November 17, 2012. http://autos.yahoo.com/news/the-worst-traffic-in-america--it-s-not-los-angeles.html.

Kapan, Durrell D., Shannon N. Bennett, Brett Ellis, Jefferson Fox, Nancy D. Lewis, James H. Spencer, Sumeet Saksena, and Bruce A. Wilcox. "Avian Influenza (H5N1) and the Evolutionary and Social Ecology of Infectious Disease Emergence." *Eco-Health* 3, no. 3 (2006): 187–94.

Kasarda, John D., and Greg Lindsay. *Aerotropolis: The Way We'll Live Next*. New York: Farrar, Straus and Giroux, 2011.

Keller, Edmond J. *Revolutionary Ethiopia: From Empire to People's Republic*. Bloomington, IN: Indiana University Press, 1989.

Kerkvliet, Benedict J. *The Power of Everyday Politics: How Vietnamese Peasants Transformed National Policy*. Ithaca: Cornell University Press, 2005.

Kim, Annette. *Learning to be Capitalists*. Oxford, UK: Oxford University Press, 2008.

La Croix, Sumner. "Economic History of Hawai'i." *EH.Net Encyclopedia*, edited by Robert Whaples, September 27, 2001. Accessed November 26, 2012. http://eh.net/encyclopedia/article/lacroix.hawaii.history.

Lapidos, Juliet. "Will My Plastic Bag Still Be Here in 2057?" *Slate*, June 27, 2007.

Laquian, Aprodicio. *Beyond Metropolis: The Planning and Governance of Asia's Mega-Urban Regions*. Washington, DC: Woodrow Wilson Press, 2005.

Larson, Krista, and Martin Vogl. "Africans Remember Gadhafi as Martyr, Benefactor." Associated Press, October 24, 2011.

Le Cong Dinh. Partner, YKVN Law Firm and White & Case LLP affiliate. Interview by James H. Spencer. Ho Chi Minh City, Vietnam, 2005.

Le Van Thanh. "Population and Urbanization in Ho Chi Minh City (Vietnam): Towards New Policies on Migration and Urban Development." Paper prepared for the IUSSP Regional Population Conference. Siam City Hotel, Bangkok, Thailand, June 10–13, 2002.

LeGrain, Philippe. *Open World: The Truth about Globalization*. London: Abacus, 2002.

Li Anshan. "China's New Policy toward Africa." In *China into Africa: Trade, Aid, and Influence*, edited by Robert I. Rotberg. Washington, DC: Brookings Institution Press, 2008, 29–30.

Lim, Dennis. "Displaced and Adrift in Los Angeles." *New York Times*, July 6, 2008. Accessed December 18, 2012. http://www.nytimes.com/2008/07/06/movies/06lim.html?_r=0.

Lindblom, Charles. *The Market System: What It Is, How It Works, and What to Make of It*. New Haven: Yale University Press 2001.

Lyman, Princeton. "China's Rising Role in Africa." Accessed November 26, 2012. http://www.cfr.org/publication/8436.

Malkin, Elisabeth. "Plan for Charter City to Fight Honduras Poverty Loses Its Initiator," *New York Times*, September 30, 2012.

Mallaby, Sebastian."The Politically Incorrect Guide to Ending Poverty." *The Atlantic*, July/August 2010.

Mann, Charles C. *1493: Uncovering the New World Columbus Created*. New York: Alfred A. Knopf, 2011.

Mbiba, B., and M. Huchzermeyer. "Contentious Development: Peri-Urban Studies in Sub-Saharan Africa." *Progress in Development Studies* 2 (2002).

McCann, Philip. "Globalization and Economic Geography: The World Is Curved, Not Flat." *The Cambridge Journal of Regions, Economy and Society* 1 (2008).

McNamee, Terence. "Africa in Their Words: A Study of Chinese Traders in South Africa, Lesotho, Botswana, Zambia and Angola." Discussion paper of the Brenthurst Foundation, 2012.

Mercer Survey. "2011 Quality of Living Worldwide City Rankings." November 29, 2011. Last accessed March 2, 2014. http://www.mercer.com/press-releases/1436950.

Merle, Renae. "Wall Street's Final '08 Toll: $6.9 Trillion Wiped Out." *The Washington Post*, January 1, 2009.

Min Zhou and Carl L. Bankston. *Growing Up American: How Vietnamese Children Adapt to Life in the United States*. New York: Russell Sage Foundation, 1998.

Ministry of Foreign Trade and Economic Cooperation. Almanac of China's Foreign Economic Relations and Trade: 2001 (Beijing. 2001). As cited in Li Anshan, "China's New Policy toward Africa."

"A More Hopeful Continent: The Lion Kings?" *The Economist*, January 6, 2011.

Mukhija, Vinit. *Squatters as Developers?: Slum Demolition and Redevelopment in Mumbai, India*. Aldershot: Ashgate Publishing Limited, 2003.

Mumford, Lewis. *The City in History: Its Origins, Its Transformations, and Its Prospects*. New York: Harcourt, Brace & World, 1961.

———. "What Is a City?" *Architectural Record* 82 (November 1937).

———. *Whither Honolulu: A Memorandum on Park and City Planning*. Prepared for the Honolulu City and County of Honolulu Park Board (Honolulu: Honolulu City and County Park Board, 1938).

Nederveen Pieterse, Jan. *Globalization and Culture: Global Mélange*. Lanham, MD: Rowman and Littlefield, 2003.

Neuwirth, Robert. *Shadow Cities: A Billion Squatters, a New Urban World*. New York: Routledge, 2005.

"New York Crime Rates, 1960–2010." The Disaster Center. Accessed December 19, 2012. http://www.disastercenter.com/crime/nycrime.htm.

Nguyen Thi Lan Huong and Luu Quang Tuan. "Policy Coherence Initiative on Growth, Investment and Employment—the Case of Viet Nam Investment, Growth and Employment." Report prepared for the International Labor Organization Regional Office for Asia and the Pacific, Bangkok, 2009.

Nguyen Xuan Thanh. "Catfish Fight: Vietnam's Tra and Basa Fish Exports to the U.S." Paper prepared for the Vietnam Program of the John F. Kennedy School of Government, Harvard University. http://www.fetp.edu.vn/Research_casestudy/CaselistE.htm, 2003.

Nielsen, Chantal Pohl. "Vietnam's Rice Policy: Recent Reforms and Future Opportunities." *Asian Economic Journal* 17 (2003).

North, Douglass. "Location Theory and Regional Economic Growth." In *Regional Development and Planning*, edited by John Friedmann and William Alonso. Cambridge, MA: The MIT Press, 1964.

Obiorah, Ndubisi, Darren Kew, and Yusuf Tanko. "'Peaceful Rise and Human Rights: China's Expanding Relations with Nigeria." In *China into Africa: Trade, Aid, and*

Influence, edited by Robert I. Rotberg. Washington, DC: Brookings Institution Press, 2008.

O'Brien, Fergal. "European Unemployment Rate Rises to Highest in Almost 15 Years." *Bloomberg News*, May 1, 2012.

Ono, Mayumi. "Long-Stay Tourism and International Migration: Japanese Retirees in Malaysia." In "Transnational Migration in East Asia," edited by Yamashita et al. *Senri Ethnological Reports* 77 (2008).

Peng Mo, Ryan J. Orr, and Jianzhong Lu. "Addis Ababa Ring Road Project: A Case Study of a Chinese Construction Project in Ethiopia." Paper prepared for the International Conference on Multi-national Construction Projects, "Securing High Performance through Cultural Awareness and Dispute Avoidance." Shanghai, China, November 21–23, 2008.

Pingali, P. L., and V.-T. Xuan. "Vietnam: Decollectivization and Rice Productivity Growth." *Economic Development and Cultural Change* 40 (1992): 697–718.

Plunkett Research Ltd. "Introduction to the Health Care Industry." Accessed November 20, 2012. http://www.plunkettresearch.com/health-care-medical-market-research/industry-trends.

"Real Estate as an Investment." Access Capital's Real Estate Sector Report, May 2010. Accessed December 18, 2012. http://www.accessrealestatesc.com/index.php?option=com_content&view=article&id=79:real-estate-as-an-investment&catid=36:general-&Itemid=55.

Reeves, Scott. "Quick Hits: Wall Street Job Losses Cause Citywide Panic." *Minyanville Business News*, October 15, 2008. Accessed November 6, 2012. http://www.minyanville.com/businessmarkets/articles/GS-lehman-aig-ms-Brothers/10/15/2008/id/19530.

"Retirement Homes in SE Asia." *Deccan Herald*. Accessed November 9, 2011. http://www.deccanherald.com/content/52065/retirement-homes-se-asia.html.

Robbins, Jim. Excellent article in the *New York Times*, July 14, 2012.

Robinson, Jennifer. *Ordinary Cities: Between Modernity and Development*. London, UK: Routledge, 2006.

Rose, Carol. *Property and Persuasion: New Perspectives on Law, Culture, and Society*. Boulder, CO: Westview Press, 1994.

Rostow, W. W. *The Stages of Economic Growth: A Non-Communist Manifesto*. Cambridge: Cambridge University Press, 1960.

Rotberg, Robert I., ed. *China into Africa: Trade, Aid, and Influence*. Washington, DC, and Cambridge, MA: Brookings Institution Press and World Peace Foundation, 2008.

Ryan, C., and C. M. Hall. *Sex Tourism: Marginal People and Liminalities*. London: Routledge, 2001.

Sachs, Jeffrey. *The End of Poverty: How Can We Make It Happen in Our Lifetime*. London: Penguin Books, 2005.

Sassen, Saskia. *The Global City: New York, London, Tokyo*. Princeton: Princeton University Press, 1991.

———. Global Networks. *Linked Cities*. New York: Routledge, 2002.

Saxenian, AnnaLee. *Regional Advantage: Culture and Competition in Silicon Valley and Route 128*. Cambridge, MA: Harvard University Press, 1996.

Scott, Allen J. *Metropolis: From the Division of Labor to Urban Form*. Berkeley and Los Angeles: University of California Press, 1988.

Sevilla, Adrienne. "Medical Tourism: An Informed Choice May Present a Safe and Realistic Alternative to Expensive Treatment at Home." *Annals of Health Law: Advance Directive* 18 (2009).

Short, John Rennie. *Global Metropolitan: Globalizing Cities in a Capitalist World*. London and New York: Routledge, 2004.

Simone, Maliqalim. *City Life from Jakarta to Dakar: Movements at the Crossroads*. New York: Routledge, 2010.

Soja, Edward. *Postmetropolis—Critical Studies of Cities and Regions*. Oxford: Wiley-Blackwell, 2000.

Soja, Edward W. *Thirdspace*. Malden, MA: Blackwell, 1996.

Southard, Dawn. "Shifting Sands." *Hana Hou, the Magazine of Hawaiian Airlines*, June/July 2012.

Spencer, James H. "An Emergent Landscape of Inequality in Vietnamese Cities." *Globalizations* 7, no. 3 (2010): 431–43.

———. "The Urban Health Transition Hypothesis: Empirical Evidence of an Avian Influenza Kuznets Curve in Viet Nam?" *Journal of Urban Health* 90, no. 2 (2013): 343–57.

———. "Water and Environmental Security in Globalizing Viet Nam: Emerging Risks in the Mekong Delta." Issue brief for the Foundation for Environmental Security and Sustainability, 2007. www.fess-global.org/.

State of Hawai'i Office of Planning, Department of Business, Economic Development and Planning. *Hawai'i Comprehensive Economic Development Strategy*. 2010.

State Planning Committee (SPC). Socialist Republic of Vietnam, UNDP, FAO, and the World Bank. *Vietnam: Agricultural and Food Production Sector Review*. Hanoi, Vietnam, 1989.

Steger, Manfred. *Globalization: A Very Short Introduction*, 2nd ed. Oxford, UK: Oxford University Press, 2009.

Storper, Michael. *The Regional World: Territorial Development in a Global Economy*. London and New York: Guilford Press, 1997.

Storper, Michael, Lena Lavinas, Alejandro Mercado-Célis. "Society, Community, and Development: A Tale of Two Regions." In *The Economic Geography of Innovation*, edited by Karen R. Polenske. Cambridge, UK: Cambridge University Press, 2007.

Teo, P., T. C Chang, and K. C. Ho, eds. *Interconnected Worlds: Tourism in Southeast Asia*. Oxford: Pergamon, 2001.

Thi Cam Van Cao and Takahiro Akita. "Urban and Rural Dimensions of Income Inequality in Vietnam." 2008. GSIR Working Papers. Economic Development and Policy Series (EDP08-2). Graduate School of International Relations, International University of Japan.

Tigabu, Tewodros and Girma Semu. "Addis Ababa Urban Profile." UN Habitat Regional and Technical Cooperation Division, 2008.

"Tough Times: Nigerians Flee to Ghana, Vietnam." *Modern Ghana*, February 16, 2009. Accessed December 17, 2012. http://www.modernghana.com/news/202691/1/tough-times-nigerians-flee-to-ghana-vietnam.html.

Trung Phan. "The Nigerian Union by Trung Phan. From the Word Ho Chi Minh." Nigerian Union of Vietnam, November 26, 2010. Accessed December 17, 2012. http://nuvietnam.blogspot.com/2010/04/nigerian-union-by-trung-phan-from-word.html.

Truong Si Anh, Patrick Gubry, Vu Thi Hong, and Jerrold W. Huguet. "Migration and Employment in Ho Chi Minh City." *Asia-Pacific Population Journal* 11 (1996): 3–22.

Tuoi Tre. "Foreigners in HCMC Settle into Fashion Business: A Group of Nigerians Have Found a Stylish New Niche in Ho Chi Minh City." *Thanh Nien News*, July 22, 2008. Accessed November 18, 2012. http://web.archive.org/web/20080822082845/http://www.thanhniennews.com/features/?catid=10&newsid=40473.

Turner, R. Kerry, Jeroen C. J. M. van den Bergh, Tore Soderqvist, Aat Barendregt, Jan van der Straaten, Edward Maltby, and Ekko C. van Ierland. "Ecological Economic Analysis of Wetlands: Scientific Integration for Management and Policy." *Ecological Economics* 35 (1995): 7–23.

"2012 Global Diaspora Forum: Moving Forward by Giving Back." Accessed November 17, 2012. http://diasporaalliance.org/featured/global-diaspora-forum/.

UN Habitat. "Urban Inequities Report: Addis Ababa." 2003.

United Nations Department of Economic and Social Affairs Population Division. Population Estimates and Projections Section. http://esa.un.org/unpd/wpp/unpp/Panel_profiles.htm.

United Nations Department of Economic and Social Affairs, Population Division. *World Population Prospects: The 2005 Revision*. New York: United Nations, 2006.

United Nations Department of Economic and Social Affairs, Population Division. *World Population Prospects: The 2010 Revision*. New York: United Nations, 2011.

United States Census Bureau. *2010 Census*. U.S. Census Bureau, 2010. Accessed March 4, 2014. http://www.census.gov/2010census/data/.

Uyen Nicole Duong. *Daughters of the River*. Las Vegas, NV: AmazonEncore, 2010.

van Arkadie, Brian, Raymond Mallon. *Viet Nam: A Transition Tiger?* Canberra, Australia: ANU Press, 2003.

Van Bui. Fulbright Economics Teaching Program. University of Economics. Interview by author (James H. Spencer, Globalization Research Center, University of Hawai'i at Manoa), Ho Chi Minh City, Vietnam, July 7, 2005.

van der Eng, Peter. "Productivity and Comparative Advantage in Rice Agriculture in Southeast Asia since 1870." *Asian Economic Journal* 18 (2004).

Waibel, Michael, Ronald Eckert, Michael Bose, and Volker Martin. "Housing for Low-Income Groups in Ho Chi Minh City between Re-Integration and Fragmentation: Approaches to Adequate Urban Typologies and Spatial Strategies." *ASIEN* 103 (2007).

White, E. B. *Here Is New York*. New York: Little Bookroom, 1999.

Wilson, William Julius. *The Truly Disadvantaged: The Inner City, the Underclass, and Public Policy*. Chicago: University of Chicago Press, 1987.

———. *When Work Disappears: The World of the New Urban Poor*. New York: Vintage Books. 1996.

Wong, Vanessa. "Which Is America's Best City?" *Bloomberg Businessweek: Lifestyle*. September 20, 2011.

World Bank. Finance, Economics & Urban Development Department. Sustainable Development Network. "Systems of Cities: Harnessing Urbanization for Growth and Poverty Alleviation." The World Bank Urban & Local Government Strategy, 2010.

World Bank. Urbanization Website. Accessed November 26, 2012. http://web.worldbank.org/WBSITE/EXTERNAL/EXTABOUTUS/0,,contentMDK:23272497~pagePK:51123644~piPK:329829~theSitePK:29708,00.html.

World Health Organization and UNICEF. *Meeting the MDG Drinking Water and Sanitation Target: The Urban and Rural Challenge of the Decade.* Geneva: WHO, 2006.

Xinhua and Dow Jones. "Xinhua-Dow Jones International Financial Centers Development Index 2012." Accessed November 7, 2012. www.djindexes.com/mdsidx/downloads/meth_info/Xinhua_Overview.pdf.

Yang Yang. "African Traders in Guangzhou: Routes, Reasons, Profits, Dreams." In *Globalization from Below: The World's Other Economy,* edited by Gordon Matthews, Gustavo Lins Ribeiro, and Carlos Alba Vega. New York: Routledge, 2012.

Youngman, Ian. "Will the Boss Pick Up the Bill for Medical Travel?" *International Medical Travel Journal,* 2009. Accessed December 18, 2012. http://www.imtj.com/articles/2009/company-funded-medical-travel/.

Zhou Jianqing. "Sino-African Economic and Trade Cooperation Develops Steadily—Survey of 2005 and Prospects for 2006." *West Asia and Africa* 1 (2006). As cited in Li Anshan, "China's New Policy toward Africa."

INDEX

Note: Page numbers in italics indicate tables and figures.

science of cities, 19–20, 38
Scientific American, 8
Scott, Allen, 31
SEA. *See* Southeast Asia
Sea-Air-Model (SAM), 113–14
Seattle Trade Development Alliance, 28
Second Green Revolution, 65–70, 74, 105
Selassie, Haile, 106–7, 112, 202
Sen, Amartya, 44
Senegal, 11, *12*
sewage or septic systems, 52, 53, 115, 141, 154–55
Shanghai, 3, 19, 36, 91, 194
Shashamene, 107
Sheba, Queen of, 106, 107, 219n28
Shenzhen, 22, 23
Short, John Rennie, 33
Sierra Club, 151
Silicon Valley, 18–19, 146, 161
silver hair and Malaysia My Second Home programs, 135
Silverstein, Larry A., 180, 181
Singapore, 28, 165
Sioux Falls, 33
sister city agreements, 28
slums, 13, 31, 53, 115
Smith, Adam, 43, 44
Snow, John, 52
soccer players, African, 3, 75, 88–90
Socialism, 107–8
Socialist Republic of Vietnam, 63, 72, 84
Soho neighborhood, New York City, 161, 173
Soho Properties, 181
Soja, Ed, 18
solid waste: in Addis Ababa, 115; in Honolulu, 152–55; in New York City, 152, 153
Solomon (king of Israel), 106, 107, 219n28

Somali refugees, 121
South Africa, 100, 133
Southeast Asia (SEA): agro-industrial processing regions in, 4, 13; retirement and, 139–40; tourism in, 132–34; urbanization in, 1, 9; urbanization trends by country, *11*. *See also specific countries*
Soviet Union, 2, 28, 104, 110
Spencer, Dao Nguyen, 216n35
SSA. *See* Sub-Saharan Africa
stadiums, 42, 213n6
stagflation, 174
starchitect developments, 22, 212n5
Steger, Manfred, 27
Stewart, Potter, 199
Storper, Michael, 31
streets: in Addis Ababa, 116–18; concentric street systems, 21–22
Sub-Saharan Africa (SSA): China and, 3, 99–105, 209n3; infrastructure in, 102; socio-environmental transformation in, 66; urbanization in, 1, 9; urbanization trends, 11, *12*. *See also specific countries*
suburbanization, 172, 197
subway system, New York City, 7–8, 16–17, 29–30
Sukhumvit neighborhood, 4
supply and demand, 50, 58, 99–105, 134, 185
sustainability, 146, 157–58, 213n7
Sydney Opera House, 155
systems-theory stance, 31

Taipei 101, Taiwan, 212n5
TARP. *See* Temporary Asset Relief Fund
telecommunications, 58, 101–2
Temporary Asset Relief Fund (TARP), 183–84
textiles, 102–3, 173

ABOUT THE AUTHOR

James H. (Jim) Spencer is the founding chair of the Department of Planning, Development, and Preservation at Clemson University. He has been a professor of urban and regional planning and of political science at the University of Hawai'i at Manoa, an adjunct senior fellow at the East West Center, and a former visiting scholar at the University of California at Berkeley's Institute for Urban and Regional Development. His research focuses on urbanization in the Global South—Cambodia, Indonesia, and other parts of Asia, as well as Ethiopia and Ghana—with a particular focus on Viet Nam. His research includes municipal services, periurbanization, water security, the urban transition, and development in fast-growing regions, as well as urban policy and inequality in the United States. Funded in part by the Ford Foundation, the National Science Foundation, and the Social Science Research Council, his work has appeared in the *Journal of the American Planning Association*, *Environment and Planning A*, *Urban Affairs Review*, *Journal of Planning Education and Research*, *Journal of Urban Health*, *Economic Development Quarterly*, and elsewhere. Prior to his academic career, Spencer worked for the Ford Foundation and numerous NGOs working in development. He earned a B.A. from Amherst College, an M.E.M. from Yale University, and a Ph.D. from UCLA. He lives in Greenville, South Carolina, with his wife, Meron, and children, Yohannes and Sabah Xuan.

   We have yet to fully understand the implications of the rapid urbanization and the global ecosystem that it is shaping. The ideas specified in this book scratch only the surface of a world of visible and latent relationships and transactions. Because of this, we are all struggling to figure out what it all means. I think the conversation is just beginning. If you would like to find others interested in the social, political, economic, and policy implications of this ongoing discussion, I encourage you to either join the Facebook page https://www.facebook.com/GlobalUrbanEcosystem or send an email to globalurbanecosystem@gmail.com. As Margaret Mead has said, *"Never doubt that a small group of thoughtful, committed people can change the world. Indeed, it is the only thing that ever has."* In today's world, a small but global network of thoughtful people interested in our shared future will inevitably shape it. The broader the conversation on these evolving relationships, the more democratic and inclusive will that shape be.